Death and Western Thought

$ 4.45

DEATH AND WESTERN THOUGHT

Jacques Choron

COLLIER BOOKS
A Division of Macmillan Publishing Co., Inc.
New York
COLLIER MACMILLAN PUBLISHERS
London

Macmillan Publishing Co., Inc.
866 Third Avenue, New York, N.Y. 10022
Collier Macmillan Canada, Ltd.

Death and Western Thought is also published in a hardcover
edition by Macmillan Publishing Co., Inc.

The poem on page 8 is reprinted from Arturo Barea,
Lorca: The Poet and His People (New York, Harcourt
Brace Jovanovich, 1949).

Library of Congress Catalog Card Number: 62-17575

First Collier Books Edition 1963
Reissued 1973
Fourth Printing 1978
Printed in the United States of America

TO VICKI

Yo quiero que me enseñen donde está la salida
para este capitán atado por la muerte.

I want them to show me where the way out
Exists for this captain shackled by death.

—FEDERICO GARCIA LORCA,
Llanto por Ignacio Sanchez Mejiás

Translated by ILSA BAREA

Foreword

THE AUTHOR hopes that this survey of what the great philosophers of the Western world have thought about death will not only be a contribution to the history of ideas but also helpful to those who, at a time when the consolations of religion have lost their force, seek to come to terms with death.

Contents

Introduction

Ein ewig buntes Fest der Himmelskinder und der
Erdbewohner, rauschte das Leben wie ein Fruehling
durch die Jahrhunderte hin . . . ein Gedanke nur
war es, ein entsetzliches Traumbild,
  Das furchtbar zu den frohen Tischen trat
  Und das Gemuet in wilde Schrecken huellte. . . .
  Es war der Tod, der dieses Lustgelag'
  Mit Angst und Schmerz und Traenen unterbrach.[1]

—NOVALIS, *Hymnen an die Nacht*

WHEN, IN ORDER TO retrace the history of man's discovery of
death, we turn to the vast store of information accumulated
by anthropologists about the idea of death and attitudes
toward it in primitive cultures, we find in the earliest stages
of human development not merely a denial of the finality of
death, but also a denial of its inevitability.
  Levy-Bruhl writes:

> In all uncivilized races everywhere, death requires to be
> explained by other than natural causes. It has frequently
> been remarked that when they see a man die, it would seem
> as if it might be the very first time such a thing had hap-
> pened, and that they never before have been witnesses of
> such an occurrence. "Is it possible," says the European to
> himself, "that these people do not *know* that everybody
> must die sooner or later?" But the primitive has never con-
> sidered things in this light. In his eyes, the causes which
> inevitably bring about the death of a man in a certain
> (fairly definite) number of years—causes such as failure of
> the body organs, senile decay, diminution of functioning
> power—are not necessarily connected with death. Does he
> not see a decrepit old man still alive? If, therefore, at a
> given moment death supervenes it must be because a mystic
> force has come into play. Moreover, senile weakness itself,

like any other malady, is not due to what we call natural causes; it, too, must be explained by the agency of a mystic force. In short, if the primitive pays no attention to the cause of death, it is because he *knows* already how death is brought about, and since he knows *why* it happens, *how* it occurs matters very little. Here we have a kind of a priori reasoning upon which experience has no hold.[2]

For the primitive, then, death is the result of the action or malign influence of an enemy in either human or spiritual form: one can be killed, or magic can induce a deadly sickness. But for these hostile acts, no one would ever die.

The various myths about the origin of death found among the primitives bear out the conclusion that during the long prehistory of the race, death was not considered a necessary attribute of the human condition.[3] Man was believed to have been created deathless. Death came into the world because of the mistake made by the messenger bearing the gift of deathlessness, who either garbled the message out of forgetfulness or malice or did not arrive on time.[4] It is interesting to note that, as Radin points out, nowhere can the idea be found among the primitives that man himself is responsible for death (as he is in the Old Testament); rather, the explanation often encountered is that the gods have sent death because they are jealous of man, who has driven them from the earth.[5]

One typical myth explaining the origin of death is that of the Nama Hottentots: The moon once sent the louse to promise immortality to man: "As I die and dying live, so you also shall die and dying live." The hare overtook the louse on its way, and promised to deliver the message. He forgot it, however, and gave the wrong version: "As I die and dying perish, etc." The moon in anger struck the hare on its lip, which has been split ever since.[6]

Although every comparison between the primitive and the child is in most cases precarious, the genesis of the child's knowledge of death may give some indication as to the probable path which the discovery of death took during the infancy of humankind.

Gesell gives us a detailed picture of the emergence of the

idea of death in children.[7] The child of five still "cannot conceive of not being alive, of dying, or of anyone living before him." There is in some cases recognition of the finality of death, but the child "may think it reversible"—that the dead can return to life—and the whole attitude to death is quite unemotional and matter of fact. In the six-year-old child, there is "a beginning of an emotional response to the idea of death"; the child may worry that mother may die and leave him. The child connects killing with death, and sometimes possibly illness and old age, but the idea of death as the result of aggression and killing is predominant. He still does not believe, however, that he himself will die; it is at the age of seven that he begins to suspect this, although only as a mere possibility that is usually denied. The decisive step toward recognizing not only that some people die when killed or stricken with illness or old age, but that all people die, including himself, occurs between the ages of eight and nine.

As a rule this information about the inevitability of death is imparted to the child by grownups.[8]

But how did mankind arrive at the conclusion that death is inevitable? To say that man knows it through experience obscures the fact that a certain stage of psychical and intellectual development must be reached before man can learn from experience. Primitive man actually had much more opportunity to observe people dying than civilized man has under normal circumstances. And since the primitive was clearly incapable of drawing from these observations the obvious conclusion, it was only when man outgrew the primitive mentality—that is, when he ceased to be a primitive—that he was able to discover the inevitability of death. In this process of growing up, the most important step was individualization. As long as primitive man was part of the clan—the horde—his most essential characteristic was the place he held in it. As Landsberg points out, "consciousness of death goes hand in hand with human individualization, with the establishment of single individualities." Once "the individual actualizes a content which is particular to him alone . . . it must overflow the limits of the clan, of the regeneration of the clan and of rebirth in the clan." [9]

The other necessary condition was the emergence of logical reasoning, which permitted him to draw from the numerous observable happenings a general rule, a law, that "all men are mortal." Once these conditions are fulfilled, the individual man knows through experience that he, too, has to die. And Voltaire, for instance, writes that a child brought up alone and transported to a desert island would no more suspect the necessity of dying than a plant or a cat.

This view has been challenged by two modern thinkers, and we shall now briefly examine their theories. That of Scheler holds that man knows intuitively that he has to die; and Landsberg maintains that the knowledge of death comes to man through a particular experience of death.

Scheler insists that man would know that death will catch up with him even if he were all alone in the world and had never seen other living beings suffer the change that leads to becoming a corpse. For in his view "death is an a priori for all observing, inductive experience of the changing contents of every real life process," since death is not a "more or less accidental 'dying' realized by this or that individual," but an integral part of life.[10]

According to Scheler, the structure of each small phase of the continuing life-process, and of the inner consciousness of it, has three dimensions (*Erstreckungen*)—the directly experienced present, the past and the future. And as we live on, the dimension of the past grows, and at the same time the dimension of the future decreases. "With each piece of life that has been lived and that is given as lived in its direct after-effect, the scope of life still to be lived becomes noticeably narrower." [11]

In this experience of a constant consuming (*Aufzehrung*) of life by the lived life, which Scheler calls the "inner experience of death directedness" (*Erlebnis der Todesrichtung*), he sees the basic phenomenon (*Grundphaenomen*) of aging, which does not exist for the world of dead things. And he maintains that even a hypothetical person who did not know his birthday or his age, who had never been sick or tired, and who did not possess the measure of his age, would still have consciousness of his age. "Death is thus not a merely empirical ingredient of our experience, but belongs to the essence of experiencing of every other life and our own life too. Thus it has the direction toward death. . . . It is not a frame that, as it were, by accident, is tacked on to the picture of various physical and physiological processes, but a frame which belongs to the picture itself." [12]

Landsberg is mistaken when he declares that Scheler is giving merely an analysis of the experience of aging.[13] For Scheler is careful to add that "even independently from aging this end is actually present to us, even if its time and mode are not." [14] Death is not a wall against which we, as it were, butt in the dark. It is not a crushing of the living being through hostile outside forces. Death can obviously come to pass through the effect of these forces. But death is contained in the process of living itself. Dying is, somehow, always an act of the living being itself.

In brief, there is, according to Scheler, an intuitive certainty of death (*intuitive Todesgewissheit*), which, however, is totally different from the premonition of death that we find in those suffering from certain diseases. It has nothing to do with different attitudes to death: with whether death is feared or desired. For this intuitive certainty of death lies much deeper than any emotion; the attitude to death is secondary and has to do with the life history of a particular individual, not with life itself. "As far as we must ascribe to all life a form of consciousness, we must ascribe to it also some kind of intuitive death certainty." [15]

An important question arises here: If there exists such an intuitive certainty of death, how is it possible that we find rather a disbelief in one's own death even among the civilized, and how can we explain that primitive man clings so persistently to the idea that death is accidental? Scheler attributes this absence of the certainty of death to man's normal and powerful repression of the idea of death.

Landsberg, however, is not satisfied with Scheler's explanation (although, as we have seen, he misinterprets it). He thinks that in order for the truth of the inevitability of death to sink in, a particular experience of death is required. This alone can produce the compelling certainty of our mortality.

There are, according to Landsberg, many varieties of this experience. They include certain kinds of fainting and deep slumber, and the living experience of death in grave accidents and in war. But the most important one is what he calls the death of the fellow creature ("la mort du prochain") and in particular of a being whom we love:

> The consciousness of the necessity of death is awakened only through participation, only through the personal love by which this experience is completely imbued. We have constituted an "us" with the dying person. And it is in this "us," it is through the specific power of this new and utterly personal being that we are led toward the living awareness of our own having to die. . . . My community with that person seems to be broken off; but this community in some degree was I myself, I feel death in the heart of my own existence.[16]

It is through just such a participation in the death of the beloved friend that the discovery of the inevitability of death takes place in the earliest document about death known to us —the Gilgamesh Epic. The discovery that Gilgamesh himself is destined for the same terrible fate goes hand in hand with the sorrow over the death of his beloved friend Enkidu: "Now what sleep is this that has taken hold of thee? Thou hast become dark and canst not hear me. When I die, shall I not be like unto Enkidu? Sorrow entered my heart, I am afraid of death." [17]

But to return to Landsberg's theory: is it necessarily only the death of someone close to us which reveals to us our mortality? As John Donne said, in his *Devotions,* "Any man's death diminishes me, because I am involved in Mankinde." It may be argued, of course, that Donne was notoriously sensitive to death. Be that as it may, we also have to consider the strange—although by now well-established—fact that no one really believes in his own death, even though no one doubts its inevitability. And it is questionable whether even an experience of death, or a direct encounter with death, will bring about a lasting awareness of our mortality. It seems that even today everyone has to discover the inevitability of death for himself in a variety of ways, either through the experience of death in Landsberg's meaning of the term, or by realizing that when the bell tolls, "it tolls for thee," or, as most often happens, by being told about it and accepting it on authority.

As far as man's original discovery of the inevitability of death is concerned, the obvious problem is to determine how the knowledge, later passed on and accepted on faith, was acquired. It is quite possible that both theories, Scheler's and Landsberg's, are correct, since individuals differ. In any case, knowledge of the inevitability of death became the common property of mankind very gradually, and it therefore must not be thought of as discovery, in the sense of a sudden event. Nevertheless, there came a time when the idea became universal. When this happened it is not possible to determine with any degree of accuracy. Interestingly, however, if we use the Gilgamesh Epic as a signpost, and even allow a few thousand years for the probability that the story itself antedates the written record, the discovery of the inevitability of death, measured against man's total presence on earth, is a relatively recent occurrence.

Learning of its inevitability is only the first stage of man's discovery of death. Although we already have in the Gilgamesh Epic most of the themes of the meditation on death— the fear of death, the intimation of the futility of life, and the problem of how to live in view of the bitter truth that this radical change from life to death is *inevitable*—Gilgamesh's encounter with death is not complete. What is destroyed is merely the belief in earthly immortality, in deathlessness; but that death may be total *annihilation* is still only suspected. In Babylonian and Assyrian speculation "death was not conceived as the absolute end of life or as affecting the complete annihilation of conscious vitality. Rather it meant the separation of body and spirit, the decay of the former and the transfer of the latter from one mode of life or existence to another —the spirit descended to the underworld to sojourn there through eternity. The evidence for this point is overwhelming." [18]

Thus, although the discovery of the inevitability of death produced a profound shock, and man did not accept without a struggle the prospect of his separation from the earth with all its splendor, or the inevitable loss of his loved ones, there was consolation in the belief in reincarnation or in immortality. Therefore, before man was able to discover death in its entirety—that is, before he could realize that it might also be total annihilation—this comforting aspect of the primitive view of death had to give way.

Primitive man does not believe that anyone dies completely. Death to him is in no case the pure and simple suppression of all forms of activity and existence. It is never absolute.[19] The dead live while awaiting reincarnation.

Sir James Frazer found that in most primitive societies "immortality has a certainty which the individual as little dreams of doubting as he doubts the reality of his conscious existence." [20]

Radin writes:

In those primitive societies of which we have any record, all individuals understood quite definitely the difference between the living person and his corpse, just as it is also clear that they did not believe that all of man's personality, i.e. everything that characterized him as a living being, disappeared upon death. His body, after all, still remained and though it decayed, some parts persisted apparently forever. Here there was visible testimony of its imperishability, and with it, of man's. . . .

Death, it must be remembered, is never looked upon as the reduction of the individual to nothingness. It is simply a change in the manner of communication of one individual and another. Essentially it is separation—just as is disease. But if disease is a temporary separation death is a permanent one. . . .

The only change in attitude, so we may surmise, that must have taken place immediately upon the occasion of a death, was the recognition on the part of the living, that the customary type of *communication* between the dead man and the living had changed. But nothing else.[21]

universe around him, as the result of the conflict between the two different theories of imperishability—one held by the man of action, the other by the thinker-poet-priest. Although for both the world was a dynamic continuity, and both recognized in this continuity conflicting disturbances and interruptions, they differed in the interpretation of these: for the one the interruption caused by death was not a break, but merely a temporary "tripping up," and therefore not fearsome; for the other it was a real break, causing "real or pretended terror," and since this was the view of the medicine-man or priest, it prevailed.[29]

However, this not very convincing theory (indeed, why would the priest consider death to be a real break?) would, at best, explain the rise of speculation about the workings of reincarnation[30] (whether after death one returns to earth or is fitted into the supernatural realm, and what one must do to be reborn), but it would not explain the emergence of doubt about survival after death.

Before this doubt could have arisen, the belief in reincarnation must have undergone a radical modification. Cornford writes:

> The essence of this belief is that the one life of the group or tribe extends continuously through its dead members as well as through the living; the dead are still part of the group, in the same sense as the living. This life, which is perpetually renewed, is reborn out of the opposite state, called "death," into which, at the other end of the arc, it passes again.

There is one homogeneous soul of the tribe, its "Daemon." It is

> in the king and the hero [that] we have found transitional forms, which make, as it were, a bridge from the Daemon of a group to the individual soul. The chief was probably the first individual. The collective authority of the tribe was vested in him, must inevitably be confounded with his in-

dividual will. . . . By a curious perversion, egoism established itself by the absorption of force derived from the
subject of its tyranny. The sense of individuality grows
strong by feeding on the collective mana.[31]

Since, however, the king is still regarded by others as a
depository of social authority—which existed before him and
will be transmitted to his successor—his soul does not begin
and end with his life span; it is immortal, primarily because
it is, in a way, still the super-individual soul of the group,
which outlives every generation of its members. There was
probably a stage in which only chiefs or heroes had immortal
souls. But this does not necessarily mean that the other members of the clan were considered mortal, only that theirs was
a collective immortality. Gradually, every one acquired an immortal soul, and as Cornford suggests, "the democratic extension of immortality to all human beings was perhaps partly
helped by the rise of the patriarchal family, as the unit of the
new social structure." [32]

Other origins of the belief in the existence of the individual
immortal soul have been suggested. Some trace it to the dream
image; others claim that the memory image was decisive. In
Homer man possesses a "breath-soul"—*thymos,* the mortal
spirit, and *psyche*—the immortal soul. Thymos appears to
have been rather a thing than a function; and it perished at
the time of death, when it left the organs on which it de-
pended. The psyche, however, escaped at death, and as late
as the fifteenth century we see it depicted, notably by Giotto
and Fra Angelico, as a naturalistic miniature of the dying
person.[33] The psyche was associated with the head and was
considered the immortal living principle, the source of the
vitality of man.[34]

It appears then that two stages can be distinguished in the
rise of the notion of the perishability of the soul. First, the
collective group soul becomes atomized into individual souls
which still feel themselves immortal, imperishable; secondly,
the breakdown of the original duality (thymos and psyche)
which led to the idea of a more complex psyche in which the

two are fused and have become localized in the body (in the head or in the chest), opened up the possibility that the psyche may not survive the body to which it was so intimately attached.

What must have equally contributed to the total discovery of death, to the realization of the inevitability of death as well as to the suspicion that it might be total annihilation, is the emergence of the lineal concept of time. Primitive man, as Plessner points out, lives in "circles, in an eternal present," and "the world which is conceived cyclically knows death only as an organic phenomenon. Where the chain does not break, or more precisely, where the past is ruled by the 'law of return,' the importance of individual death remains limited and so to speak obscured. Only with the transformation of the mythical time-consciousness from its cyclic into its eschatological form appears the perspective of 'never more' and the separation into the past, present and future." [35]

Not until lineal time replaced cyclic time did every event receive the character of uniqueness and of unrepeatability, and it is its combination with the already dawning individualization of the members of the primitive group that makes death appear as a real threat.

The realization of the possibility that death may be total annihilation probably came very gradually. For many primitives the skeleton is conclusive proof that one is not totally destroyed by death. We do not know when and how the association between death and decay originated. This association was, perhaps, a decisive factor in leading to the conception of death as total destruction.

It is possible that the first hint that death may be complete annihilation comes from the spectacle of human death. Here the change is so unexpected and overwhelming that it cannot fail to convey the idea of the real and irrevocable end. Still, there is the soul, the spirit, which may continue to exist.

How the dependence of one's psychic life on that of one's body is experienced appears, therefore, to be of decisive importance. As long as we experience the autonomy of our spiritual being, which either directs or dominates our body or is independent of it, or even as long as we simply feel that we possess a soul, its continuation after physical death will appear to be self-evident.

If, however, the experience in which we identify our being with our corporeal substance predominates, if we "feel" our bodily life as the only life—and man seems more and more inclined to do so[36]—it is obvious that we will tend to assume, or even expect, that our personality will be completely destroyed with our bodies. For there will be nothing to oppose the impression conveyed by the corpse that man is completely annihilated in death.

With the realization that death is total annihilation, man's discovery of death is complete. And under the impact of this total discovery of death, the sense of the futility of life overwhelms man with unprecedented force. If man is to perish for all eternity, if there is no hope for a hereafter,

> what does a busy man gain from all his toil? . . . What is the use of all my wisdom? . . . Man's fate is a beast's fate. One fate befalls them both; as the one dies so the other dies; the same breath is in them all; man is no better than a beast, for both are vanity, both are bound for the same end; both sprang from dirt, and to dirt they both return.[37]

This mood of despair and frustration seized not only the peoples of the old civilizations of the valley of the Nile, of Mesopotamia and of Palestine, but also those inhabiting the Greek colonies of Asia Minor.

> The Ionians, as we can see from their literature, were deeply impressed by the transitoriness of things. . . . We find Mimnermos of Kolophon preoccupied with the sadness of the coming of old age, while at a later date the lament of Simonides, that the generations of men fall like leaves of the forest, touches a chord that Homer had already struck.[38]

With the probability, bordering on certainty, that death is total annihilation of the human personality, the problems of death—the fear of dying and the sense of futility of life—which made their appearance already with the realization of the inevitability of death, become more urgent and more acute. Although the primitive's firm conviction of the impossibility of total destruction is now reduced to a mere hope of immortality, the nature of death remains the central issue, and the history of the death problem in philosophical thought is on the one hand the story of attempts to ascertain that—as man wants to believe and as myth and religious doctrine assert—death is not the absolute end, and that survival after death is not an illusion.

But it is also the story of growing scepticism as to these assertions and beliefs. The problem shifts more and more from that of demonstrating the unreality of death to that of a reconciliation, emotional and intellectual, with the fact that, with the last fluttering of our pulse, all is ended.

The two main aspects of this problem are mastery of the fear of dying, and the neutralization or refutation of the seemingly unavoidable conclusion that our brief sojourn under the sun is a senseless joke, an absurd tragicomedy. The question of the meaning of human existence in the totality of Being, this fundamental question of philosophy, gains its true and practical importance through man's total discovery of death.

BOOK I
ANTIQUITY

Chapter 1

The Pre-Socratic Philosophers

WHAT WAS THE SITUATION, as far as death is concerned, when philosophy began in the Greek colonies of Asia Minor around the year 600 B.C.? In his famous treatise "Wie die Alten den Tod gebildet" Gotthold Ephraim Lessing (1729-1781) asserts that "death was not terrible for the peoples of Antiquity." Lessing based this opinion on his discovery that the skeleton represented "larvae," the souls of evil men, and not death, as it did in later times. Death was pictured as a youth holding a torch turned downward and it is this representation that gave him the idea of the reconciliation with the fact of death in ancient Greece.

Later scholars, however, have disproved this view. Schelling speaks of the "sorrow over the unconquerable finitude of existence" which permeates like a "sweet poison" the works of art of the Greeks. Erwin Rohde says that nothing was so hateful to the Greeks as death. Cornford writes that "the overwhelming consciousness of mortality darkens the whole main current of Greek reflection." [1] And, as we have already seen, Burnet points out that "the Ionians . . . were deeply impressed by the transitoriness of things. There was, in fact, a fundamental pessimism in their outlook on life. . . ." [2] Edith Hamilton, stressing the joy of life as a special mark of the Greek spirit, admits that "the Greeks were keenly aware, terribly aware of life's uncertainty and the imminence of death. Over and over again they emphasize the brevity and the failure of all human endeavor." [3] And precisely because for them the world was beautiful and delightful to live in, death seemed so terrible.

There are many instances that bear out these statements. Homer makes the shadow of Achilles express the prevalent opinion:

Speak not smoothly of death, I beseech you, O famous Odysseus, Better by far to remain on earth the thrall of another . . . rather than reign sole king in the realm of bodyless phantoms.[4]

Death is the greatest evil. "Gods so consider it," says Sappho, "else they would die." And Anacreon is terrified by approaching death: "Death is too terrible. Frightening are the depths of Hades. There is no return."

The prevailing view of death could not appease this acute consciousness of mortality. Death was neither peaceful sleep nor the better and happier existence in the hereafter, although some held such views. Generally the dead were thought to become bloodless shadows wandering listlessly in the Underworld, which was more dreadful than anything known on earth. To this distressing view of death the Greeks opposed the ideal of the heroic attitude to it. As Bowra writes, "the exponents of the heroic ideal regard death as the climax and completion of life, the last and most searching ordeal to which a man is subjected and the true test of his worth." [5]

It is doubtful, however, whether we can consider the heroic outlook anything but an exception. It is true that there was among the Greeks a high sense of duty to the city and readiness to sacrifice one's life for its welfare. Great value was also set on fame for glorious deeds in battle as a means of achieving token immortality in the minds of future generations. But the hero was honored and glorified precisely because he was an exception to the rule.

What is even more relevant in connection with the prevailing view of death among the Greeks is the obvious despair and sadness that underlie the heroic outlook. Bowra himself points out that it is "a gesture of defiance," in which the hero throws away his life in some splendid act of bravery. And because he is so close to the gods in his deeds and achievements, he is more keenly and painfully aware that he is, nevertheless, mortal. "But over me stands death and fate's overmastering power," says Achilles. The hero accepts his human condition, but with melancholy resignation. The need for a more satisfying view of death than the one offered by

of their depriving each other of the possibility of existence, as Nestle suggests, apparently thinking in terms of *Lebensraum,* the terrible fact that things perish must have greatly impressed Anaximander.[11] And to insist that "things perish into those things out of which they have their birth" may well represent an attempt to neutralize death, and may be an expression of the hope that somewhere and somehow death shall have no dominion. Anaximander seems to have posited an infinite and inexhaustible "boundless," the *apeiron,* because the great, the disturbing and tantalizing question for him was why all that comes into existence, all that has a right to exist, has to perish. What is existence worth when it is momentary and fleeting?

His answer to death, then, already contains the nucleus of the philosophical answer that was subsequently favored by all who were unable to side wholeheartedly either with the view of traditional religions or with the view that death was final annihilation. Accepting their individual deaths, they pin their hopes on the everlastingness of the Whole, in which death cannot be senseless perishing.

Heraclitus (533–475 B.C.) was affected by the spectacle of the impermanence and transitoriness of things perhaps even more than Anaximander. His concern with human death is very obvious in the considerable number of fragments that deal with it.[12] And this most radical, conspicuous, and shocking change must have impressed upon him the idea of change as the basic characteristic of reality:[13] "We step and do not step into the same rivers; we are and are not." [14]

But Heraclitus does not remain in this state of bewilderment and despair over the apparent instability of reality. He has the revelation that although becoming is a strife, in this strife the opposites form, nevertheless, a unity, like two poles of a magnet or two fighters in the arena, and that this war of opposites is not an injustice, but the highest justice,[15] for the many are one, and the one is many. This is not, however, a retreat to the position of Anaximander. For Heraclitus the many perceived qualities are neither the essences themselves, as Anaxagoras thought later on, nor products of our imagination, as Parmenides taught; and the "boundless" of Anaximander, to which things return as a penalty for this strife, gives way to a substance that would pass into everything, and into which everything in turn would pass. This substance was, for Heraclitus, fire: "All things are an exchange for Fire, and Fire for all things, even as gold is exchanged for wares, and wares for gold." [16] And precisely because everything flows and changes, death itself is not permanent, for man's soul is part of the eternal Fire which transforms itself but abides eternally. Through respiration the soul is nourished by the outward atmospheric evaporation as well as by the inner evaporation that comes from the blood. The alternations of humidity and dryness produce the alternations of the life rhythm, of sleeping and waking, of life and death. The drier the soul, the closer it is to wisdom. But the soul can also become wet, and this spells death to the soul. However, and this is the crucial point, although water becomes earth, the process is reversible. As Fragment 68 states: "For it is death to souls to become water, death to water to become earth. But water comes from earth; and from water, soul." [17] There is no question of the survival of the individual soul. Instead, there is the identity of life and death, which is repeatedly stressed in Fragments 66, 67, and 78:[18]

The bow [biòs] is called life [bíos] but its work is death.

Mortals are immortals and immortals are mortals, the one living the other's death and dying the other's life.

And it is the same thing in us that is quick and dead, awake and asleep, young and old; the former are shifted and become the latter, and the latter in turn are shifted and become the former.

How is this identity of life and death to be understood?

That Heraclitus actually speaks not of life and death, but of living and dead, and that these opposites appear together with the opposites of sleeping and waking, may, according to Kirk, indicate that Heraclitus "could have assumed that living and dead were reciprocal extremes of the type of waking and sleeping. Such reciprocity is adduced to illustrate a quite different truth, namely, the unity of opposites in general." [19]

Another possible explanation suggested by the same author is that Heraclitus was thinking of the quasi-religious belief, widely held by the ordinary people of Greece and found in many undeveloped societies today, that the grandchild is the continuation of the life of the grandfather, after whom he is often named. "In this simple way, life may be said to succeed death, and the infant the old man. Or simpler still: from whence are babies born?—from nothing, from a condition of not-life, which could be named death. This idea alone may explain the fragment." [20] But does such an interpretation do justice to Heraclitus? [21]

It seems certain that the famous Fragment 27—"there awaits men when they die such things as they look not for nor dream of"—means neither a threat of punishment nor a promise of blissful immortality.[22] It is nevertheless doubtful whether it means simply the end.

One may ask, however, why Heraclitus did not follow the road Pythagoras took in line with the Orphic tradition, and instead rejected the alluring promise of immortality? There seems to be only one possible answer, namely that Heraclitus was certain of having found an answer to death that was free of the onus of the repulsive rites of mystery cults[23] and at the same time did not offend reason. If this view is correct, the disputed question of Heraclitus' place in the history of philosophical thought appears in a new light. Heraclitus is neither continuing what appears to some to be the sole task of the Milesians, to carry forward the scientific tradition, nor is he, as Cornford asserts, the exponent of the "undisguised revolt against rational science." [24]

If we assume that all that Heraclitus means by the identity of life and death is that the individual perishes but the species survives, his answer would be an anticipation of the answer Aristotle[25] and subsequent biology have given to the problem of death: There is, nevertheless, an important difference, for modern science acknowledges that the species can die out and even that all life may cease. Heraclitus, however, although he conceives the world process not as circular but as an "upward and downward path," does not teach "general conflagration," which the Stoics later attributed to him.[26] Thus, the chain of life cannot, as far as he is concerned, be broken; and the process of creation of life from dead matter will go on in all eternity. Life did not emerge from inorganic matter accidentally, but of necessity, because of the very nature of Fire as the all-pervading spirit of life.

To one who taught that "this world which is the same for all, no one of Gods or men has made; but it was ever, is now, and ever shall be an ever living Fire, with measures of it kindling, and measures going out," and to whom nature appeared to be alive and the human soul intimately bound up with the whole world process, death could not be final or total annihilation.[27]

Moreover, it is significant that it is "in studying himself" that Heraclitus discovers the "Logos," that is, reason, thought, or word, which tells him that a rational principle rules the world, and that there is a unity between divine and human reason.

It appears, then, that we have in Heraclitus an attempt to facilitate the acceptance of death as a necessary and natural event, through the realization that strife, the tension of the opposites—and among these the tension of life and death—is precisely what makes and upholds the universe. Moreover, he minimizes death by insisting that all change is only apparent, that death is not the absolute and irreversible cessation, but that there is a unity of life and death that means not only that life dies, but that death generates life. And precisely because everything flows and changes, death itself is not final, for man's soul is part of the eternal Fire and as such returns and passes again and again into everything. Thus, in a sense, it is the doctrine of "the eternal return of the same" that was revived twenty-five hundred years later by Nietzsche—Heraclitus' answer to death.

Parmenides (flourished around 495 B.C.), the antipode of Heraclitus, had one point in common with his elder contemporary: the denial of the possibility of total and final destruction in death. Since he does not, like Heraclitus, "prize the most the things that can be seen and heard" but bases himself on "reasoning," he is not only less affected by the spectacle of change, but can argue and demonstrate (and not merely assert on the basis of a broad vision of the cosmic process) that there is permanence behind the constant flux. He finds that ". . . there is not, and never shall be, anything besides what is, since fate has chained it so as to be whole and unmovable," for:

One path only is left for us to speak of, namely that *It is.*[28] In this path are very many tokens that what is, is uncreated and indestructible; for it is complete, immovable and without end. Nor was it ever, nor will it be; for now *it is,* all at once, a continuous one. For what kind of origin for it wilt thou look for? In what way and from what source could it have drawn its increase? . . . I shall not let you say nor think that it came from what is not; for it can neither be thought nor uttered that anything is not. . . . How, then, can *what is* be going to be in the future? Or how could it come into being? If it came into being, it is not; nor is it if it is going to be in the future. Thus is becoming extinguished and passing away not to be heard of.[29]

We are not concerned here with Parmenides the alleged father of logic, but with the implication which his assertion that *It is*—which, according to Burnet, "amounts just to this, that the universe is a plenum"—has for the problem of death. That the universe is a plenum means, as Burnet further points out, "that there is no such thing as empty space, either inside or outside the world. From this it follows that there can be no such thing as motion. Instead of endowing the One with an impulse to change, as Heraclitus has done, and thus making it capable of explaining the world, Parmenides dismissed change as an illusion."

And if change is an illusion, so is death—as perhaps the most flagrant change: "Coming into being and passing away have been driven afar, and true belief has cast them away." [30] It is "true knowledge" that shows Parmenides what the vision of the unity of life and death revealed to Heraclitus: passing away is impossible.

What can be distilled from the philosophies of Heraclitus

and Parmenides as the first philosophical answer to death fell far short of the promise of personal immortality.

In the meantime we have in Empedocles (495–435 B.C.) an odd mixture of Pythagorean doctrine of immortality and of the scientific spirit. In the poem, "Purifications," he affirms the transmigration of the soul and its divine origin. And in the "Poem on Nature" he declares that the psychic forces are functions of matter, that thought is nothing but "the blood round the heart," [31] and that living organisms arise from a mixture of four elements into which, at death, they are again resolved. This contradiction is not really explained by saying that Empedocles was a weird combination of a scientist and a mystic. Nor, as E. Frank has pointed out, can it be explained away by an alleged change of mind in favor of mysticism in the philosopher's old age.[32] Frank's own suggestion that this inconsistency is due to the fact that the early Greek philosophers did not see the irreconcilability of the two because their way of thinking was different from ours appears to be more plausible. Where death is concerned, such contradictions are not at all unusual, even among modern philosophers.

Somewhat later we find the first appearance of the detached attitude to death, which was subsequently exalted as the only attitude becoming a philosopher and a scientist. Anaxagoras (500–428 B.C.) is the prototype of the man of science, of the detached observer. It is reported of him that when asked why he preferred existence to non-being he answered: "Because I can study astronomy and investigate the order which pervades the cosmos." Neither the obvious miseries of existence nor the brevity of life should interfere with the aim of life, which consists of intellectual pursuits. Moreover, Anaxagoras not only finds encouragement and comfort in the order he discovers in the universe around him, but particularly in his view that "Nous"—Mind—ordered the world, was the cause of all things and of motion.[33]

The deliberate disregard of death comes to the fore combined with, and perhaps as the result of, the conviction that death is total dissolution. Already in Leucippus (flor. 440 B.C.) animals at death are resolved into "atoms." But even more important for the formation of such an attitude was the emergence of the view of death as a necessary and natural change. Leucippus' great disciple, Democritus (460-370 B.C.), affirms the mortality of the soul,[34] since the fine atoms of which it is constituted, according to him, are dispersed at death. And he drew from it the same consolation that we find later in Epicurus. He says that some people, who have a bad conscience, and do not realize that there is total dissolution everywhere in Nature, live in fear because of concern with what they imagine happens after death. Democritus' goal in life is *eudemia*—joy, gaiety, which is attainable only if we desire nothing but the possible, are moderate in all things, avoid strong emotions and strive for *paideia*—education, which is a treasure when luck smiles on us and a refuge in misfortune. Still, "a life without feasts is like a long road without an inn." As for death, man had better realize that life is perishable and of short duration, afflicted with many hardships and miseries, and that we almost always die in fear.

Democritus does not take death lightly, but realizes that it is a necessary part of life and so he can bear it more easily. However, he sees not only the dark clouds, but also the bright skies. As opposed to Heraclitus, the weeping philosopher, he is the laughing one, even though his laughter may be mixed with tears.

It is possible that acceptance of the fact of our mortality, with the help of the realization of its naturalness and necessity, does succeed in some instances. But even then it is difficult to imagine that it is considered a happy solution of the problem of death; and it may turn out to be only a little more satisfactory and stable than the other solution, which consists of keeping the scientific evidence and the answer offered by religion separated as if in watertight compartments of the mind, thus protecting the latter from the impact of the former. It is therefore understandable that an attempt of reconciliation between the scientific and religious answers had to be made. And philosophy comes into its own as a mediator between the two in the teaching—and death—of Socrates.

Chapter 2

Death May Be Better Than Life

THE ACUTE DEATH-CONSCIOUSNESS given eloquent expression in the literature and legend of the eighth, seventh, and sixth centuries B.C. is evident also in the Greek drama of the following century.

In Euripides, complaints about the transitoriness of life are constantly heard, sometimes taking the form of the regret that it is denied to man to be young twice, for "there is nothing sweeter than to behold the light of the sun." [1] And "when death approaches, no one wants to die anymore, and old age is no burden." [2]

These constant laments over the necessity of having to die are paradoxically combined with the insistence of the misery of life. Aeschylus praises death as a cure for life's misery, but nevertheless esteems as a divine gift the ability not to think of death. Even the hope for an after-life is no real consolation: "The life of man is all misery and trouble and there is nowhere salvation and peace. Surely there is a better, a blissful existence, but it is hidden in mists and darkness. So we cling desperately to the deceptive splendors of this world only because we know nothing of another life. No human eye penetrates the shadows of death and we are misled by the delusions of belief." [3]

Sophocles, however, goes beyond mere lamentation or resignation. Although he too recognizes that death is all-powerful ("Of all the great wonders, none is greater than man. . . . Only for death can he not find a cure" [4]), there are situations when other considerations are more important than the preservation of life. There is duty, there is honor, neither of which can be compromised even though in obeying their dictates one may incur death.[5] "Is there something more you want? Or just my life?" Antigone asks. Even premature death is bearable when life is full of trouble, which here means not only physical pain and misery but moral conflict. "We all die anyway," says Antigone, "and if this hurries me to death before my time—

Why, such a death is gain. Yes surely gain
To one so overwhelmed with trouble.
Therefore, I can go to meet my end
Without a trace of pain. . . ." [6]

Man is a finite and contingent being, but he has greatness which consists in accepting his human condition with responsibility, and pitching force of character against death.

This is, essentially, also the position of Socrates. After the judges have decided for the death penalty, Socrates points out to them that he could have escaped death by using his wits, but did not chose to do so: "But I suggest, gentlemen, that the difficulty is not so much to escape death; the real difficulty is to escape doing wrong." [7]

As far as immortality is concerned, Socrates is anything but dogmatic in his interpretation of the nature of death. In what we now call Socratic spirit, he points out that it would be "the pretense of wisdom" to make the claim of knowing it. He leaves the choice open between the two possibilities: death is either dreamless sleep or migration of the soul to another world. [8] What he asserts, however, is that in either case fear of death is unfounded, and that it is only under the influence of this fear that death appears to be the greatest evil. Yet as dreamless sleep "Death will be an unspeakable gain." And if it is "a journey to another place . . . what can be greater than this?" But how could he convince his listeners that death is not to be feared? There is ample evidence in Plato's report of the trial of Socrates that he could have talked his way out and gained acquittal, or at least have avoided the death penalty. We are also given to understand that he could have escaped, and his pupil Crito repeatedly advised such a step. Socrates, however, chose death, for only in this way could he convince his followers that death is not to be feared.

What gave him courage in the face of death? The great majority of Plato-scholars consider that the agnostic views about after-life expressed toward the end of *Apology* correctly reflect Socrates' thought. This brings up, however, the problem of reconciling with the discussion of the same topic by Socrates in the *Phaedo*, where Plato has him advance arguments for immortality of the soul and present the theory of *Ideas*. The usual conclusion is that in the latter dialogue Plato has arbitrarily combined the factual account of Socrates' last hours with his own doctrine of immortality.

This is not a very satisfactory answer to the puzzle. Walter Kaufmann suggests therefore that "Socrates' complete equanimity in the face of death *reminded* Plato of the Pythagorean, originally Orphic, dictum that the body is the prison of the soul: death is not—may not be, cannot be—the end." [9] But is it not more plausible to assume that Socrates himself, when death was really at hand, remembered the Pythagorean teachings, or, even more probably, that, seeing the distress of his disciples, he attempted to console them over his imminent (and their prospective) death by asserting and offering proofs of immortality? In that case, the only addition Plato made to what Socrates might actually have said was the theory of Ideas, as a firmer basis for the doctrine of immortality, in that it provided another world as a home for the soul before birth and after death.

But even if Socrates himself did not really believe in an immortality that would afford him intercourse with the great and wise men of the past, he appears in the *Apology* as deeply religious:

> For I do believe that there are gods, and in a sense higher than that in which any of my accusers believed in them. And since there is God, no evil can happen to a good man, neither in life, or after death. [10]

But there is also another factor that would explain his courage. Socrates was seventy years old when he was sentenced to die, and this fact had considerable bearing on his attitude to death.

"When a man has reached my age," he says in *Crito*, "he ought not to be repining at the approach of death."

This last motive, which in Plato's accounts plays a secondary role, assumes a central position in the report of the trial of Socrates that Xenophon left for posterity. The problem of immortality is not even mentioned in this classic of ancient journalism. In Xenophon's opinion, the main reason for Socrates' uncompromising attitude before his judges was that death would permit him to avoid the disabilities and miseries of old age. "He had now come to the conclusion that for him death was more to be desired than life." In this connection it is well to remember that the fear of a miserable old age obsessed many a Greek, and that an easy death, without having to inflict it upon oneself, was an often-voiced wish. Moreover, looking back on his life, he was content:

> Do you not know that I would refuse to concede that any man has lived a better life than I have up to now? For I have realized that my whole life has been spent in righteousness toward God and man, a fact that affords the greatest satisfaction; and so I have felt a deep self-respect and have discovered that my associates hold corresponding sentiments toward me. But now, if my years are prolonged, I know that the frailties of old age will inevitably be realized. . . . Perhaps God in his kindness is taking my part and securing me the opportunity of ending my life not only in season but also in the way that is easiest.[11]

His desire to leave a favorable image of himself in the hearts of his companions was paramount.

> When dissolution comes while he still possesses a sound body and a spirit capable of showing kindliness, how could such a one fail to be sorely missed? If I am ending my life when only troubles are in view, my own opinion is that you ought all to feel cheered, in the assurance that my state is happy.[11a]

It is the naturalness of death which is the final argument of Socrates as related by Xenophon: "Have you not known all along that from the moment of my birth nature has condemned me to death?"

The two different answers to death that Plato and Xenophon[12] give us as those of Socrates have both been developed by subsequent philosophers: accordingly some see him primarily as the prophet of immortality and others as the ideal of the stoic wise man.

But neither the agnostic position nor popular religion (which, although it asserted an after-life, depicted it in a far from pleasant manner) was able to give satisfaction to man's deepest craving to see his conscious personality continuing after death. The philosophical teachings of Heraclitus and Empedocles could not fulfill this desire either. It was Plato who, by presenting apparently conclusive arguments for the immortality of the soul, gave a new and consoling answer to death.

Chapter 3

Plato (427-347 B.C.)

Death Is the Release of the Soul from the Body

WE HAVE SEEN that another—more satisfying—answer to death than that of Homeric religion was in existence, namely that of the Orphic mysteries. Their adherents claimed to possess secret knowledge of the spiritual world, taught the immortality of the soul, and asserted that death was merely a door to another, better life.

This position is reflected in two fragments of Euripides: "Who knows if this life be not death, and death be not accounted life in the world below?" and "Who knows if what is called death is not life and life not death?"

The soul is held to be of heavenly origin, and it dwells in the body as if imprisoned; it can escape, at death, and regain its divinity. As Cornford points out, there is no gulf here between the divine and the human, as in the Homeric theology, and "immortality in this sense is to be sharply distinguished from the mere continuance." [1] As we have seen, this doctrine has found its way into philosophy through Pythagoras; and it strongly influenced Plato, who attempted to cast it into a logically consistent system. The assertion of the immortality of the soul means that "when attacked by death it cannot perish." Plato realized the doubts that existed in the minds of his educated contemporaries. He makes Cebes, one of Socrates' disciples, formulate the contrary view of the perishability of the soul:

> But in what concerns the soul, men are apt to be incredulous; they fear that when she has left the body her place may be nowhere, and that on the very day of death she may perish and come to an end immediately on her release from the body . . . vanishing away into nothingness. . . .

But much persuasion and many arguments are required in order to prove that when man is dead the soul yet exists, and has any force and intelligence.[2]

The arguments for immortality that Plato advances in *Phaedo* are:

(a) The soul existed before birth. This pre-existence of the soul is based on the contention that knowledge is recollection (*real* knowledge is considered here not to be empirical, but *a priori*). This, however, established only the existence of the soul before birth. Does it exist after death? [3]

(b) There are eternal and immutable "forms," or "ideas," and since the soul is capable of apprehending them, it must be itself eternal and divine ("nothing mortal knows what is immortal").[4]

(c) The soul rules the body, and therein resembles the immortal gods.

(d) The soul is simple; it is uncompounded, and therefore incapable of dissolution (what is simple cannot change, begin or end—the essence of things is simple, indivisible, unseen and eternal).

(e) The soul, whose essence is life and thus the very opposite of death, cannot be conceived of as dying, any more than fire can be conceived of as becoming cold.[5] And additional proof is given in *Phaedrus:* the soul, being self-moved and the source of life and motion, can never cease to live and move.[6]

As to these "proofs," a host of questions remain unanswered and have perplexed philosophers ever since. The famous translator and commentator of Plato, Jowett, has brought together these problems in his Introduction to *Phaedo:*

What idea can we form of the soul when it is separated from the body? Or how can the soul be united with the body and still be independent? Is the soul related to the body as the ideal to the real, or as the whole to the parts, or as the subject to the object, or as the cause to the effect, or as the end to the means? Shall we say with Aristotle that the soul is the entelechy or the form of an organized living body? Or with Plato, that she has a life of her own? Is the Pythagorean image of the harmony, or the monad, the truer expression? Is the soul related to the body as sight to the eye, or as the boatman to his boat? And in another state of being is the soul to be conceived as vanishing into infinity, hardly possessing an existence she can call her own, as in the pantheistic system of Spinoza and others? Or as an individual spirit informed with another body and retaining the impress of her former character? Or is the opposition of soul and body a mere illusion, and the true self neither soul nor body, but the union of the two in the 'I' which is above them? And is death the assertion of this individuality in the higher nature, and the falling away into nothingness of the lower? Or are we vainly attempting to pass the boundaries of human thought?

Plato himself was aware of the inadequacy of his arguments about the immortality of the soul. What has been demonstrated is that death is a process that affects only the bodily organism, and that the soul is undying. But this still does not prove that the soul continues to live after the body has died. It is true that *dead* cannot be predicated of the soul; but it can either be annihilated or it can withdraw. That it withdraws is, in the last resort, not demonstrated but rests on faith, as does the assertion that the soul is imperishable. And this reaches a high degree of probability because of the soul's divinity. But actually the divinity of the soul and the existence of eternal "forms" require further investigation.[7] (Thus it is a hope of immortality, and not a certainty, that we are given in Plato—but a reasonable, a plausible hope.)[8]

What should be the true philosopher's attitude to death? "The true philosopher is ever pursuing death and dying" because he is a seeker after truth. And since the body is "a hinderer of acquirement of knowledge," because our senses merely disturb our mental vision which alone can behold the light of truth, the attainment of true knowledge is possible only when the soul is liberated from the chains of the bodily prison, which is what death is to Plato. It is because of his thirst for knowledge and truth that the philosopher has "the desire for death all his life long." [9]

It is therefore a mistake to attribute to Plato, as is so often done, the definition of philosophy as "meditation on death." As Taylor expressly points out, the Greek word Μελετη does not mean meditation but *rehearsal,*

> . . . the repeated practice by which we prepare ourselves for a performance. . . . The thought is thus that "death" is like a play for which the philosopher's life has been a daily rehearsal. His business is to be perfect in his part when the curtain goes up. . . . It is implied throughout the argument that "philosophy" has the special sense, which is clearly Pythagorean, of devotion to science as a way *to the salvation of the soul.*[10]

This rehearsing, then, is not, or is only incidentally, learning to die in the sense of the later Stoics—becoming accustomed to the necessity of having to die and thus mastering the fear of death. For Plato it is first and foremost a preparation for an existence freed from the restraint of the bodily frame.

It is obvious that such a conception of the philosopher's life as the pursuit of death, and of death as the ideal state in which alone true knowledge can be attained, is possible only when there is a firm conviction of immortality. Yet we have seen in our discussion of Plato's arguments for the immortality of the soul that he was not completely satisfied with them. Must we also conclude that Plato was shaken in his belief in immortality? If this were so it would mean that the above described vision of the philosopher's life and death must be given up. It seems, however, that Plato's scepticism refers only to the arguments and implies at the most the impossibility of finding incontrovertible proofs of immortality, but that Plato himself was convinced of it, and the arguments were mostly for the benefit of others.

But if Plato firmly believed in the immortality of the soul, on what grounds did he believe? In this connection we have to consider the assertion that he believed in the eternal Ideas and the immortality of the soul "because he was afraid to die." [11] The main argument advanced in support of this assertion refers to a purported episode in the life of Plato when as a youth he came under the influence of the philosopher Cratylus. A disciple of Heraclitus, Cratylus is said to have outdone his master not only in his greater emphasis on change (he is reported to have insisted that "you cannot step into the same river even once"), but also in the intensity of his grief over the impossibility of escaping it. There is, however, no evidence that Plato was deeply affected by the spectacle of change and death. Aristotle, who is the source of all we know about Plato's acquaintance with Cratylus, does not mention it and what he does tell seems rather to indicate the contrary. He reports that the discovery "that all sensible things are ever in a state of flux" led Plato to the conclusion that "since there is genuine science its object must be something other than flux." [12]

That fear of death was the "inspiring genius" of Plato's philosophy is also contradicted by Plato's statement (in *Theaetetus* 155 D) that "philosophy begins in wonder." Of course, "wonder" may be aroused also by the phenomenon of death. But the issue here is not whether Plato was intrigued by death or afraid of it, which, like most people, he presumably was, but whether he believed what he believed because he was afraid to die.[13]

The most telling objection against the above assertion is, however, that fear of death does not of necessity result in the belief in immortality. A great many among those who are afraid to die are nonetheless unable to embrace this consoling belief.

But if it is more than doubtful that Plato believed in eternal Ideas and the immortality of the soul because he feared death, it does not mean that death was not an important motive and motif of his philosophizing.[14] One death in particular, that of his teacher and friend Socrates, played a decisive role in determining the direction of his whole philosophical effort. That a good and wise man could have been falsely accused and condemned to die inspired his preoccupation with the problem of justice, of good government, and of education, which led to the writing of the *Republic* and the *Laws*. And Socrates' last hours, his courage and serenity in the face of death, and his discussion of the nature of death led Plato to elaborate and develop the arguments for immortality of the soul in *Phaedo* and *Phaedrus*.

Chapter 4

Aristotle (384-322 B.C.)

The "Immortality" of Reason

PLATO'S GREATEST PUPIL, Aristotle, was in many respects the very opposite of his teacher. Aristotle's standing on two feet in the world of fact, as against Plato's interest in the super-sensible world, made him seek his answer to death in the natural world and with the means of the natural endowment of man, rather than through recourse to the invisible.

In his earlier writings Aristotle was still a true disciple of Plato. His dialogue *Eudemos* not only follows Plato in theme, which is the immortality of the soul, but it also asserts the pre-existence of the soul and its migration from body to body, and as a matter of course the survival after death of the in-dividual, conscious personality. And in *Protrepticos*, which Cicero imitated in his *Hortensius*, Aristotle speaks of the body as the prison of the soul.[1]

After Aristotle developed his own philosophical system there emerged, however, a radical departure from Plato. In *De Anima* the migration of the soul from one body to another is dismissed as a *mythos*. The soul appears as the *entelechy* of the physical organism and is as closely bound to it as the power of sight is to the eye. All psychical phenomena includ-ing the effects depend on the body.[2] Man, like most other living beings, survives only in so far as he continues in his offspring:

. . . for any living thing that has reached its normal de-velopment and is unmutilated, and whose mode of genera-tion is not spontaneous, the most natural act is the production of another like itself, an animal producing an animal, a plant a plant, in order that, as far as its nature allows, it may partake in the eternal and divine. That is the

53

goal towards which all things strive, that for the sake of which they do whatsoever their nature renders possible. The phrase "for the sake of which" is ambiguous; it may mean either a) the end to achieve which, or b) the being in whose interest the act is done. Since then no living thing is able to partake in what is eternal and divine by uninterrupted continuance (for nothing perishable can for ever remain one and the same) it tries to achieve that end in the only way possible to it, and success is possible in varying degrees; *so it remains not indeed as the self-same individual but continues its existence in something like itself—not numerically but specifically one.*[3]

Aristotle is very skeptical about Plato's doctrine of Ideas. And he thinks it impossible that the soul in its entirety can survive.

Plato was not far wrong when he said that there are as many Forms as there are kinds of natural objects (if there are Forms distinct from the things of this earth). The moving causes exist as things preceding the effects, but causes in the sense of definitions are simultaneous with their effects. For when man is healthy, then health also exists; and the shape of bronze sphere exists at the same time as the bronze sphere. (But *we must examine whether any form also survives afterwards.* For in some cases there is nothing to prevent this; e.g. the soul *may be* of this sort—not all soul but the reason; for presumably it is impossible that all soul should survive.) Evidently then there is no necessity, on this ground at least, for the *existence of the Ideas.* For man is begotten by man, a given man by an individual father; and similarly in the arts; for the medical art is the formal cause of health.[4]

But Aristotle was nevertheless aware of the profound difference between animal and man. What distinguishes man from the animals is his reason (*nous*), his ability to think. Reason comes to man "from the outside," it is the divine element in man, and it alone does not perish in death.

Aristotle's views on the immortality of reason have led to prolonged and bitter disagreements about interpretation. Did he believe in personal immortality, and, if not, what did he mean by the survival of reason? The way he expressed himself is not unambiguous:

And in fact mind as we have described it is what it is by virtue of becoming all things, while there is another which it is by virtue of making all things: this is a sort of positive state like light; for in a sense light makes potential colours into actual colours. Mind in this sense of it is separable, impassible, unmixed, since it is in its essential nature activity (for always the active is superior to the passive factor, the originating force to the matter which it forms). Actual knowledge is identical with its object; in the individual, potential knowledge is in time prior to actual knowledge, but in the universe as a whole it is not prior even in time. Mind is not at one time knowing and at another not.

When mind is set free from its present conditions it appears as just what it is and nothing more; this alone is immortal and eternal (we do not, however, remember its former activity because, while mind in this sense is impassible, mind as passive is destructible), and without it nothing thinks.[5]

When Aristotle says in this key passage that at death the mind is "set free from its present conditions," one is reminded of Plato's view of the liberation of the soul from the bodily chains. But does it mean that the individual consciousness continues, or that the divine part of man is reabsorbed into its original source? Or does it mean that man attains immortality (apart from indirect survival in his offspring) only when, following his own true nature, he leads a "life of reason"?

In any event, for Aristotle, to lead such a life is not only a possibility open to man, but also his duty.

If reason is divine, then, in comparison with man, the life according to it is divine in comparison with human life.

But we must not follow those who advise us, being men to think of human things, and being mortal, of mortal things, but must, so far as we can, make ourselves immortal, and strain every nerve to live in accordance with the best thing in us; for even if it be small in bulk, much does it in power and worth surpass everything. This would seem, too, to be each man himself, since it is the authoritative and better part of him. It would be strange, then, if he were to choose not the life of his self but that of something else. And what we have said before will apply now; that which is proper to each thing is by nature best and most pleasant for each thing; for man, therefore, the life according to reason is best and pleasantest, since reason more than anything else is man. This life therefore is also the happiest.[6]

As for the fear of death, the occasions for it are infrequent, and even the most atrocious and painful death, as for instance the one described in the poem Aristotle dedicated to the memory of his friend Hermeias, cruelly put to death by Artaxerxes III, can be overcome by courage and virtue.

Plainly the things we fear are terrible things, and these are, to speak without qualification, evils, for which reason people even define fear as expectation of evil. Now we fear all evils, e.g. disgrace, poverty, disease, friendlessness, death, but the brave man is not thought to be concerned with all; for to fear some things is even right and noble, and it is base not to fear them—e.g. disgrace. . . . With what sort of terrible things, then, is the brave man concerned? Surely with the greatest; for no one is more likely than he to stand his ground against what is awe-inspiring. Now *death is the most terrible of all things;* for it is the end, and nothing is thought to be any longer either good or bad for the dead. But the brave man would not seem to be concerned even with death in *all* circumstances, e.g. at sea or in disease. In what circumstances, then? Surely in the noblest. Now such deaths are those in battle; for these take place in the greatest and noblest danger. . . . Properly, then, he will be called brave who is fearless in face of a noble death, and of all emergencies that involve death. . . .[7]

Fear may be defined as a pain or disturbance due to a mental picture of some distinctive or painful evil in the future. Of destructive or painful evils only, for there are some evils, e.g. wickedness or stupidity, the prospect of which does not frighten us: I mean only such as amount to great pains or losses. And even these only if they appear not remote but so near as to be imminent: we do not fear things that are a very long way off: for instance we all know we shall die, but we are not troubled thereby, because death is not close at hand. . . .[8]

Professional soldiers turn cowards, however, when danger puts too great a strain on them . . . while citizen forces die at their posts. . . . For to the latter flight is disgraceful and death is preferable to safety on those terms. . . .[9]

What did Aristotle oppose to death, this "most terrible of all things," except courage? It was his amazement before the wonders of the universe. His insatiable curiosity drove him to study heavenly bodies, minerals, plants, animals, and man. He gathered, ordered, and classified facts and information from all over the globe, and what sustained him in this enormous task was the over-all view of the totality of things: the world is not only eternal and indestructible, but there is plan and purpose in it, as evidenced especially by the purposeful arrangement of the living organisms. "God and Nature do nothing without a plan." [10] And although there is no providence that cares for the well-being of each single individual being, and man's personality does not survive death, Aristotle felt very strongly that human existence is meaningful and important in this cosmic plan. Death may be evil, but not yet absurd.

Chapter 5

Death Is Nothing to Us

IT IS OBVIOUS not only that Aristotle's philosophical faith was
beyond the intellectual grasp of most men of his day, but also
that it must not appear to be an altogether satisfying answer
to those who feel intensely the shock of having to die. And
most men do not have, or do not believe they possess, the
courage he was talking about. Moreover, the spectre of Hades
was apparently still very much a reality for most people.

Another philosophical system, evolved partly to meet this
situation and to facilitate the coming to terms with death,
is characterized not only by its endeavor to achieve this objective without challenging the view of the nature of death as
it is given us in sense-experience, but also precisely by emphasizing the mortality of the soul and its total annihilation
in death.

For Epicurus, knowledge is not an end in itself, as it was
for Democritus, but a "remedy for the soul." He calls the
résumé of his Fundamental Doctrines (*kyriai doxai*) the *Four
Remedies,* which are: "We need not fear God. Death means
absence of sensation. The Good is easy to obtain. Evil is easy
to bear." [1] And he says that "vain is the word of a philosopher
which does not heal any suffering of man." [2]

Philosophically speaking, Epicureanism, together with
Stoicism, represents a reaction to the dualism of Plato. But
it is also a reaction to certain aspects of popular religion, and
in a narrower sense, it is clearly a reaction to the apparently
unavoidable side effect of every doctrine that denies the
finality of death: the fear of the hereafter. How great and
widespread this fear must have been can be judged from the
success of Epicurus' argument that the soul dissolves after
death. And his disciple Lucretius exalts Epicurus as "the glory

58

of the Greek race" and as a benefactor of mankind for having "cleansed men's breasts with truth-telling precepts and fixed a limit to lust and fear," so that the "dread of Acheron . . . [is] driven headlong forth, troubling as it does the life of man from its innermost depths and overspreading all things with the blackness of death, allowing no pleasure to be pure and unalloyed." [3]

Epicurus takes over the materialism of Democritus. This materialism is, however, a *Hylozoism*, that is, it holds that matter contains somehow the seeds of life. For Epicurus, as for Democritus, the world is composed of indivisible, eternal atoms, differing in size, weight and shape. And special round, fiery atoms located in the chest make up the soul. The important thing is, that it is the product of an accidental encounter of atoms, and that it is formed with the body and perishes with it. What obviously attracted Epicurus in this doctrine was the perishability of the soul along with the body, since it makes all the apprehensions of the soul's post-mortem tribulations and sufferings groundless.

But while the soul exists it is afflicted by a sickness which is caused by religious beliefs and consists of the fear of the gods and of the hereafter. Gods exist, but they are not what the masses think they are. Their idea of the gods arose out of fright before awesome natural phenomena, which they explain as manifestations of the divine wrath; and their image of the beyond, where evildoers are punished, grew out of man's bad conscience. For Epicurus the gods possess entirely different attributes from those usually ascribed to them. They lead a blissful existence in the interplanetary spaces, but they do not care about the world of man, since this world disturbs their bliss. Thus Epicurus' view, according to which gods are virtually in retirement, amounts to practical atheism, in spite of his vehement denial of this imputation.

The world from which gods are thus absent is ruled by chance. Man has no hope of improving the world, and must resign himself to making, by his own efforts, the best of his own existence. For although he is, like the animals, subject to the forces of nature, he possesses relative freedom of action, and for him "there is no compulsion to live under compulsion." [4] He can achieve peace of mind and extract from life the maximum of pleasure. But there is no contradiction between Epicurus' insistence, on the one hand, that pleasure is the goal of life and, on the other, that the ideal of the sage is the attainment of a worry-free state, of *ataraxía*, which one can reach through suppression of desires and conquest of fears. For *ataraxía* is not an end in itself and is valuable only as a means of attaining pleasure.

It is this emphasis on pleasure that caused Epicurus' ethics to be misunderstood. He anticipated this, however, and was careful to stress that "when, therefore, we maintain that pleasure is the end, we do not mean the pleasures of profligates and those that consist in sensuality, as is supposed by some who are either ignorant or disagree with us or do not understand, but freedom from pain in the body and from trouble in the mind." [5] The famous "eat, drink, and be merry, for tomorrow we die" (*edite, bibite post mortem nulla voluptas*) is a pseudo-epicurean slogan of a popular misinterpretation of Epicurus' teachings.

For Epicurus the main obstacle to peace of mind is the fear of death. But it can be eliminated, for it is totally unfounded:

Become accustomed to the belief that death is nothing to us. For all good and evil consists in sensation, but death is deprivation of sensation. And therefore a right understanding that death is nothing to us makes the mortality of life enjoyable, not because it adds to it an infinite span of time, but because it takes away the craving for immortality. For there is nothing terrible in not living, so that the man speaks idly who says that he fears death not because it will be painful when it comes, but because it is painful in anticipation. For that which gives no trouble when it comes, is but an empty pain in anticipation. So death, the most terrifying of all ills, is nothing to us, since so long as we exist death is not with us, but when death comes, then we do not exist. It does not then concern either the living, or the dead, since the former it is not, and the latter are no more. [6]

This is the famous Epicurean argument against the fear of death.

While trying to alleviate the fear of death, Epicurus opposes also those who deprecate life and assert that not to be born is the highest good. For Epicurus life can be good, if only man will learn how to live and how to die.

> I have anticipated thee, Fortune, and entrenched myself against all thy secret attacks. And we will not give ourselves up as captives to thee or to any other circumstances; but when it is time for us to go, spitting contempt on life and on those who here vainly cling to it, we will leave life crying aloud in a glorious triumph song that we have lived well.[7]

It is in Lucretius Carus (96-55 B.C.), Epicurus' outstanding disciple, who elaborated in detail Epicureanism's answer to death, that the inadequacy of the Epicurean argument against the fear of death becomes manifest. In Book III of *De Rerum Natura,* he advances a series of arguments for the mortality of the soul and comes to the conclusion that "death is nothing to us, concerns us not a jot . . . since the nature of the mind is proved to be mortal." [8] He tries to dispel the apprehension even of those who believe in the existence of an independent soul that survives death.

> And even supposing the nature of the mind and the power of the soul to feel, after they have severed from our body, who by the binding tie of marriage between body and soul are formed each into a single being, yet that is nothing to us. And if time should gather up our matter after our death and put it *once more into the position in which it now is,* and the light of life be given to us again, this result even would concern us not at all, when the chain of our self-consciousness has once been snapped asunder.

Hence he makes much moan that he has been born mortal, and sees not that after real death there will be no other self to remain in life and lament to self that his own self has met death, and there to stand and grieve that his own self there lying is mangled or burnt.[9]

However, the Epicurean argument as a remedy for the fear of death has limitations, for it applies only to *one* aspect of this fear, namely, the fear of what happens after death. There are, however, at least two other aspects of this fear. Of the fear of the process of dying Lucretius says that it is unfounded because death comes swiftly and painlessly—it is "quickcoming death." On the most important aspect of this fear, however, the reluctance to cease living, his argument is totally unconvincing. When men complain that "short is this enjoyment for poor weak men; presently it will have been and never after may it be called back," Lucretius retorts that they act "as if after their death it is to be one of their chiefest afflictions . . . that craving for anything will best them."[10]

This argument obviously avoids the main issue, since to most people it is precisely the fact that "we do not exist when death comes" that is the first object of fear. Epicurus glances over this,[11] taking for granted that no one really minds not existing, and treats the whole matter as if it were simply like not being home when an unwelcome visitor arrives.[12]

Lucretius must have become aware that fear of death arises mostly from the fact that "man's mind is mortal," and that this fear had not been adequately countered by him. For we find him suddenly abandoning his ironic scorn of those who fear the void and nothingness of death, and taking up the argument of the emptiness and monotony of life. In order to make death acceptable he uses—and in this he differs from Epicurus—the device of deprecating life.

> Moreover we are ever engaged, ever involved in the same pursuits, and no new pleasure is struck out by living on; but whilst what we crave is wanting, it seems to transcend all the rest; then, when it has been gotten, we crave something else, and ever does the same thirst of life possess us, as we gape open-mouthed. . . ."[13]

To this argument Lucretius adds still another: "Quite doubtful it is what fortune the future will carry with it or what chance will bring us or what end is at hand"—as if man would give up living out of fear of future miseries; or console himself about having to die *now* because it is doubtful "what end is at hand," as if that end could be anything but death, quick and painless.

It is only because life is painful and full of suffering that the sleep of death is so consoling to Lucretius.

> For thou shalt sleep, and never wake again,
> And quitting life, shalt *quit thy living pain* . . .
> The worst that can befall thee, measured right,
> Is a sound slumber, and a long good-night . . .
> One being, worn, another being makes;
> Changed, but not lost; for nature gives and takes:
> New matter must be found for things to come,
> And these must waste like those, and follow nature's doom.
> All things, like thee, have time to rise and rot,
> And from each other's ruin are begot:
> For life is not confined to him or thee;
> 'Tis given to all for use, to none for property . . .
> But all is there serene in that eternal sleep.
> For all *the dismal tales, that poets tell,*
> *Are verified on earth,* and not in hell.[14]

Chapter 6

Stoicism, Greek and Roman

The Older Stoa

STOICISM, the other great philosophical system of antiquity, is much more elaborate than Epicureanism. And although both arose at the same time, the scope of problems with which Stoicism concerned itself originally was much broader than that of Epicureanism.

With the destruction of the old city-states and the formation of an Empire by Alexander the Great, two sets of problems became acute. On the one hand, a vision of "one world" in which the differences of origin and custom could be brought under one denominator became imperative; here the comprehensive frame of reference was found, following the Sophists, who opposed convention and emphasized human nature. On the other hand, the individual, deprived of the emotional security and self-evident meaningfulness of existence in and for the sake of the city-state and confronted with a wide and strange world, was not only in need of support and guidance on how to live in it; he also became conscious of being an isolated individual, and this new awareness of his individuality of necessity brought into a sharper focus the old problem of death. Whereas the Epicureans concentrated on the individual himself and tried to cope with the new situation by building up self-reliance and inner strength, to control fears and anxieties from within (whether it is because of this that they preferred an image of the world as a mere concatenation of atoms indifferent to man, or whether they thought such an image to be correct, is a moot question), the Stoics, although equally mindful of building up the individual's resistance to the vicissitudes of the outside world—their ideal of *apátheia* was even more extreme than the Epicurean *ataraxía*—sought to root man in Nature. And their universe, of which man was an integral part, was as well-ordered as the Epicurean world was chaotic.

The older Stoics followed Heraclitus' view of the creative Fire as the material as well as the spiritual principle. According to them, the world is not at the mercy of chance, but obeys universal laws; and *pronoia,* the divine providence, rules there supreme. Periodically the universe returns through cosmic conflagration (*ekpyrósis*) to its original state and is reabsorbed again into the divine fire. Then the process of formation of the world and everything that occurs in it repeats itself.[1] God is immanent in the world, and in this pantheism we have a middle position between the anthropomorphism of popular religion and epicurean atheism.

The human soul is "of corporeal nature, and arises together with the body, but its matter is the purest and noblest." [2] It is a particle of the divine breath and is not completely perishable; it merely becomes reabsorbed into the divine spirit from which it issued, at the end of the world.[3] Thus the Stoics, in radical opposition to the Epicureans who separated man from the gods, bring him into direct connection with the divine principle.

Man has to live and act "according to Nature." Death belongs to the cosmic order of things as much as birth does. And, inasmuch as it is a universal law applicable to all living beings, it too is "according to nature," and therefore it is just and there is no ground for complaint and protest. Nature, or *physis,* means, however, more than what we understand today by this term, and life "according to nature" is therefore much more than the simple life or that of naturist cults. Reason is a natural endowment of man, and living according to nature implies the full use of reason, and means living by its lights. And it is reason that not only shows us the inflated worth of many things commonly valued, but enables us to gain mastery over our passions. Zeno, the founder of the school (335-265 B.C.) agrees with Epicurus that control of emotions is the only way of achieving the good life; but he goes further in stipulating as his ideal not merely peace of mind, but complete impassibility, total imperviousness to harassment—a kind of apathy. It appears, then, that the Stoics should have been in a much better position to deal with the problems confronting man than the Epicureans. Thus the problem of the fear of death, which gradually came to occupy as prominent a place in the reflection of the Stoics as it did in that of Epicurus and Lucretius, could be—in principle—attacked from two directions: psychologically, by building up indifference; and metaphysically, through a pantheistic world view, the hope of a benevolent providence, and possibly even (at least as long as it was held) through the doctrine of eternal recurrence.

However, because the ideal of complete impassibility has been from the start a superhuman and unattainable goal, and because death became more and more the central problem of Stoicism, we find considerable changes in this philosophy throughout the five hundred years of its history. The views of each of the great exponents of late (or Roman) Stoicism —Seneca, Epictetus, and Marcus Aurelius—differ not only from each other but from the original Stoic doctrine as well.

Nevertheless, there is a strong common bond between all of them, namely their conception of philosophy as an art of right living and of dying well. And as Benz points out, for all of them death deserves attention less as a phenomenon than as an act; [4] it becomes the central problem of the Stoic ethics because it is the one manifestation of life the attitude to which serves as a decisive measure of the philosopher's moral stature.

Seneca

Seneca (4 B.C.-A.D. 65), the tutor of Nero and one of the most influential Romans of his day, states in one of his famous letters to his friend Lucilius the questions that preoccupy him:

> May I not inquire into the beginnings of all things, who shaped them, who sorted out matter that was heaped in an indiscriminate mass? May I not ask who the artificer of this universe is? . . . Should I be ignorant of the region whence I descended? Am I to see all this once, or undergo repeated births? Where am I to go from the bondage of humanity? [5]

But philosophy, which Seneca expects to provide the answers to these questions, can also teach us how to die. He recommends the study of the great thinkers because "none of these will force you to die, but all will teach you how." [6] In the famous dialogue, *The Shortness of Life,* he acknowledges that it is a general complaint among mankind that

> . . . our allotted span is brief, and the term granted us flies by with such dizzy speed that all but few exhaust it just when they are beginning to live. And it is not only the unthinking masses who bemoan what they consider the universal evil: the same sentiment has evoked complaints even from men of distinction. . . . Hence Aristotle's grievance against Nature—an incongruous position for a philosopher: Nature has been so lavish to animals that they vegetate for five or ten human spans, whereas man, with his capacity for numerous and great achievements, is limited by so much shorter a tether." [7]

Seneca argues that such complaints are unjustified, for the true length of life cannot be measured in years. If it appears short it does so only because "we make it so; we are not ill provided but use what we have wastefully." People waste their lives in many ways, they spend it on "groundless regrets, foolish gladness, greedy desire, polite society." And then they realize that their death will be premature. Life appears short because people live as if they would live forever and "the thought of human frailty never enters their heads. They all say that they are going to retire and relax sometime." But "what stupid obliviousness to mortality to postpone counsels of sanity to the fifties and sixties, with the intention of beginning life at an age few have reached." [8]

It is for the preoccupied man that life is shortest of all. Seneca means not only those who are "always preoccupied with work so that they may be in position to live better; they spend life in making provision for life"; he means also those who are preoccupied "even in their leisure," of those whose life is in reality "a busy idleness"—the art-collectors, the sports-enthusiasts, the dandies, who "pass many hours at the barber's," and those who are preoccupied "with composing, hearing and learning songs." Finally, "among the worst offenders I count those who give all their time to drink and lust." He concludes that "The only people really at leisure are those who take time for philosophy. They alone really live. . . . Unless we prove ingrate, it was for us that the illustrious founders of divine schools of thought came into being, for us they prepared a way of life. . . ." Seneca goes on to say that only those who make "Zeno and Pythagoras and Democritus . . . their daily familiars, who cultivate Aristotle and Theophrastus can properly be said to be engaged in the duties of life." Not only will felicity and fair old age await such a person but he "will have friends with whom he can deliberate on matters great and small, whom he may consult about his problems every day. . . ." But even more, communion with philosophers "will open the path to eternity," and "will raise you to a height from which none can be cast down. This is the sole means of prolonging your mortality, rather of transforming it into immortality. Honors, monuments . . . will speedily sink to ruin; there is nothing that the lapse of time does not dilapidate and exterminate. But the dedications of philosophy are impregnable; age cannot erase their memory or diminish their force."

Such is the way of life Seneca acknowledges as the only one able to neutralize the saddening thought of death.[9]

Philosophy shows that man's life and even his personality are "temporary holdings" and that he must live "as if he were on loan to himself, and is ready to return the whole sum cheerfully on demand." [10]

But very obviously this is not sufficient to overcome the fear of death. Although "the good life (which is the gift of philosophy) is a handsomer gift than mere life," and "life is not to be bought at all costs," the thought of death pursues Seneca.[11] He wants to learn how to die without fear and regret and how to prevent the thought of mortality from poisoning his days, and he is aware that this art is not easily mastered.

It is something great and one has to learn it for a long time to be able to depart with equanimity, when the inevitable hour strikes. <u>Who does not have the will to die</u>, <u>does not have the will to live</u>; for, <u>life has been given to us only under the condition of death.</u> It moves toward death. Therefore it is folly to be afraid of it.[12]

<u>Seneca</u>'s famous recipe to <u>avoid fear of death</u> is "<u>One must think of it constantly.</u>" [13] But although he reiterates what amounts to the Socratic position in the *Apology*—"Death is either end or transition. I do not fear ceasing to be, for it is the same as not having begun to be; nor am I afraid of transition, for no alternative state can be so limiting" [14]—he wants to believe in immortality of the soul. He realizes that "the great authorities . . . promised rather than proved so great a boon." But he does not want to abandon what he calls "his charming dream." [15] He departs from the Stoic tradition and follows Plato. He speaks of the <u>soul</u> being "<u>imprisoned in</u> this dark and gloomy domicile" that is the <u>body</u>.[16] His main argument for its <u>immortality</u> is the <u>greatness of the human mind</u>: (A great and noble thing is the human mind) . . . Its fatherland is all the arch that encompasses the height and the sweep of the firmament, this whole dome within which lie sea and land, within which the ether separates human and divine and also joins them to one another. . . ." Neither will the mind tolerate a restricted time span: "All centuries are mine," it says: "no era is closed to great intellects, no epoch impassable to thought. When the day comes which will separate this mixture of human and divine I will <u>leave the body here</u> where I found it and <u>betake myself to the gods.</u>" [17] This <u>earthly existence</u> is but a <u>preparation of another.</u> "Just as the mother's womb holds us for ten [sic!] months not in preparation for itself but for the region to which we seem to be discharged when we are capable of drawing breath and surviving in the open, so in the span extending from infancy to old age we are ripening for another birth. Another beginning awaits us, another status." [18] "The <u>day which you dread as the end is your birth into eternity.</u>"

Seneca answers the rejoinder that in that case there is no

reason to delay "the departure" by pointing out that it is natural to resist change: "At your other birth, too, it required a great effort of your mother to thrust you forth. You weep and wail; weeping, too, is incidental to birth." [19]

And returning to the fear of death, he argues that at birth into the earthly existence it was pardonable to weep "for you came without knowledge or experience." But when the time comes for the "new birth," we should "look to it unfalteringly," for this "decisive hour is the body's last, but not the soul's."

This conviction not only facilitates dying but assures freedom in life. "Thinking at this level allows nothing sordid to find lodgment in the soul, nothing base, nothing cruel. . . . And the man who has conceived eternity in his mind cringes from no army, is alarmed by no trumpet blast, is intimidated by no threats. How can man not be free of fear if he hopes for death?"

Seneca, and this has been repeatedly stressed by his critics as early as his own time, did not live by his own preachings of a simple life dedicated exclusively to philosophy. But he died by them. When, after a career of great brilliance as a virtual co-ruler of the Roman Empire, he was suspected of participating in a political conspiracy and was ordered by Nero to commit suicide, he unhesitatingly did so.[20] His last moments are not less impressive than those of Socrates. Tacitus tells us in his *Annals* (15.62) that Seneca asked for writing material in order to make his will. When his request was turned down by Nero's messenger, he turned to his friends and reminded them of the "philosophical precepts" that they studied together in order to be prepared for precisely such an event. And when his wife expressed the wish to die with him, he tried to dissuade her, but finally consented that she join him "in the glory of death." And they simultaneously slashed their wrists.

Seneca was pessimistic about man's moral nature: "We must admit, we are evil, were evil, and I hate to admit, will remain evil." It is on this point especially that he differs from the other great representative of later Stoicism, Epictetus.

Epictetus and Marcus Aurelius

Epictetus (A.D. 60-117) argued that there was no evil in the universe: "As a mark is not set up to miss it, there is nothing intrinsically evil in the world." [21] "Bring whatever you please, and I will turn it into Good. Bring sickness, death, want, reproach, trial for life. All these, by the rod of Hermes, shall turn to advantage. What will you make of death? Why, what but an ornament to you; what but a means of your showing, by action, what that man is who follows the will of Nature?" [22]

Virtue is defined by him as "living according to nature," which means that man must accept everything that takes place as good or "indifferent" and he lays great stress on *kartería* —endurance. "All things serve and obey [the laws of] the Universe: our body likewise obeys the same, in being sick and well, young and old, and passing through the other changes decreed. It is therefore reasonable that what depends on ourselves, that is our own understanding, should not be the only rebel. For the universe is powerful and superior, and consults the best for us by governing us in conjunction with the whole. And further, opposition, besides that it is unreasonable, and produces nothing except a vain struggle, throws us into pain and sorrow." [23]

Epictetus reduces the demand for apathy to one for peace of mind and internal calm. These can be attained through proper use of impressions, which involves keen discrimination between the things in our power and those not in our power. This is the task of philosophy, which is worth nothing if it is merely theoretical speculation without reference or applicability to the business of living.

Death is nothing terrible, "else it would have appeared so to Socrates. But the terror consists in our notion of death, that it is terrible. It is not death or pain which is a fearful thing, but the fear of pain or death." [24]

"I ask you, where am I to escape death? Point me to the place, point me to the people among whom I am to go, on whom it does not light, point me to the charm against it. If

I have none, what would you have me do? I cannot escape
death: am I not to escape the fear of it? Am I to die in fear
and trembling?" [25]

One has to think of life as a thing given us by God on loan,
for temporary use only. It is similar to a banquet at which
one takes one's modest place. When death approaches, we
have to resign ourselves to our fate and play to the end the
role God assigned to us, as best we can. We have to leave the
feast of life quietly and gracefully, giving our thanks to God
for having invited us to participate in it and to admire his
works.

Epictetus' philosophy is one of resignation and quiet hero-
ism. It is not a philosophy of despair, because he loved life
and men, and possibly also because he too departed from the
original Stoic world view. He speaks of God in a manner that
goes far beyond a purely pantheistic position; and, although
he does not say what the destiny of the soul will be after
death, he speaks of its desire to return to a better existence
with God in a way that makes it appear as if he expects to
find this wish fulfilled. It is significant that Marcus Aurelius
quotes him as being fond of speaking of man "as a little soul
bearing about a corpse." [26]

In Marcus Aurelius (A.D. 121-180) we find this trend away
from the materialism of the Stoics even more pronounced.
Already Seneca saw the body and the soul as opposed to each
other, and distinguished in the soul a *pars rationalis* and a
pars irrationalis. And Epictetus considered the soul the carrier
of the divine *logos*. Aurelius rediscovers the *nous,* the pure
spirituality, which alone is capable of true knowledge and is
completely emancipated from the body: "Whatever this is
that I am, it is a little flesh and breath, and the ruling part.
. . . " [27] And again: "The things are three of which thou
art composed, a little body, a little breath [life], intelligence.
Of these the first two are thine, so far as it is thy duty to take
care of them; but the third alone is properly thine. . . ." [28]

But Marcus Aurelius, who follows Aristotle in this, does
not go so far as to believe in the immortality of even this
intelligent part of the soul. And one wonders whether his
obsession with the transitoriness of all things would allow such

a belief to take hold or to be of real assistance in checking his constant preoccupation with mortality.

Perhaps no ancient philosopher is as painfully conscious of perishability and transitoriness as the Emperor-philosopher. Death darkens his entire world outlook and extends beyond individual destiny to the destiny of mankind. For him, the supreme law of history is the transitoriness of earthly greatness. He constantly refers to the downfall of great rulers and empires. And death is not only, as it was with the other Stoics, the center of philosophical reflection as an event against which the moral greatness of a life is measured; it becomes the test of every single act and event.

His *Meditations* are meditations on death and almost nothing else. The contemplation of human activity becomes for him the revelation of transitoriness and death, a constant demonstration of dissolution and decay. To see life *sub specie mortis* was not only the essence of his philosophy, but of his daily life:

> When we have meat before us and such eatables, we receive the impression, that this is the dead body of a fish, and this is the dead body of a bird or of a pig. . . . Just in the same way ought we to act all through life, and where there are things which appear most worthy of our approbation, we ought to lay them bare and look at their worthlessness and strip them of all the words by which they are exalted.[29]

It is the transitoriness of life that makes it utterly worthless: "Of human life the time is a point, and the substance is in a flux, and the perception dull, and the composition of the whole body subject to putrefaction, and the soul a whirl, and fortune hard to divine, and fame a thing devoid of judgement. And, to say all in a word, everything that belongs to the body is a stream and what belongs to the soul is a dream and vapour, and life is a warfare and a stranger's sojourn, and after fame is oblivion."[30]

Like Lucretius, he stresses the boredom of existing. "As it happens to thee in the amphitheater and such places, that the continual sight of the same things and the uniformity make the spectacle wearisome, so it is in the whole of life; for all the things above, below, are the same and from the same. How long then?" [31]

The thought of death has a moralizing effect: "And thou wilt give thyself relief, if thou doest every act of thy life as if it were the last, laying aside all carelessness and passionate aversion from the commands of reason, and all hypocrisy and self-love and discontent. . . ." [32]

"Since it is possible that thou mayest depart from life this very moment, regulate every act and thought accordingly. But to go away from among men, if there are gods, is not a thing to be afraid of. . . ." [33]

But his exhortation against the fear of this possibility does not sound very convincing.

He tries to argue himself out of the horror of death that grips him:

What dost thou wish? To continue to exist? Well, dost thou wish to have sensations? movement? growth? and then again to cease to grow? to use thy speech? to think? What is there of all these things which seems to thee worth desiring? But if it is easy to set little value on all these things, turn to that which remains, which is to follow reason and God. But it is inconsistent with honoring reason and God to be troubled because by death a man will be deprived of the other things.[34]

How small a part of the boundless and unfathomable time is assigned to every man? . . . Reflecting on all this consider nothing to be great, except to act as thy nature leads thee, and to endure that which common nature brings."

Everything else, whether it is in the power of thy will or not, is only lifeless ashes and smoke.

This reflection is most adapted to move us to contempt of death.[35]

Yet, even though man may realize his insignificance, the thought of mortality is difficult to bear. And few men have felt this aspect of the human condition as acutely as Marcus Aurelius. It is to what he calls "philosophy" that he takes refuge in his distress:

What, then, is that which is able to conduct a man? One thing and only one—Philosophy. But this consists in keeping the daemon within a man free from violence and unharmed, superior to pains and pleasure . . . accepting all that happens and all that is allotted, as coming from thence, wherever it is, from whence he himself came; and finally, waiting for death with a cheerful mind, as being nothing else than a dissolution of the elements of which every living being is compounded. But if there is no harm to the elements themselves in each continually changing into another, why should a man have any apprehension about the change and dissolution of all the elements? For it is according to nature, and nothing is evil which is according to nature.[36]

Philosophy, then, for Marcus Aurelius is not the quest for knowledge but the ability to look at life and death philosophically. In his conclusion Marcus Aurelius reiterates the necessity of accepting man's fate as a mortal being:

Man, thou hast been a citizen in this great state the world: what difference does it make to thee whether for five years or three? For that which is conformable to the laws is just for all. Where is the hardship then if no tyrant nor yet an unjust judge sends thee away from the state, but nature who brought thee into it? The same as if a praetor who has employed an actor dismisses him from the stage. "But I have not finished the five acts, but only three of them." Thou sayest well, but in life the three acts are the whole drama; for what shall be a complete drama is determined by him who was once the cause of its composition, and now of its dissolution; but thou art the cause of neither. Depart then satisfied, for he also who releases thee is satisfied.[37]

But was he, the great emperor and tragic human being, really satisfied? Is philosophy really effective in the face of such profound, such desperate disillusionment with life and such maddening fear of death? St. Augustine, who was, for a short time, in a similar state of mind ("there was in me a great weariness with life and at the same time fear of dying" [38]), needed a stronger refuge than intelligence alone could provide. Such an answer to death was offered in the new religion of the Christ who died and was resurrected.

Before we turn to the Christian answer to death, we must mention the revival and clarification of Platonism by the last great thinker of antiquity—Plotinus (A.D. 204-270). His great influence on Christian thought is of less concern for the present survey than the way in which he was able to surmount—or rather sweep aside—the inconsistencies of Plato's doctrine of the immortality of the soul. It is based on the "mystical" experience of "ecstasy," in which Plotinus is aware of the soul's independence from the bodily frame it inhabits. "Many times this happened: lifted out of the body into myself; becoming external to all other things and self-centered; beholding a marvelous beauty, then, more than ever, assured of community with loftiest order . . . ." [39]

The problem is, how did the soul ever enter the body, and in what manner should their relationship be conceived? Is the soul in the body in the same way as a pilot is in a ship? Or in the same way as art is in the instrument of art? Or in the same manner as light is with the air? But "this when present is (in reality) not present. And being present through the whole, is mingled with no part of it. Hence, here also, it may be rightly said, that air is in light, rather than light in air. . . . He who knows will know what I say, and will be convinced that the soul has then another life. . . ."

The soul will desire to participate in divinity and "hence it is necessary to hasten our departure from hence, and to be indignant that we are bound in one part of our nature. . . ."

If we can trust his disciple and biographer, Porphyry, Plotinus was ashamed to be in the body. And he refused to sit for a sculptor, saying that it was enough to have to bear the image into which nature had wrapped him, without consenting to perpetuate the image of an image.

His last words were in keeping with his philosophy and his attitude to earthly existence and death: "I am making my last effort to return that which is divine in me to that which is divine in the universe."

BOOK II

THE CHRISTIAN ANSWER
TO DEATH

THE MANNER of Socrates' death inspired the Platonic, as well as the Stoic, answer to death. Meanwhile, more than a hundred years before Marcus Aurelius sought consolation in a philosophical attitude to mortality, another death occurred that served as the point of departure for a great new religion. As the result of the victorious march of Christianity, which—in part at least—succeeded because of its answer to death, the Christian solution supplanted all others in the western world and enjoyed a virtual monopoly for a period of almost a thousand years. It is still one that finds wide acceptance in the Occident; and many philosophers, even though not able or willing to accept it on philosophical grounds or under normal circumstances, take refuge in it when the thought of death overwhelms them or when death appears close at hand. Before we turn to this answer, we must briefly consider the conception of death in the Old Testament.

Chapter 7

Death in the Old Testament

IT WOULD BE VAIN to seek in the Old Testament comfort and consolation for the fact of death in terms of belief in immortality. Not that Israel was oblivious of death; on the contrary, one could even say that death occupied an important place in the thoughts of the ancient Hebrews. It is significant that at the very beginning of the Old Testament we find a theory of the origin of death. And, as we shall see, it was the difficulty many felt in becoming reconciled to death that precipitated a heretic trend in Judaism, which found its expression in the Jewish Gnosis.

Renan points to the passage in Daniel 12:2, "and many of them that sleep in the dust of the earth shall awake, some to everlasting life, and some to shame and everlasting contempt," in order to prove that the idea of immortality and resurrection was not alien to the Jews. Some refer also to Isaiah 26:19, "Thy dead men shall live, together with my dead body shall they arise." And finally some writers cite Job 19:25-26.[1] But these passages are out of tune with the dominant view, of which Ecclesiastes is much more representative: "Go thy way, eat thy bread with joy, and drink thy wine with a merry heart; for God now accepteth thy works. . . . Whatsoever thy hand findeth to do, do it with thy might; for there is no work, nor device, nor knowledge, nor wisdom, in the grave whither thou goest." [2]

The world is good, there is no doubt about it: "God saw every thing that he had made, and, behold, it was very good." Therefore, the rabbis argued, if God praises His creation, who can blame it? And evil—including the greatest evil, death—came into the world through the fault of man. He was created to live and not die. God imparted to man the divine spark of life and destined him to live on the earth He had prepared for him. He even warned man what not to do in order not to fall prey to death: "But of the tree of knowledge of good and evil, thou shalt not eat of it."

There was, however, another tree in the Garden of Eden besides the tree of knowledge—the tree of life—and no divine prohibition was connected with it. It plays no part in the story of the fall itself, but because it is there, and because he could regain immortality by eating its fruit, man was driven from the Garden of Eden. Frazer suggests an ingenious hypothesis to explain why there was such a tree at all, in addition to the tree of knowledge. In the original story intended to explain man's mortality, man appears to be created neither mortal nor immortal, but as having been given the choice between the fruits of either tree. Misled by the serpent, he chose the tree of knowledge, which is actually the tree of death.[3] What is remarkable in the biblical account of the origin of death is that, since death came to man through his own fault, the protest against it as an injustice on the part of the Creator is thereby effectively forestalled.

Once death appeared, the only thing God could do for man was to prolong his life, as a reward for obedience to His law. But this is as far as it can go. There is no escape from death, and there is no other life. It is in his children that man can find a pale semblance of immortality. For even the sojourn in *Sheol,* the kingdom of shadows, which was part of the popular beliefs, is but a poor substitute for the existence on earth.

But even before the Christian era, however, not only the belief in the immortality of the soul but also the belief in the resurrection of the dead at the end of time became a fundamental doctrine of the Pharisees. As far as resurrection is concerned, a person was regarded by them as a heretic, forfeiting his share in the world to come, not merely if he denied this doctrine, but even if, believing it, he denied that the Torah was the authority for the belief. It was one of the important differences between the Pharisees and the Sadducees, the latter denying it.

Even transmigration found its way into Judaism, although it was generally attacked by Jewish philosophers. It appears in the *Cabala;* it is found systematized in the *Zohar;* on the whole, however, beliefs in the hereafter never became dogmas in

Judaism. This subject belongs to those "hidden" matters on which it is better not to speculate.

It was faith in the unique and all-powerful Creator that brought solace in the face of death. We cannot even begin to fathom the intensity of this faith and the complete reliance on the will of God and the absolute surrender to Him. Herbert J. Muller remarks: "The authors of the Old Testament had no philosophy, they had a simple, absolute faith, that the Lord *was,* that the whole universe testified to Him, and that all this was *self-evident*. They did not have to find Him through introspection or mystical experience; they did not have to formulate a creed or rationalize their faith. If, like Job, they were troubled by Yahwe's behavior, they never dreamed of questioning His existence or His majesty. The logic of their faith was simply that Yahwe had declared himself to Abraham, to Jacob, and most completely to Moses." [4] That is why, in mortal peril, the Jew does not ask anything, he just repeats his confession of faith and trust: God is One, God is our God. God's ways are obscure to the poor creature, man, but he can have complete confidence in Him. "He hath shewed thee, O man, what *is* good; and what does the Lord require of thee, but to do justly, and to love mercy, and to walk humbly with thy God?" [5] This means unlimited trust. It means the unquestioned acceptance of God's will: "The Lord gave, and the Lord hath taken away; blessed be the name of the Lord." [6] Out of this burning faith, the conviction begins to emerge that everything is possible for God, and that, in the words of the prophet Isaiah, through His benevolence and charity and pity, "He will swallow up death in victory; and the Lord God will wipe away tears from off all faces. . . ." [7]

Chapter 8

Death in the New Testament

THE NEW TESTAMENT proclaims the victory over death. The essence of the answer to the problem of death in the New Testament is that death is the last and greatest enemy, but that this enemy is already conquered. The Christian doctrine teaches the resurrection of the dead on the Last Day of Judgment. The graves will be opened, saint and sinner will stand before the Son of God and be judged. It is the resurrection of the body, and not the immortality of the soul; this latter is not Christian, but pagan.[1]

Acts 17:32 tell us that when St. Paul was preaching in Athens, his audience listened with interest. But when he mentioned the "resurrection of the dead" (or, more literally, "the uprising of the corpses"), some mocked. "They were familiar with the doctrine of the immortality of the soul, but when this eloquent Asiatic tent-maker began to explain that the dead bodies would get up and walk, they could not take him seriously." [2] And when St. Paul appeared before King Agrippa, and the Roman Resident Festus heard him speak of resurrection, he could not hold back his indignation: "Paul, thou art beside thyself: much learning doth make thee mad." [3]

Why did St. Paul speak as he did? In Gilbert Murray's opinion it was because the physical resurrection of the body was the only form in which the doctrine of immortality could be grasped by the very ignorant populations of the villages and big manufacturing towns of Asia Minor.[4]

But is it not more realistic to assume that the doctrine of the resurrection was propounded by St. Paul because he believed it to be true, and because it is a more satisfying one? Here at last man was promised the fulfillment of the next best choice after the impossible dream of deathlessness, for he would become deathless once he passed through the gates of death. And not only his soul would live on, but also his body. Here were indeed "glad tydings." What tremendous impression this message must have made can be realized when we consider that preoccupation with death and fear of it were at their peak. It was a time when in Rome the commerce in pills of immortality was thriving, and mystery rites to cleanse the body and prepare it for transfiguration and elevation were a daily occurrence. It is into this troubled and horror-filled world that the news burst that resurrection was actually witnessed. Death, this great terror, was after all not what it appeared to be—the invincible power, the inescapable fate. It had been conquered—the dead will rise again.

This resurrection of the flesh, which was the object of derision on the part of pagan philosophers, can be understood only if one considers St. Paul's view of man. His distinction between natural (*sarkical* and psychical) man and spiritual man is here fundamental. The natural man is, however, not the good or bad savage; on the contrary he is highly civilized. But no matter how great his wisdom and how high his morals, he remains within the boundary of the merely human. Opposed to him is the *pneumatic* man who received the Spirit of God, and knows himself as the recipient and guardian of the divine spark. The pneumatic man is not a different species of man, however, but arises from natural man through a sudden conversion, through rebirth.

What is important to remember is that this rebirth, which St. Paul has himself experienced on the road to Damascus, cannot be attained, no matter how much one desires it and no matter what one does for it; it remains a gift of God. And it is significant that the pneumatic man can be, in every respect, intellectually and morally inferior to the natural man, but is nevertheless far superior to him as God's child, the temple of the Divine spirit.

The pneumatic man is two men at once. *Flesh* and *Spirit*, the *outward* and the *inward* man, are the terms used to underline this dual nature. There is in this conception of man a similarity with the Platonic image of the bodily vessel that is inhabited by the immortal, that is, the divine, soul. But whereas in Plato the soul is the pure and divine principle, and

the body the only source of evil, for Paul the whole natural
man, body and soul, is sinful. The decisive difference is that
for Paul the soul represents (as in the Old Testament) the
vital principle—life—and body and soul are both natural.[5] We
are not concerned here with the subsequent attempts to reconcile the Platonic and the Pauline views. But once we realize
that Pneuma is not the Platonic Psyche, that it is not simply
opposed to body-soul, and that there is no dualism, but that
the pneumatic man is a totality and includes the body, the
resurrection of the flesh loses its foolishness and ceases to be
the stumbling block it appeared to be to the Greeks and the
Jews.

Accordingly, the Christian theologians, when speaking of
death, give it a three-fold meaning. There is, first of all, the
physical death, which is the end of the biological life. Then
there is spiritual death, which is the condition of humanity
outside of the Christian faith. Finally, there is mystical death,
which is the participation already in effect during this earthly
existence, and despite physical death, in the divine life made
accessible by Christ. St. Paul says: "Ye died, and your lives
are hid with Christ in God." The mystical death is the victory
over physical death; and resurrection is but another phase of
this mystical death, which is, at the same time, eternal life.

For the pious Christian the basis of this view of death, the
rock of reliance, is the resurrection of Jesus. Christ is risen,
therefore we shall rise in Christ. No other proof is required.

But doubt lifts its ugly head: God Christ was victorious
over death, but can miserable man be sure that this applies
equally to him? And how can we reconcile this belief with
the testimony of our senses and with common sense? Ter-
tullian's well known answer was: precisely because it does
not make sense.

Mortus est dei filius; prorsus credibile est, quia inemptum
est. Et sepultus resurrexit; certum est, quia impossibile est.
(The Son of God died; this is believable because it does not
make sense. And after he was buried, he rose again; this is
quite certain, because it is impossible.)[6]

Where, however, such belief is present, death appears merely as a necessary and preparatory event for another existence. Death is a crisis, however, one that leads not into nothingness but into true being.

John Donne, in his last sermon, *Death's Duell, a consolation to the soul against the Dying Life and the Living Death of the Body,* speaks of the triple deliverance—*a morte, in morte, per mortem* (from Death, in Death and through Death)—which is in God's power to give us.

It is this view of death that makes it possible for many to look death in the face "with a quiet glance" and to say:

"If I die, it will be glory; if I live, it will be grace." [7]

Chapter 9

The Crisis of the
Christian View of Death

IT IS IN PART the unbearable tensions that developed in connection with the Christian answer to death that have not only
led to the undermining of the Christian answer, but contributed to the decline of the absolute domination of Christianity
over Western thought. They were "tensions of incertainty"
(Lecky) about the promise of immortality and resurrection,
and "tensions of certainty" about the eternal tortures in the
hereafter.

The hereafter has become, through the efforts of the
Church, a source of terror and not consolation. Instead of
reward, most people could expect only retribution. In order
to secure a blissful existence in the other world, and not to
be condemned eternally to unimaginable torture so vividly
depicted by Hieronymus Bosch and others, it was necessary
to lead such a life in this world as was beyond the endurance
of most people, except for a few over-zealous ascetics. At
the same time, as a result of the activity of priests and of
monastic orders, an acute death consciousness became widespread. It is best expressed in the words *Media in vita in morte
sumus* (in the midst of life we are in death).[1]

Huizinga writes:

No other epoch has laid so much stress as the expiring
Middle Ages on the thought of death. An everlasting call of
memento mori resounds through life. . . . In earlier times,
too, religion had insisted on the constant thought of death,
but the pious treatises of these ages only reached those
who had already turned away from the world. Since the
thirteenth century, the popular preaching of the Mendicant
orders had made the eternal admonition to remember death
swell into a sombre chorus ringing throughout the world.[2]

Despite the constant reassurance that *mors melior vita* (death is better than life), the horror of death was all-pervading. In fact, it became so general and intense that neither the sweet reasonableness of philosophical arguments nor religious belief was of any avail. The only means of counteracting this fear was to give in to it, to display it openly.[3] It was a complete reversal, in the sense that now everybody gave up trying to show why death should not be feared and was bent on showing why it should be feared—an apologia for the fear of death, as it were.

The dominant theme of the perishable nature of all things appeared, according to Huizinga, in three main versions. "The first is expressed by the question: where are now all those who once filled the world with their splendour? The second motif dwells on the frightful spectacle of human beauty gone to decay. The third is the death-dance: death dragging along men of all conditions and ages." [4] Both latter motifs had attained toward the end of the fourteenth century a prominent place in painting, sculpture and literature. Typical is François Villon's (born 1431) *Ballade des Dames du Temps Jadis* with its famous refrain: "Mais où sont les neiges d'antan?" (But where are the snows of bygone years?) And in his *Les Regrets de la Belle Heaulmière* an old woman bewails her lost youth and beauty. Representations of decomposing corpses and dancing, grinning skeletons served as vivid illustrations of the sermons heard from the pulpits and on street corners. And the "Triumph of Death," showing it as the great equalizer, became a theme of many a great painting.

Another factor, in addition to the widespread representation of the horrible aspects of death, contributed to keeping the fear of death alive. The moment of death became of the utmost importance, since the deathbed came to be seen as the battleground of the last and desperate fight which the Devil and his cohorts waged for the soul of man. Because of this contest between the forces of Good and Evil in the last hour it was indispensable to avail oneself of the help the Church was ready to extend; and this was the reason why sudden death was a manner of dying dreaded above all others.[5]

A story making the rounds illustrates the deep gloom and

despair of the times—the *Story of the King Who Never Laughed*. When asked the reasons for this sadness, he replied, "Because four spears are directed against my heart and would pierce it if I only show the slightest sign of joy; the first spear is the bitter suffering of Christ; the second—the thought of death; the third—the uncertainty of the hour of death and the possibility of sudden death without absolution; the last spear is the fear of the last judgment." [6]

In this revealing story we find strikingly illuminated the rift that developed gradually in the heretofore unified and grandiose world-view of the Middle Ages. The peace of the soul was disturbed. Everything, it is true, lives and exists in God and is secure in Him. But can man do right by God? Can he live up to His commands?

It is impossible to assess correctly the extent to which the urge to escape the all-pervasive thought of death and the conflicts assailing the conscience of believers contributed to the appearance of the entirely new consciousness that is characteristic of the Renaissance. Several other factors were involved in these revolutionary changes, which arose out of an apparently spontaneous interest in the world, the discovery of its beauty and the sudden feeling that life was wonderful. This new *Welt- und Lebensgefühl* could not but deeply influence man's attitude toward death. Death could wait. *Memento vivere* (Guicciardini) became the slogan of the man of the Renaissance.

The changes that culminated in the Renaissance actually began to sprout with the empirical revolt and the victory of nominalism over "realism." Abelard (1079-1142) had already contested Plato's notion that Ideas are more real than things. He argued the formation of concepts by abstraction from observation of particulars. Implicit in such a position is the encouragement of direct observation of particular things. The new respect for empirical knowledge begins to take shape in Abelard's disciple, John of Salisbury (1115-1180), and challenges Augustine's disregard of the world of sense in favour of the only thing that mattered to him: *Deus et anima*—God and the soul. The majestic world of faith, the world seen as the domain of supra-natural forces, as a *Theatrum Dei,* begins to give way to the natural world. To be sure, it was still God's world, and its wonders still clearly sang the glory of its Creator. But the new feeling for nature is strong enough to create in Petrarca (1304-1374) the conflict between the withdrawal from this world, preached by the Church fathers, and the keen interest in it. It is this interest that compels him to ascend Mount Ventoux and, as he reports to his teacher, "nothing but the desire to see its conspicuous height was the reason for this undertaking." [7] Yet, although he admired "every detail . . . relishing earthly enjoyment" he nevertheless "thought it fit to look into the volume of Augustine's Confessions," which he carried with him. Opening it at random, he hit upon the famous passage: "And men go abroad to admire the heights of mountains, the mighty billows of the sea, the broad tides of rivers, the compass of the ocean, and the circuits of the stars—and pass themselves by." Petrarca closed the book "angry with myself that I still admired earthly things. Long since I ought to have learned, even from pagan philosophers, that nothing is admirable besides the mind; compared to its greatness nothing is great."

It is also in Petrarca that we see the role the rediscovery of antique thought played in the creation of the new spirit. He reports that he was seized by the impulse to accomplish the ascent: "while I was reading Roman history again in Livy . . . I hit upon the passage where Philip, the King of Macedon . . . ascends Mount Haemus in Thessaly, since he believed the rumour that you can see two seas from the top —the Adriatic and the Black Sea." In Petrarca we also see the beginnings, if not yet of changing attitude toward death, then at least of a different notion of its nature. The greatest weight attributed to empirical evidence, as well as the rediscovery of the views of ancient philosophers, notably Aristotle and Lucretius, made the possibility of the finality of death as total annihilation of the person reappear on the horizon. As Kallen writes:

Petrarch believed himself to be not only a priest but a true believer in the Christian hope; and so, when pondering death, he was. Nevertheless, the consolation of the Christian, that the dead continue to live when they are dead, was no sure consolation to him. In his heart Petrarch felt that death was surer than immortality, and that against this death not even beauty can prevail. Such was the burden of his song: that life, alas, is short, and beset with dangers: that the spirit must not be misled by the "pride of beauty." [8]

The following passage shows clearly Petrarca's struggle with the problem we mentioned earlier: how can one be sure of deserving immortality? [9] And it also shows his preoccupation with death: how to face it with equanimity—a question that is indicative of the gradual shift from the fear of afterlife to the fear of extinction:

I . . . asked myself: suppose you succeed in protracting this rapidly fleeing life for another decade, and come as much nearer to virtue, in proportion to the span of time, as you have been freed from your former obstinacy during these last two years as a result of the struggle of the new and the old wills—would you then not be able—perhaps not with certainty but with reasonable hope at least—to meet death in your fortieth year with equal mind and cease to care for that remnant of life which descends into old age? [10]

Petrarca's own solution is given in his famous *Trionfi*, where death triumphs over love, but fame and time triumph over death, and time itself is overcome in the eternity of Divinity.[11]

In the following centuries, not only the Christian answer to death but also the doctrine of the immortality of the soul became questionable. The interpretation of Aristotle's position by Alexander of Aphrodisias (around A.D. 200) as denying personal immortality, which found support in the leading Arab thinker Averroës (1126-1198), became with the publication of the "Alexandrist" Pietro Pomponazzi's *De immortalitate animae* (1516) the prevailing view of philosophical thought newly emancipated from theology.[12]

Whatever disappointment there might have been because of loss of the hope for a "personal" after-life was compensated by a combination of unbounded *joie de vivre* with a radically new conception of man's relationship with God, of his place in the universe and an unprecedented faith in man's own forces and unlimited possibilities.

In his famous *Oration on the Dignity of Man,* Pico della Mirandola (1463-1494) makes God say to man: "I have put thee in the center of the universe in order for thee to see better what is there. I did not make thee either a heavenly or an earthly creature, either mortal or immortal; I created thee so that as thine own sculptor thou makest thine own features. Thou canst degenerate into an animal; but thou canst also be reborn, through the free will of thine own spirit, into the image of God."

This manifesto of the Renaissance is a far cry from the passive attitude of the Christian and of the Stoic; it replaces that attitude with active resistance to fate, and with a drive towards self-fulfillment and self-realization. The man of the Renaissance experiences a boundless vitality, a sense of almost superhuman power, and a feeling of being part and parcel of a wonderful wide world where there is no decay and destruction but only change and transformation. These experiences and feelings also made the desire for personal survival less urgent. In living one's life fully and creatively, and giving it intensity and *élan,* man could make death not only lose its terrors but even its annihilating power.

The denial of personal survival after death appeared to have the distinct advantage of freeing men from the oppression of the fear of Hell and eternal perdition. It was being prompted also by moral considerations. First of all, there was the need to conform to a new (or rather, rediscovered) criterion of truth: the empirical evidence and natural reason made immortality (either as eternal life or as the immortality of the soul) appear improbable. Secondly, the belief in "everlasting life" seemed to an emancipated mind to corrupt rather than promote virtue. Not so long before, Dante still insisted that the disbelief in an after-life was the most foolish, the vilest, and the most dangerous position,[13] and Thomas More made King Utopus decree "that no man should conceive so vile and base an opinion of the dignity of man's nature as to think that the souls do die and perish with the body."

Now however, Pomponazzi holds that "those who maintain the mortality of the soul can be shown to save the essence and reason of virtue better than those who believe the soul immortal: for the hope of reward and the fear of punishment imply a certain servility which is incompatible with true and rational virtue." [14]

Similarly, Shakespeare expresses scorn for those who are driven to a belief in immortality by their fear of death and who "want nothing of a god but eternity" (*Coriolanus*, Act V, Scene IV).

And Montaigne argues against all those who are frightened into the belief in immortality, and insists that true faith should be independent of the promise of eternal life: "What kind of faith could it be that cowardice and feebleness of heart plant and establish in us? A pleasant faith that believes what it believes only for want of courage to disbelieve it." [15]

The impersonal immortality, made acceptable because of the feeling of exaltation and exuberance, was nevertheless not an answer to death which could appeal to everyone. Many were still seeking reassurance that man's personality does not completely disappear at death, and were either clinging to the religious view of death or trying to rehabilitate the doctrine of the immortality of the soul by new arguments. We shall see how Giordano Bruno finds them in his new vision of the universe as infinite. In every instance, however, whether one was sure of an after-life, doubtful of it, or convinced of its impossibility, there was a clearly felt need for an *ars moriendi*—the art of easy dying—and, especially, of finding a way of preventing the fear of death from poisoning the enjoyment of life. It is this problem which became one of the main concerns of Michel de Montaigne.

Chapter 10

Montaigne (1533-1592)

On How to Learn to Die

WITH MONTAIGNE an answer to death appears in the Western world that became perhaps the most frequent alternative to the Christian answer to death. What distinguishes this answer from those reviewed in Book I is that the *nature of death* ceases to be the principal issue. Death is seen as it appears to common sense—total annihilation. It is not correct, however, to consider Montaigne's position as merely a revival of Stoicism, as is so often the case. Montaigne's thinking on death and his answer to it fall into two distinct periods, and whereas the first is identical with the Stoic position, the second represents a decisive step beyond Stoicism and is distinctly modern in its vigorous affirmation of life and resolute turning away from the preoccupation with and preparation for death.

In his *Essays* Montaigne confesses that he was tormented for a long time by the fear of dying, even when he was, as he himself points out, in robust health. His whole thinking was permeated by the awareness of what he calls *la nullité de la condition humaine:* Life is destined for death, which threatens it at every moment. What can one do against this obsession with the thought of death and the paralyzing effects of the fear of dying? One has to learn to live with this thought, and it is his acquaintance with the writers of antiquity, especially Cicero and Seneca, which shows him the way: it is philosophy that can teach man how not to fear death and dying. "To philosophize is to learn how to die." [1]

Montaigne repeats all the arguments of the later Stoics in order to show that death is not to be feared. It is but an instant. It is natural: "Your death is part of the order of the universe . . . it is the condition of your creation, a part of yourself . . . death is the goal of your existence." [2] Why should we resent the fact that in a hundred years we shall be no more, if the thought that we were not alive a hundred years ago leaves us unperturbed?

To suppress the thought of death is the remedy of the vulgar. The philosopher is aware of death, knows that it waits for him everywhere. Montaigne repeats Seneca's advice that to think of it constantly is the best method of conquering the fear of it. One must familiarize oneself with death, for nothing that is familiar can be frightening. But at the same time one should keep oneself free from all attachments, and not consider anything too important. "One must keep one's boots on all the time and be ready to depart at a moment's notice." [3]

Montaigne knows very well what advantages the acceptance of death will give us: *"qui apprendroit les hommes à mourir, leurs apprendroit à vivre."* And "Whoever has learned to die, has forgotten how to serve. . . . *Le savoir mourir* liberates us from all constraint and slavery, and whoever has understood that to be deprived of life is not an evil will know how to enjoy life."

Gradually, however, Montaigne comes to realize that this constant preparedness does not solve anything. One cannot live in a permanent state of alert; and in trying to liberate oneself in this manner from the oppression of the thought of death, one becomes, on the contrary, enslaved to it. We find in the 1588 edition of the *Essays,* the significant passages indicating this change in Montaigne's position: "We trouble life by our concern with death, and we trouble death by our concern with life." [4] Montaigne sees now "that it is certain that the preparation for death has created more trouble than death itself."

Many events occurred in the life of Montaigne after the first edition of the *Essays* in 1580 that must have contributed to this change in his view. There was the death of his infant daughters; civil war spread to the Bordeaux region in 1585; and the plague broke out the same year. Instead of remaining an abstract idea, death breathed down his neck and became a very real danger. [5]

He had occasion to observe the attitude of the common

people toward death and was greatly impressed by it: no one seemed unduly concerned with it; people "expected death the same night or the next day, with a calm face and as if they were reconciled to it and had understood the necessity of this universal and inevitable event."

In the posthumous edition of 1595 we find this change completed: "Philosophy orders us to have death constantly before our eyes, to foresee it and to reflect on it before its time, and gives us rules so that this thought should not hurt us. . . . However, if we have known how to live, it is not proper to teach us how to die. . . ." [6] He realizes now that death is merely the end of life, and not, as he thought before, its goal. Whereas he said before that "the aim of our pursuit is death, it is the necessary object of our design," [7] he now says, "but it has become clear to me that it is really the end, not the aim of life, it is the termination, its last moment, and not its object."

But what about the fear of death? "I have never seen a peasant meditate on the manner in which he would spend this last hour. Nature teaches him not to think of it except when he actually dies. . . . Should we say that it is stupidity that gives him his patience toward present evils and his profound indifference toward the sinister accidents of the future? If this should be so, let's all learn from stupidity."

Originally Montaigne felt that life was completely devalued by its finiteness. Now he discovered that, precisely because of this, life has its own intrinsic value. It is our reason that rebels against our finitude because it commits the error of substituting for what we are an imaginary reality, a mere concept, formed by the simple trick of denying life's most fundamental trait, its temporality. This unreasonable claim to eternity, in his unfounded feeling of having been cheated, makes man depreciate the gift of life he has received.

This gift, Montaigne now sees clearly, is nothing else but the concrete individual himself, and he alone can determine the value of this gift. In particular, the certainty of having to die some day does not give us any ground for the depreciation of life, for we have no experience whatsoever of a life that is not mortal, of an existence that does not have the character of transitoriness. It is the sickness of reason, "the most savage of sicknesses," that induces us to *betray* our true being and makes us despise it (*mépriser notre être*), whereas he feels that we must not only accept it but love it and make the most of it.[8]

"The value of life is not in its extension, but in its use. It is not the number of years that determine whether you have lived enough," he writes, following closely what Seneca already said. But he adds something radically new:

> I enjoy life twice as much as others do. . . . Now that I see my life limited in time, I want to extend it in weight. I want to arrest the speed of its flight by the speed of my grasp and by the vigor of my use to compensate for the haste of its flow. To the extent that the possession of life is short, I have to make it the more profound and full.[9]

This is, of course, something quite different from the Stoic position. We have here the new Renaissance spirit, with its appreciation of the exciting and wonderful world surrounding man, and of the new feeling that life can be pleasant and must be enjoyed. And with this new attitude toward life we find here the notion that one's life must not be tolerated and suffered, but can be changed, can be molded, according to one's freely chosen plan, can and should be lived more intensely and vigorously, so that one is almost tempted to see in Montaigne's position the first anticipation of Nietzsche's appeal to "live dangerously."

This new approach to life—this new way of living—is, as it were, self-sufficient. The skeptic Montaigne lacked the imaginative sweep of a Mirandola, who believed man should strive to come as close as possible to being "an image" of God. And there was no certainty for Montaigne of life eternal that is open to the Christian believer. Even at the death-bed of his dearest friend, La Boëtie, who was certain that he was going to "rejoin the abode of the blessed," he could not suppress his skepticism. "Why, my brother," he reports poor La Boëtie exclaiming, "you want to scare me?"

His definition that "philosophizing is learning to die" clearly has an entirely different meaning from the one it had for the Platonist Cicero, whom Montaigne quotes as having said that to philosophize is nothing else but preparing for death. But whereas, for Plato, as we have seen, philosophizing was a rehearsal for dying, and death the great moment of fulfillment when the soul separates from the body, for Montaigne it means learning to accept death as final annihilation of the human personality. His ultimate wisdom is that "one should lead human life in accordance with the human condition." And the highest achievement of which man is capable consists for Montaigne in what he says on the last page of the *Essays:* "It is absolute perfection and as if divine, to know how to enjoy one's own being loyally."

What gives him support and comfort at the thought of death is not only the suppression of needless brooding about the mysteries of life and death.[10] Even though he seems to have been a Christian in name only and his scorn for the clergy is limitless, he is sharply opposed to atheism.[11] But more often than not he identifies God with "Nature" or "Fortune."

He considers nature "our great and powerful Mother." She even arranged it so that death should not be too difficult. But although like the Stoics he advocates "giving in" to Nature, although he does not revolt but adapts himself,[12] adjustment is for Montaigne not an end in itself, but merely a means to what he calls "loyal enjoyment of one's own being." As for death, his final conclusion is: "If we have known how to live properly and calmly, we will know how to die in the same manner."

But what happens to the "nihilité de l'humaine condition," to the futility of life that death seems to proclaim? Montaigne was not a "metaphysician." Once the fear of dying ceased to torment him, the whole problem lost its urgency for him. Living the good life according to Nature was apparently quite enough for Montaigne.

Chapter 11

Giordano Bruno (1548-1600)

Death Is Not Possible in the Infinite Universe

A CERTAIN SIMILARITY between Bruno's views on Nature and those of Montaigne has been pointed out.[1] Montaigne speaks of "our universal mother Nature" and says that "he only can value things according to their essential greatness and proportion" who views himself in her: "this great universe is the true looking-glass wherein we must look, if we will know whether we be of a good stamp, or in the right bias." [2]

There is, however, a basic difference between the two thinkers, for in the final count it is to *human* nature that Montaigne looks for guidance and on the basis of which he seeks to formulate a philosophy of life; he cares very little for the universe. For Bruno, however, cosmology was "the passionate faith of his life," and it is by it that he was led to a new ethic and a new philosophy.[3]

Temperamentally Bruno was at the opposite pole from Montaigne, the cautious compromiser. He was a born rebel, "as fiery as Vesuvius" (Dilthey), in the vicinity of which he saw the light of day. What the two really had in common, however, was their concern with death. "Who gives me wings and who removes my fears of death and torture?" Bruno asks in a poem prefacing one of his main works, *On the Infinite Universe*. This universe, as he imagined it to be and as we gradually came to know it, differs greatly from that of Copernicus, which for all the revolutionary displacement of the earth from the center of it, was still a closed universe. It was enclosed by "the sphere of fixed stars, containing itself and all things, for that very reason immovable; in truth, the frame of the Universe, to which the motion and position of all other stars are referred. . . . Of the moving bodies first comes Saturn, who completes his circuit in XXX years. . . . Fourth in order an annual cycle takes place, in which we have said is contained the Earth, with the lunar orbit as an epicycle. . . . In the middle of all dwells the Sun. Who indeed in this most beautiful temple would place the torch in any other or better place than one whence it can illuminate the whole at the same time? Not ineptly, some call it the lamp of the Universe, others its mind, and others again its ruler. . . . And thus rightly in as much as the Sun, sitting on a royal throne, governs the circumambient family of stars. . . ." [4]

Bruno, as he puts it himself, broke through this "frame of the universe." He dethroned the sun, considering it not the center of the universe but merely another star, and the stars as so many suns. The universe, he insisted, is not surrounded by "the sphere of fixed stars," but is infinite, with an infinite number of worlds. "Whoever thinks there are no more planets than we already know, is as smart as the one who thinks there are no other birds flying through the air than those he just saw from his little window." [5] Since the universe is infinite, there are as many centers as there are worlds. And he argues that "as it is good that this world exists, so it is not less good that each of the other innumerable worlds exist." [6]

Bruno went even further: "Only a complete fool can believe that in the infinite space, in the innumerable worlds, most of which surely enjoy a better fortune than ours, there is nothing but the light we perceive. It is simply silly to assume there are no living creatures, no other minds and no other senses than those known to us." [7]

This prophetic anticipation is the more impressive in that it was made before the invention of the telescope, at a time when the number of stars visible to the naked eye did not exceed 1,500. Bruno's vision, which shows great similarity to the Indian cosmology with its worlds upon worlds and endless aeons of time, reveals a universe so immense as to stagger the imagination. Bruno's idea of infinity, however, comes from Christian sources. He was familiar with the concept of infinity—in St. Thomas, in St. Bonaventura, and in Duns Scotus—as an attribute of God, and he admired Cardinal Nicolas of Cusa (1401-1464), who assigned to the created universe a kind of infinity, while still maintaining the positive infinity of God alone.[8]

While, as we shall see, for Pascal infinity of the universe was a source of profound uneasiness, for Bruno it was the magic formula to conjure the dread of change, decay, and death. Precisely because of the infinity of the universe there can be no real end to anything; even the smallest part of it merely changes its appearance, merely transforms itself, but cannot perish. This infinite universe is a plenum, there is no emptiness in it, no Nothingness which could engulf things.

"Against the madness of the dread of dissolution, nature cries out with a loud voice, assuring us that neither bodies nor souls should fear death, since both matter and form are absolutely constant principles." Fortified by this belief, Bruno —a modern version of Socrates—fearlessly died a horrible death at the stake.

We can only indicate here Bruno's basic philosophical position and some of the arguments with which he tried to justify it. He is passionately opposed to Aristotle, for whom infinity has meaning only as an extension of that which is finite and determined, a potential that can never be realized. The infinity mysticism of Neo-Platonism was more congenial to his poetic temperament.

In contrast to Cusanus, who called the universe "explication" of the infinite God, Bruno calls it the "extensive" infinite (as against the "intensive" infinity of Substance) and the living reflection of the infinite Substance.

His idea of God was that of a universal, unifying substance from which all things come of necessity. As God's manifestation the universe must be infinite. In his defense before the Inquisition he says: "I hold the universe to be infinite, as the effect of the infinite divine power and goodness. . . . I place in this universe a universal providence whereby each thing grows and moves according to its nature. . . ."

In *On the Cause* he writes: "The Universe is one, infinite, immobile. . . . It comprises all and is not affected by one or another being, and does not bear within itself nor in itself any mutation, is consequently all that [it] can be." [9]

Following Cusanus, Bruno points out that in an infinite

universe there can be no absolute position, neither higher nor lower, right nor left, center nor circumference.[10] And in it "the act is not different from potency. If the potency is not different from the act, it is necessary that in it the point, the line, the surface and the body are not different; for then, that line is surface, as the line, in moving itself can become surface; then the surface is moved and becomes body. . . . It is necessary, then, that in the infinite, the point, since it is in potentiality a body, does not differ from being a body. . . . Therefore, the indivisible is not different from the divisible, the simplest from the infinite, the center from the circumference . . . the finite from the infinite. . . ."[11] The universe is also eternal. Therefore there is no difference in it "between the century and the year, and the year and the moment."[12]

In this infinite and eternal universe Bruno finds, again following Cusanus, the "coincidence of contraries" (*coincidentia oppositorum*). "Being though logically divided into that which is, and that which can be, is really indivisible, indistinct and one . . . without difference of part and whole, principle and principled. Everything is in everything, and consequently all is one . . . unity in multiplicity and multiplicity in unity."[13] To understand this, Bruno holds, is "the indispensable key" for the true comprehension of Nature, that is, who has found this unity has discovered the indispensable key.

This insight allows him to advance his particular solution of the problem of change and to find his answer to death.

But you would ask me: Why then do things change? Why does particular matter force itself to other forms? I answer you—there is no mutation that seeks *another being,* but rather *another mode of being.* And this is the difference between the universe and the things of the universe—because that comprises all the being and all the modes of being; and of the latter, each one has all the being, but not all the modes of being. . . . Of these (things), each one comprises all the being, but not totally, because beyond each there are infinite others. Therefore, it is to be understood that all is in all, but not totally in all the modes in each one. Therefore understand that everything is one, but not in the same mode. . . .

Everything we see of difference in bodies, in relation to formations, complexions, figures, colours and other properties or common qualities, is nothing else than a diversity of appearance of the same substance; a *transitory, mobile, corruptible appearance* of an immobile, stable and eternal being. . . .[14]

To clarify his thought he says:

As in the art of carpentry there is a substance of wood, subject to all measures and figures, which are not the wood, but of wood, in wood and about wood, [so] all that makes for diversity of genus, species, difference, properties, all which consists in generation, corruption, alternation and change—is not being or existence, but a condition and circumstance of being and existence which is one, infinite, immobile, subject, matter, life, soul, true and good.[15]

As Dorothea Singer points out, "Bruno envisaged an eternal process of what we may call cosmic metabolism. Death was but a stage in this process, while life was a quality inherent to a lesser or greater degree in every part of nature." [16]

According to Bruno, through the contemplation of the infinite universe man achieves his greatest good. It is the means by which he rises to the understanding of the true infinite being; and through it he can fulfill his supreme end—unity with the eternal source of Being. Moreover, "from these reflections . . . we find the true path to true morality; we will be high minded, despising that which is esteemed by childish minds . . . and follow the divine laws which are engraved upon our hearts. . . . We will be beyond the reach of jealousy, liberated from vain anxiety. . . ." At the same time, these thoughts give Bruno the assurance that "we must not fear that any object may disappear, or any particle veritably melt away or dissolve in space or suffer dismemberment by annihilation." For "when we consider . . . the being and substance of that universe in which we are immutably set, we shall discover that neither we ourselves nor any substance doth suffer death; for nothing is in fact diminished in its substance, but all things, wandering through infinite space, undergo change of aspect." [17] Bruno continues:

Pythagoras, *who does not fear death* but awaits change understood this. Salomon who says that there is nothing new under the sun, but which is, always was, has understood this. You have therefore, this fact: that all things are in the universe, and the universe is in all things—we in that, that in us; and, therefore, all things concur in a perfect unity. You see by this, then, that we ought not to *torment our spirit, for there is no thing by which we ought to become vexed.*[13] We do not have to fear that by the violence of some erring spirit or by the wrath of a thundering Jove, that which is accumulated in our world could become dispersed beyond this hollow sepulchre or cupola of the heavens, be shaken or scattered as dust beyond this starry mantle. In no other way could the nature of things be brought to nought as to its substance save in appearance . . . For in the world as known to us, object succeedeth ever to object, nor is there an ultimate depth from which as from an artificer's hand things flow to an inevitable nullity.[19]

What gives Bruno solace and comfort at the thought of death and dissolution, which tormented his soul and "bruised his heart," was the conviction of the impossibility of death as total annihilation. The unquenchable thirst for knowledge and virtue that animates him is for Bruno also a confirmation of the infinity of the universe, the contemplation of which is the "high calling of man." Striving toward the "most noble and most lawful" goal of infinite perfection, man is in tune with the Universe where "there waits for each being eternity and realization." In Bruno's infinite universe death simply has no dominion, and "it is in vain that time raises itself to a cruel stroke, stretches the menacing hand armed with the scythe." [20]

BOOK IV

THE ANSWERS TO DEATH
IN MODERN PHILOSOPHY

Chapter 12

Our Souls Outlast Our Bodies

IN HIS INTERESTING STUDY on the father of modern philosophy, Leon Roth asserts that René Descartes' primary interest "was not in theology or metaphysics, and far less in the pure concepts of consciousness. . . . He himself avers a passion for truth; but the truth he was seeking was, to quote the title of the Discourse, 'the Truth in the Sciences,' and the sciences for Descartes have a definitely practical aim, the harnessing of nature to the purposes of man. The will o' the wisp of his life was the conquest of death not only for the soul but also for the body. . . ." [1]

There is no doubt that Descartes was greatly interested in medicine most of his life and was ever ready to give consultations, but medicine was for him much more than the art of healing or alleviating suffering. He assigns to it a much larger task, for he is convinced that, through better knowledge of the human body and through proper diet, it will be possible to extend the span of human life to last several centuries. This idea of his was so well known that Queen Christina of Sweden could not help commenting on it sarcastically when Descartes died at the age of fifty-three, while her guest in Stockholm.

But no matter how concerned he might have been with the prolongation of life, Descartes finally came to realize the utopian character of his expectations. In a letter of June 15, 1646 to Chanut, in which Descartes refers to the book he was working on at the time (*On the Passions of the Soul*) he states that "instead of finding means to conserve life I have found another, an easier and a surer one, which is not to fear death."

In an earlier letter, written in 1642 to his friend Constantin

Huygens, the father of the famous physicist, we find that this remedy against the fear of death is his firm conviction that "our souls outlast the body," and that it is based, not on the teachings of religion, but on "very evident natural reasons":

> I know well . . . that you have a strong mind, and that you know all the remedies to appease your sorrow, but I cannot abstain from telling you of one that I have found to be very powerful, not only to make me bear patiently the death of those I loved, but also to prevent me from fearing my own, although I belong to those who love life very much. It consists in the view of the nature of our souls, of which I believe I know so clearly that they outlast the body, and that they have been born for joys and bliss much greater than those we enjoy in this world, that I cannot conceive of those who die anything else but that they go to a life more peaceful and sweet than ours, and that we are going to rejoin them some day, and this with the memories of the past; for I recognize in us an intellectual memory, which is certainly independent of the body. [2]

At the same time he emphasizes that even though he wants to believe and even believes that he believes, he realizes he is convinced only by "natural reasons."

The evidence of natural reason shows, according to Descartes, that the body belongs to the world of matter (*res extensa*), subject to the laws of motion and which can therefore be understood as a mechanical system, whereas the mind is unextended, thinking substance (*res cogitans*). There is a radical dualism between the two kinds of substance, and what gives life to the body is not the mind or soul, but "animal spirits." The mind or soul inhabits the body, and the question of their interaction is the crucial problem that Descartes attempts to solve.

In Article 2 of the *Passions of the Soul,* Descartes states that in order to understand the passions we have to distinguish the functions of the soul from those of the body, and in Article 3 he continues:

We shall not find much difficulty in doing this, if we take note that whatever we experience as being in us, and which, we find, can also exist in completely inanimate bodies, has to be attributed to our body, and on the other hand that all which is in us, and which we cannot anywise view as appertaining to a body has to be attributed to the soul.[3]

The important point is that "it is an error to believe that the soul gives the body its movement and heat" (Article 5):

From observing how all dead bodies are devoid of heat, and consequently of movement, it has been thought that it is the absence of the soul which has caused these movements and this heat to cease; and thereby, without reason, we have come to believe that our natural heat and all the movements of our body depend on the soul. What, on the contrary, we ought to hold is that the reason why the soul *absents itself* on death is that this heat ceases and that the organs which operate in moving the limbs disintegrate.[4]

This insistence that the soul has nothing to do with the movement and heat of the body and that it leaves the body when it becomes "uninhabitable," obviously aims at proving the soul's independence from the body, which in turn enhances the probability of its survival after the body's disintegration. The difference between a living and a dead body (Article 6) consists in that "death never comes through failure of the soul, but solely because some principal parts of the body disintegrate." Descartes continues,

Let us hold that the body of a living man differs from that of a dead man just as any machine that moves of itself (e.g., a watch or other automaton when it is wound up and thereby has in itself the corporeal principle of those movements for which it is designed, together with all else that is required for its action) differs from itself when it is broken and the principle of its movement ceases to act.[5]

It is in Article 30 that Descartes' views of the nature of the soul as radically opposed to that of the body, and of the soul's ability to persist unharmed and complete after the body dies, are made explicit:

> The soul is united to all parts of the body conjointly, is really joined to the whole body, and . . . we cannot, properly speaking, say that it is in any one of its parts to the exclusion of the others—the body being unitary, i.e. in some fashion indivisible, in virtue of the disposition of its organs which are so related each to the others, that when any one of them is removed, the whole body is rendered defective. Again, the soul is of such a nature that it has no relation to extension, nor to the dimensions or other properties of the matter composing the body, but only to the whole assemblage of its organs, as appears from our stability to think of the half or the third of a soul, or of its occupying a space. It does not become smaller on the removal of a part of the body. When, however, the assemblage of the bodily organs disintegrates, it itself, in its entirety, *withdraws* from the body.[6]

So far, so good. However, once Descartes so carefully separated body and mind, the difficulty arose of explaining how they interact, since it was evident that they do interact. Descartes' answer is (Article 31):

> that there is a small gland in the brain in which the soul exercises its function more specifically than in its other parts: although the soul is joined to the whole body, there is yet in the body a certain part in which it exercises its functions more specifically than in all the others. It is a matter of common belief that this part is the brain. . . . But on carefully examining the matter I seem to find evidence that the part of the body in which the soul exercises its functions immediately is in no wise the heart, nor the brain as a whole, but solely the innermost part of the brain, viz. a certain small gland, situated in a midway position, and suspended over the passage by which the animal spirits of the anterior cavities communicate with those of the posterior cavities. . . .[7]

This is, of course, pure fancy. The difficulties of explaining how the soul is able to affect the material body are indeed insurmountable; Descartes himself finally takes refuge in the not very convincing excuse that it is perhaps unwise to spend too much time on such matters.

In the last resort it was not the evidence of natural reason which led to his view of our souls as immortal. It was rather the hope that after we die we are going to enjoy the bliss of another life which decisively influenced this view.

Chapter 13

Pascal (1623-1662)

The Best in This Life Is the Hope of Another Life

PROPERLY SPEAKING, Pascal does not belong in a survey of philosophical answers to death, since he himself was of the opinion that philosophy is not worth even an hour's study.[1] Moreover, his answer is merely a reiteration of the Christian position, and his main concern is to demonstrate the truth of the Christian doctrine.

What makes Pascal nevertheless relevant within the framework of our investigation is his extraordinarily intense awareness of the "human condition," his obsession with the thought of death, his terror at this thought, and his conviction that if life is annihilated in death, it is a meaningless joke:

We run toward the precipice, after we have put something before our eyes in order not to see it. . . .

Death, which threatens us at every moment, will irrevocably put us in a few years into the horrible predicament of being either annihilated for eternity, or eternally unhappy. *. . . There is nothing more real than this, nor more terrible.* We may whistle in the dark as much as we like: this is the end which awaits even the most beautiful life on earth. . . .

The last act is cruel, no matter how pleasant was the comedy: *In the end a little earth is thrown on one's head and all is over for good.*[2]

Pascal does not understand the indifference of so many to the all-important question of whether death annihilates them completely and forever.[3] In his view "the immortality of the soul is something which is so important to us, which affects

116

us so deeply, that one has to have lost all feeling in order to remain indifferent to the question whether there is any truth to it, or not." [4]

Accordingly, we find the scientist and mathematician Pascal singularly unmoved by the controversy over the new world view. "I consider it proper that one should not explore the opinion of Copernicus. But . . . it is important for the whole life to know whether the soul is mortal or immortal." [5] For, "the science of external things is not going to help me in time of affliction.[6] . . . There is no good in the life except the hope of another life, and one is happy only to the degree that one approaches it, and just as there will be no further misfortunes for those who possess a firm assurance of eternity, there is no happiness for those who have no inkling of it." [7]

For Pascal, the problem of immortality is the most profound and the most pertinent question, and he is ready to help others find the answer he himself found, in his religious faith. He begins with the statement that no one can blame a Christian for not being able to prove his beliefs rationally, because God, if he exists, is "infinitely incomprehensible . . . we are incapable of recognizing not only *what* He is, but even *whether* He is." [8]

To those who deserve to be helped to make up their minds about God's existence, Pascal expounds his famous "wager": Either God exists, or He does not exist. Neither proposition, Pascal argues, can be proved. The only thing to do is to wager. If we wager that God exists, we win all—"the infinity of infinite bliss." And if it should turn out that God should not exist, we lose nothing. But maybe the right thing to do is refrain from making the wager? This, Pascal holds, we cannot do, for we are committed. And since one has to choose, one has to see where one's interest lies, and it is obvious that this self-interest dictates belief in God's existence.[9]

It is not a theoretical argument: the truth of either position —God exists—God does not exist—is not being investigated or subjected to analysis. His approach in the wager is purely pragmatic, it is a weighing of risks; and the accent is on what is more useful, on what brings the greatest advantage in terms of peace of mind and infinite happiness.

Bell remarks about Pascal's application of the theory of probabilities in the wager that the expectation in a gamble is the value of the prize multiplied by the probability of winning the prize.[10] According to Pascal, the value of eternal happiness is infinite, and even if the probability of winning eternal happiness by leading a religious life were very small indeed, nevertheless, since even the smallest fraction of infinity is infinite, it would pay anyone to lead such a life. But, as Bell remarks, Pascal himself was not very certain of his argument. In another place in the *Pensées* he jots down this thoroughly skeptical query: "Is probability probable?"

It has been pointed out, and correctly, that the underlying premise of the wager is the pessimistic view of life. And indeed, as Pascal saw it, earthly existence was not worth much to a true Christian. Therefore, to renounce such a life would not be a sacrifice. Consequently Pascal reasons as if the game has practically no stake: one could win all, but lose very little or nothing.

What he considered to be the true Christian life we find defined in a passage of his biography, written by his sister. When suffering great pain and discomfort, he used to say:

Do not pity me; sickness is the natural state of the Christian, because it is one *in which he should always be*, in suffering and privation of all the pleasure of the senses, exempt of all passions . . . without ambition, without avarice, in a continuous expectation of death. Is it not the way Christians should spend their lives? Is it not a great blessing when one finds oneself through necessity in a condition in which one should be and one has no other choice but to submit humbly?

This continuous expectation of death is, however, not of death merely as liberator from pain and suffering of earthly existence. The Christian knows that the death of the body is the beginning of a new life in God.

In a letter of October 17, 1651, to his sister Gilberte, on the occasion of the death of their father, he writes:

We should not look at death like pagans, but as Christians, that is with hope, for this is the special privilege of the Christians. We should not look at the corpse as deceptive nature shows it to us, as a putrefying piece of flesh but as the inviolate and eternal temple of the Holy Spirit. . . . The mistake of the philosophers is to consider death natural to man. This is a childish and base view. For man as animal is born and dies, and death, according to the laws of nature, leads to the total destruction of the body. But man is created by God so that he should live with Him, and as such man does not die. Death must be seen in this perspective, and the believer has the extraordinary advantage of knowing that in reality death is punishment imposed for having sinned, and necessary for man in order for him to be able to expiate his crime.

Only the Christian view of death can help to overcome the fear of death: "Without Jesus death is horrible, but in Christ it is holy, kind, and the joy of the true believer . . . ." We should, therefore, take into account this true view of death and "correct the mistaken sentiments and feelings of horror so natural to man."

Pascal gives an explanation of the origin of this natural horror of death: God has created man with two loves—the love of God and the love of himself. But with the advent of sin, man lost the first love and only the second remained, so that man came to love himself without limit. As long as Adam was innocent, the horror of death was natural to him, since it terminated a life that was conformable to the will of God. But after Adam sinned, his life became corrupted, his body and his soul became enemies, and both became enemies of God. And what was just for Adam before the fall—to love life and to fear death—is unjust and criminal in believing Christians. However, they should not abandon the love of life completely, for it has been implanted in them by God; but this love should concern the innocent life only; even Christ loved his innocent life and was reluctant to suffer death. But a true Christian should not fear the death of a vicious and guilty body.

But how can one become a true Christian? Not through reason, but through what Pascal calls the heart, which "has reasons that reason does not know." Heart is for Pascal more than a faculty of the soul. It is the soul itself, insofar as it is capable (and was created) to receive the revelation of eternal verities. And religion is the heart's direct experience of God.

Pascal had such an experience.[11] But what should those who have no mystical experiences do? Pascal's advice, "il faut s'abêtir"—one has to renounce reason—is more than most people are prepared to do. And his other suggestion that since belief comes through habit, "Do as if you believed," more often than not fails to work.

Chapter 14

Spinoza (1632-1677)

The Human Mind Cannot Be Absolutely Destroyed

AMONG the great philosophers of the seventeenth century, Spinoza occupies a very special place. He too was seeking salvation, but his road to it was in direct opposition to that of Pascal and the Christian tradition in general. Still, he was not as uncompromising a rationalist and as dispassionate a thinker as he appears to many. But it is in keeping with this image of Spinoza that he is often cited as the very voice of philosophical wisdom with regard to death, counselling us not to think of it, and the example of the true philosopher in his total indifference to it.

The main argument for this view of Spinoza rejecting death as an object of the philosophical reflection and being himself wholly unconcerned with mortality is based on the famous proposition LXVII of the fourth part of his *Ethics:* "A free man thinks of nothing less than death and his wisdom is a meditation not of death but of life." [1]

But already Spinoza's insistence that not to think of death is preferable to thinking of it ought to make us skeptical about his own indifference to death. And his definition of the free man, which he gives in the proof for the above-mentioned proposition, clearly shows that not to think of death is not simply a matter of turning one's back on it, of simply ignoring it. In this proof Spinoza says that a free man is "one who lives under the guidance of reason, who is not led by fear, but who directly desires that which is good, in other words, who strives to act, to live, and to preserve his being on the basis of seeking his true advantage: wherefore such a one thinks of nothing less than of death, but his wisdom is a meditation of life."

121

The free man is then the wise man, that is, one who, under the guidance of reason, has conquered his passions and fears. And proposition LXVII is not an admonition or well-meaning advice not to think of death because no wise man does such a foolish thing; it is the assertion that the ability not to think of death comes as the result of the proper use of reason. Spinoza does not say "a free man should not think of death"; he says "he does not think of death," indicating thereby that it is a consequence of being free or wise, which is altogether different from saying that one must not think of it. And this ability not to think of death is obviously conceived by Spinoza as a reward for having become free, that is, as an incentive for pursuing wisdom.

Spinoza's free man differs, as he himself points out, from the wise man of the Stoics in that for the latter virtue consists of the exercise of the will, whereas the wisdom of Spinoza's free man comes from his intellectual insight: "for insofar as we understand, we can desire nothing other than what is necessary. . . ."

Spinoza knows that one cannot by a simple act of volition stop thinking of death, and he is fully aware of the great difficulty of becoming wise. At the end of *Ethics* he says that "the way which I pointed out as leading to this result seems exceedingly hard. . . . But all things excellent are as difficult as they are rare."

As for Spinoza's own alleged unconcern with death, one may ask why he attributed such value to the ability not to think of it? The eagerness with which he sought a way of mastering and controlling thoughts when they turn to the prospect of death indicate that he himself was disheartened by it and not at all immune to the fear of death.

Nevertheless, it would seem unwarranted to go to the extreme of claiming, as for instance Dixon does, that Spinoza was obsessed by the thought of death: "He desired not to think of it, and never ceased to think of it." [2] The truth lies somewhere in the middle. Spinoza's main motive in philosophizing was, as he states explicitly at the beginning of *On the Improvement of Our Understanding,* to discover the possibility of the attainment of "continuous, supreme and unending happiness." But at the same time, death is for Spinoza the great evil to be avoided as long as possible. The things "commonly pursued by men" are "vain and futile" because they only hasten or cause death.

> All the objects pursued by the multitudes not only bring no remedy that tends to preserve our being, but even act as hindrances, causing the death not seldom of those who are possessed by them. There are many examples of men who have suffered persecution even to death for the sake of their riches, and of men who in pursuit of wealth have exposed themselves to so many dangers, that they have paid away their life as a penalty for their folly. Examples are no less numerous of men, who have endured the utmost wretchedness for the sake of gaining or preserving their reputation. Lastly there are innumerable cases of men, who have hastened their death through over-indulgence in sensual pleasure.[3]

Spinoza's concern with death is also evident from the attention he gives to the problem of mastering the fear of it. He emphasizes that the mind which attains "higher" knowledge is "less subject to those emotions which are evil, and stands in less fear of death" (*Ethics,* Prop. XXXVIII, Part 5).

Had he tried to counter this fear with the assertion of personal immortality, he would have flagrantly contradicted his view of the unity of Nature and the uniformity and universality of Nature's laws. Spinoza therefore seeks to overcome the fear of death without the help of the belief in afterlife. And he argues that even "if men had not this hope and this fear [of being horribly punished after death], but believed that the mind perishes with the body, and that no hope of prolonged life remains . . . men do not have necessarily to return to their own inclinations, controlling everything in accordance with their lusts, and desiring to obey fortune rather than themselves. Such a course appears to me not less absurd than if a man, because he does not believe that he can by wholesome food sustain his body forever, should wish to cram himself with poisons and deadly fare; or if because he

sees that the mind is not eternal or immortal, he should prefer
to be out of his mind altogether, and to live without the use
of reason; these ideas are so absurd as to be scarcely worth
refuting." [4]

But if Spinoza asserts that the belief in an after-life is not
a necessary condition for ethics, it doesn't mean that death
as total annihilation is acceptable to him. Thus, what could be
called his doctrine of immortality is clearly a compromise between the desire to find consolation with regard to death and
that of avoiding a position involving a break in the unity of
Nature. To have carried out uncompromisingly this principle
of unity and to have done away with the inconsistency of other
philosophers who, although asserting this principle, still could
not bring themselves to relinquish completely the idea of
man's autonomous position within Nature, is Spinoza's great
achievement; this is what gives his system its impressive
coherence.

What then is Spinoza's position with regard to the immortality of the soul? In proposition XXIII of the fifth part
of *Ethics* he states: "The human mind cannot be absolutely destroyed with the body, but there remains of it something which
is eternal." In the proof to this proposition Spinoza says "we
have not assigned to the human mind any duration, definable
by time, except insofar as it expresses the actual existence of
the body, which is explained through duration and may be defined by time—that is we do not assign to it duration, except
while the body endures. Yet, as there is something, notwith-
standing, which is conceived by a certain eternal necessity
through the very essence of God, this something, which
appertains to the essence of the mind, will necessarily be
eternal."

In the note to proposition XXIII he says "it is not possible
that we should remember that we existed before our body,
for our body can bear no trace of such existence." But "although we do not remember that we existed before the body,
yet we feel that our mind, *insofar as it involves the essence of
the body, under the form of eternity,* is eternal, and that thus
its existence cannot be defined in terms of time, or explained
through duration." Some light is thrown on this proposition

by what Spinoza says in the previous proposition (XXII), where he states: "Nevertheless in God there is necessarily an idea which expresses the essence of this or that human body under the form of eternity."

In the note to proposition XXIX (Part 5) Spinoza explains that "things are conceived by us as actual in two ways; either as existing in relation to a given time and place, or as contained in God and following from the necessity of the divine nature. Whatsoever we conceive in this second way as true or real, we conceive under the form of eternity, and their ideas involve the eternal essence of God. . . ."

Existence of all beings, including man, is, as we have seen, of two kinds: In so far as man exists "contained in God" [5]—the body still has "ideal" existence even after it has actually ceased to exist, for "in God, nevertheless, there is necessarily granted an idea which expresses the essence of this or that human body under the form of eternity." And this idea or conception *in* God that expresses the idea of the human body is something that pertains to the essence of the human mind, for the human body is the object of the idea constituting the human mind.[6] What then remains of the human mind and "cannot be absolutely destroyed with the body," the something that is eternal, is that part of the mind that is its thinking essence, which is a mode of the eternal and infinite attribute of thought.

Wolfson says that "Spinoza's conception of the immortality of the soul may be regarded with respect to other conceptions of the hereafter as either an affirmation of immortality or a denial of it. Insofar as it denies that the soul continues to exist after death in its entirety and as an individual entity, it is a denial of immortality; insofar, however, as it denies the utter destructibility of the soul it is an affirmation of immortality." [7]

But even within this circumscribed immortality there are degrees. For Spinoza says: "The mind's essence consists in knowledge; therefore, in proportion as the mind understands more things by the second and third kind of knowledge the greater will be the part of it that endures" (Proof to proposition XXXVIII, Part 5). Only those who attain the higher kind of knowledge or what Spinoza calls the "intellectual love of God"—*amor Dei intellectualis*—will be immortal in a sense similar to that which is traditionally associated with this term.

In his book on Spinoza, Pollock uses as motto for the chapter in which he discusses Spinoza's doctrine of immortality a quotation from Rabelais: "I believe, said Pantagurel, that all intellective souls are immune to the scissors of Atropos." [8]

Pollock summarizes Spinoza's views as follows: "The eternity of the human mind is a *function* of pure intellect, and depends on the mind's power and habit to exact knowledge. Its perfection goes along with the statement of the most perfect kind of knowledge, and its degree is different in different individuals. It has no relation to time and therefore is not a future life or continuance of personal consciousness in the ordinary sense. At the same time it is, in some sense individual; the active and understanding mind is an eternal mode of thought which is part of the infinite intellect, but is not lost in it. . . . It seems to me that we cannot but trace in this a direct connection with Aristotelian doctrine of immortality taken up and developed by the Averroists in the middle ages." [9]

In proposition XX of the fifth book of *Ethics*, Spinoza says that "our mind insofar as it knows itself and the body under the form of eternity, has to that extent necessarily a knowledge of God, and knows that it is in God, and is conceived through God." Even though for Spinoza God is Substance, Nature (*Deus sive Natura*), that is, neither the God of Abraham, Isaac, and Jacob, nor even the "God of the philosophers," he sets out to prove, as Wolfson remarks, "not only the depersonalized God, but also that such a God, depersonalized as He is, not only does not cease to be a force and power for goodness in man's life but also, like the God of tradition, a rock of salvation and a refuge in the day of evil." [10]

And, according to Wolfson, Spinoza's conception of immortality is that ". . . which is commonly held by medieval philosophers."

Morin, however, points out that "although in the framework of Cartesian logic, [Spinoza] echoes the main theme of Hinduism. There are very remarkable analogies between his 'something which is the essence of the soul' and the *atman*, between the pantheistic Deity and the *Brahman*, between

Spinozistic 'beatitude' or 'perfect knowledge' and the ecstatic knowledge of Brahmanism of the Raja Yoga." [11]

Spinoza says that it is idle to speculate about the actual state of the human mind after the dissolution of the body. What we know of it is by analogy with the experience of the state of immortality during our lives—that union with God, which is sometimes described as "the love for God."

In particular we experience this kind of intellectual love in philosophic contemplation, through which we achieve the highest possible peace of mind. Even the common mass of people is conscious of the eternity of their minds, but they confound it with duration, and attribute it to imagination or memory, which they believe to remain after death (*Ethics,* V, prop. XXXIV, Schol.).

There is nothing supernatural in Spinoza's conception of immortality. His God is self-conscious of His infinite perfection through His attribute of thought, and of His being the cause of Himself (*causa sui*). The mind is part of God's attribute of thought, and such a mind will love God— which love will be "part of the infinite love with which God loves Himself" (prop. XXXVI). And although Spinoza previously said that "God loves no one" (*Ethics,* V, prop. XVII, Corol.), he says now that "in so far as He loves Himself, He loves man."

The state of immortality—be it called salvation, blessedness, or regeneration—consists of the reciprocal love of God and man. This, as Wolfson points out,[12] is nothing new—theologians before him have said this and Spinoza acknowledges this by saying that "this blessedness is called Glory in the sacred writings, and not without reason." (*Ethics,* V, prop XXXVI, Schol.)

Spinoza's vision in which the individual is merely a dependent and transitory *mode,* a tiny part of an immeasurably great Whole in which everything that happens takes place with absolute necessity and where human personality with its desires, fears, and hopes is without significance or value for the impersonal whole, has appeared to many as oppressive and gloomy. Nevertheless, there is in it a strange power to give, if not consolation, at least inner peace, which comes partly because it does not offend the intellect and partly because death no longer appears to be a catastrophe and injustice, but a necessary and unimportant factor in a scheme of things that is just and good, not in human terms, but in those of Nature, which Spinoza calls God.

For modern man, however, the real problem about Spinoza's answer to death is, as Nietzsche already knew, whether "something like Spinoza's amor dei could be experienced again!" [13]

Chapter 15

Leibniz (1646-1716)

No Living Creature Perishes Completely . . . There Is Only Metamorphosis

LEIBNIZ, "one of the supreme intellects of all time" (Russell), represents a reaction to the mechanistic conception of nature that dominates the systems of Descartes and Spinoza. He attempts to combine their mechanistic position with a teleological view of nature and to reconcile religion and philosophy.

He feels that "the moderns carried the reform too far, since they reduced everything to a machine." Although the difference between mind and body does not exclude the possibility of their being qualities of the same substance, as Spinoza thought, there is not one substance but an infinite number of substances, and the nature of these *monads* has to be conceived as analogous to that of the souls of men and animals.

Each one of these individual substances is an idea of God, actualized by means of a continual "emanation"; and that the monads should be found to be in harmony with each other is due to universal harmony. This universal harmony was the object of Leibniz's faith.

In *The Principles of Nature and of Grace* (the title is indicative of Leibniz's endeavor to reconcile religion and philosophy) where he attempts a solution of the mind-body problem that had caused so much difficulty for Descartes, he asserts that "all nature is a *plenum*." And

since the world is a plenum, all things are connected together and each body acts upon every other, more or less, according to their distance, and each, through reaction, is affected by every other. Hence it follows that each Monad is a living mirror, or a mirror endowed with inner activity, representative of the universe, according to its point of view, and as subject to rule as is the universe itself. And the perceptions in the Monad are produced one from another according to the laws of desires (appetite), or of the final causes of good and evil, which consists in observable perceptions, regular or irregular, as, on the other hand, the changes of bodies and external phenomena are produced one from another, according to the laws of efficient causes, that is to say, of motions. Thus there is a perfect harmony between the perceptions of the Monad and the motions of the bodies, a harmony pre-established from the beginning between the system of efficient causes and that of final causes. And it is in this way that soul and body are in agreement and are physically united, while it is not possible for the one to change the laws of the other.[1]

In pointing out the necessity of making a distinction between *"perception,* which is the inner state of the Monad representing the outer things, and *apperception,* which is *consciousness* or the reflective knowledge of this inner state, and which is not given to all souls nor to the same soul at all times," and attributing the omission of the Cartesians to make this distinction to their mistaken belief that lower animals have no soul, he argues that one must avoid "confounding a *prolonged unconsciousness,* which comes from a great confusion of perception, with *absolute death,* in which all perception would cease. This has confirmed the ill-founded opinion that some souls are destroyed, and the bad ideas of some who call themselves free-thinkers and who have disputed the immortality of our soul." [2]

Leibniz argues that "modern" science has shown us that plants and animals do not spring from putrefaction as has hitherto been assumed, "but from seeds, and consequently from the transformation of pre-existing living beings." [3]

But he holds that "general animals are not entirely born in conception or generation" and, therefore, "no more do they entirely perish in what we call death; for it is reasonable that what does not come into being by natural means should not any more come to an end in the course of nature."

This is applicable not only to large animals. It applies

also to the generation and death of spermatic animals themselves, that is to say, they are growths of other small spermatic animals, in comparison with which they in turn may be counted large, for everything in nature proceeds *ad infinitum*. Thus not only souls but also animals are ingenerable and imperishable; they are only developed, enveloped, clothed, unclothed, transformed. Souls never put off the whole of their body, and do not pass from one body into another body which is entirely new to them. Accordingly, there is no metempsychosis, but there is metamorphosis.[4]

The human soul is, however, much more than "simple" soul. It is rational soul, or spirit:

As regards the rational soul or mind (esprit), there is in it something more than in the Monads or even in mere (simple) souls. It is not only a mirror of the universe of created beings but also an image of the Deity. The mind (l'esprit) has not merely a perception of the works of God, but it is ever capable of producing something which resembles them, although in miniature. For, to say nothing of the wonders of dreams, in which we invent without trouble (but also without willing it) things which, in our waking hours, we should have to think long in order to hit upon, our soul is architectonic also in its voluntary activities, and discovering the scientific principles in accordance with which God has ordered things (pondere, mensura, numero, etc.), it imitates, in its own province and in the little world in which it is allowed to act, what God does in the great world." [5]

Leibniz, as Descartes before him, wants to justify the teachings of religion by the evidence of natural reason.

But in order to judge by natural reason that God will always conserve not only our substance, but also our person, that is the memory and the knowledge of what we are (even though the distinct knowledge of it may be sometimes suspended in sleep and in fainting), it is necessary to join moral consciousness to those of metaphysics: that is one has to consider God not only as the principle and the cause of all the substances and of all the Beings, but also as the chief of all the persons or intelligent substances, or as the absolute Monarch of the most perfect city or Republic which is that of the Universe. . . .[6]

Chapter 16

The Denial of Immortality

PERHAPS no other period shows a more intense preoccupation with what follows death than the eighteenth century. At the same time, however, it was a time of hardheaded *denial* of immortality.

The first trend is evidenced not only by an unceasing flow of writings dealing with after-life, some of them even "letters from the departed" describing in detail the condition of the dead in the "beyond," but by the prominence that the problem of the immortality of the soul held in philosophical writings. Moses Mendelssohn's *Phaedon* (1767), ostensibly patterned after Plato's, was widely read and commented on. There was also a marked revival of interest in the doctrine of transmigration, to which the sober Lessing lent a sympathetic ear, and even the skeptical Hume found it to be worth discussing.[1] This preference for the doctrine of transmigration points already to the growing doubt about the immortality of the soul as hitherto conceived. A search began for new arguments in its favor.

Of particular interest in this respect is the treatise written in 1792 by the Russian Alexander Radishchev.[2] He considers the arguments for the mortality of the soul more convincing than those for immortality. Surveying the latter as they appeared in contemporary writings (he does not seem, however, to be acquainted with those of Kant) he comes to the conclusion that the purely metaphysical and rationalistic arguments are inadequate and that one therefore has to include "reasons of the heart." Even so, he leaves it to his readers to ponder the evidence pro and contra immortality and to come to their own conclusion. As far as he himself is concerned, the weightiest arguments are the "powers of the soul," and man's striving for perfection. He believes that "the all-merciful Creator did not create man in order that he should find this purpose to be in vain."

The opposing trend, that of denying the immortality of the soul, began to assert itself in the seventeenth century. We have to be careful, however, not to mistake it for a correct reflection of the real answer to death for a philosopher. Thomas Hobbes (1588-1679) is a case in point. We find here the same situation as with Pietro Pomponazzi. Where death is concerned, all the materialistic conclusions to which rational thought leads Hobbes are forsaken in favor of the promise of resurrection that Christian religion holds out to the true believer. The soul is not immortal, Hobbes maintains, but on the Day of Judgment God will raise the faithful with glorious and spiritual bodies, whereas the sinners will suffer a second and everlasting death. Of course this is a miracle, but "God, that could give life to a piece of clay, hath the same power to give life again to a dead man, and renew his inanimate, and rotten, carcass into a glorious, spiritual, and immortal body."

If we want to look for a possible explanation of this inconsistency, Hobbes' autobiography provides a possible clue. He confesses that all his long life he was plagued by his "twin brother" fear ("my mother . . . gave birth to twins, to myself and to fear"), and it is quite probable that the fear of death must have been not the least among his anxieties. If authentic, his last words, "I take a fearful leap into the dark," seem to confirm this view; they may be interpreted as expressing his awareness of the conflict between his philosophy and his religion, and of his religious doubts—unless he was referring merely to what might await him in after-life.

With the French materialists of the eighteenth century, the denial of the immortality of the soul became the philosophical position par excellence. As for the Humanists of the Renaissance, for the *philosophes* the accent was on life, and death was merely the unavoidable and unpleasant "natural accident," [3] the thought of which had better be kept in the background. And in keeping with the spirit of Enlightenment, with its extravagant and fervent belief in the powers of reason, life could be improved and happiness attained in this life, the only one there can be and therefore the only one that matters. Immortality was a "priestly lie" which had to be unmasked and destroyed in order to achieve a better life in freedom and happiness for all here and now, or at least for future generations. This, and not salvation of the soul, was the paramount goal. But what about death? For the enlightened man of the world, to know how to die correctly—the *ars moriendi*—is part of the art of living.

Thus La Mettrie (1709-1751), the celebrated author of *L'Homme Machine,* gives this answer to death: "These are my plans for life and death: throughout life and until the last breath, be a sensual Epicurean; but a firm Stoic, at the approach of death."

D'Holbach (1723-1789), author of the influential *Système de la Nature,* relies on philosophy, which, according to him, is truly defined as meditation on death. We have to familiarize ourselves with the inevitable and face death serenely. The main thing is not to let it spoil the enjoyment of life. Fear of death is the only true enemy that has to be conquered, and that there is no after-life makes us free from the power of the priests.

But Condorcet (1743-1794) is not satisfied with mere acceptance of death. Like Descartes, he is very much concerned with the problem of prolongation of life and proclaims the new ideal of "natural" death, which would come only after all the vital forces are exhausted,[4] and when death will be welcome. In his *Outline of the Progress of the Human Mind* (1794) Condorcet anticipates that "a period must one day arrive when death will be nothing more than the effect either of extraordinary accidents, or of the slow and gradual decay of the vital powers; and that the duration of the interval between the birth of man and his decay will have itself no assignable limit. Certainly man will not become immortal; but may not the distance between the moment in which he draws his first breath, and the common term, when in the course of nature, without malady, without accident, he finds it impossible any longer to exist, be necessarily protracted?"[5]

However, postponement of death is not a solution to the problem of the fear of death. It is true that for those who will die a natural death in advanced old age this fear may be spared at the hour of death, but there still will remain the fear of dying prematurely. Condorcet's own Socratic fortitude in the face of death is due not only to his personal courage but to a considerable extent to what has become—thanks to him—the official credo of the following century: the belief in progress. For even for him just "the living of life" was not enough. Life had to have a purpose, it had to be dedicated to an ideal, which in Condorcet's case was the ideal of *humanitas,* of furthering the welfare of all men, of relieving pain and suffering and misery, the former through more knowledge, the advance of science, the latter through liberation from political and economic enslavement. And beyond that, as with Goethe's Faust, there is satisfaction and consolation in this ideal, that even though death is the irrevocable end and total annihilation of the person,

> Never in ages can be worn away
> The traces of my mortal day.

The doctrine of the immortality of the soul has been subjected to a scathing attack from another direction as well. To David Hume (1711-1776),[6] the doctrine of immortality is suspect since it is so obviously favored by our passions. Man would not cling so tenaciously to the hope of survival did he not fear death. But the very fact that man *fears* death speaks rather in favor of the assumption that death ends all, for since "Nature does nothing in vain, she would never give us a horror against an *impossible* event." But what is the point of giving us a horror against an *unavoidable* event? Hume answers that without the aversion to death mankind could not be preserved.

Hume's main arguments against immortality of the soul are the following:

Why does Nature confine our knowledge to the present life, if there is another? "By what arguments or analogies can we prove any state of existence which no one ever saw and which in no way resembles any that ever was seen?" The arguments from analogy to nature—and these are the only ones admissible here, as in any other question of fact—are "strong for the mortality of the soul."

The body and the mind are "exactly proportioned" in infancy, in manhood, in sickness, and in old age, where they decay *together*. "What reason then to imagine that an immense alteration, such as is made on the soul by the dissolution of the body, and all its organs of thought and sensation, can be effected without the dissolution of the whole?" There is, however, still a possible answer to that, which Hume does not overlook, and this is that of the pre-existence of the soul. If there were immortality it could be possible only in the form of transmigration of the soul: "Metempsychosis [transmigration of the soul] is therefore the only system of this kind that philosophy can hearken to." [7]

But Hume has no sympathy for it. Nor can he follow those who, acknowledging that we are unable to prove rationally this "state of existence which no one ever saw," claim another kind of logic and "new faculties of the mind, that they may enable us to comprehend that logic." He leaves no doubt about what he thinks of these new faculties and this logic. We can therefore assume that it was with his tongue in his cheek that he concluded that ("nothing could set in a fuller light the infinite obligations which mankind have to Divine Revelation; since we find that no other medium could ascertain this great and important truth.")

This devastating critique of the doctrine of immortality is still further deepened by Hume's repudiation of the concept of *substance* as far as our psyche is concerned. He accomplishes this by showing that there is no such *thing* as *the Self*. "When I enter most intimately into what I call *myself*, I always stumble on some particular perception or other. . . . I never catch myself at any time without a perception, and never can observe anything but the perception." Since the Self is never perceived, we can, according to Hume, have no idea of it. We believe in it only because we habitually relate our sensations and impressions to the same subject, thus forming the notion of an unchangeable bearer of these impressions. What we term "I," what we cherish and expect to survive, is nothing but a "bundle of perceptions."

The force of Hume's attack on the belief in immortality is not diminished by the interesting psychological reasons that made him wish it were not true. He suffered from a peculiar variant of death-fear, quite common in his day—fear of what comes after death. The "unaccountable terrors with regard to futurity which arise in some minds" of which he speaks are his own.[8] That they "would quickly vanish, were they not artificially fostered by precept and education," was, however, (not true in his case.) When he fell gravely ill in Turin in 1748 (he was thirty-seven at the time), his Calvinist upbringing played tricks on him. Lord Charlemont reports that "in the Paroxysm of his Disorder he often talked, with much seeming Perturbation, of the Devil, of Hell, and of Damnation." His much admired later equanimity, even serenity in the face of death, when he was struck by intestinal cancer at the age of sixty-four, was due to the successful destruction of the belief in survival. Death as annihilation of his conscious personality he did not fear at all. He was almost looking forward to it. Although he was "reckoning upon a speedy dissolution," he retained "the same ardour in study, and the same gaiety in company. . . ."[9] And Adam Smith reports that his friend's "cheerfulness was so great . . . that many people could not believe he was dying."

Chapter 17

The "Moral" Argument for Immortality

KANT was well aware of the weaknesses of the immortalist positions. He took issue with Moses Mendelssohn, when the latter, realizing that the usual argument for the immortality of the soul based on its "simplicity" is insufficient because the soul can "vanish," presented in his *Phaedon* (1767) the new argument that this vanishing, which would be equivalent to true annihilation, cannot take place, since the soul cannot be diminished or reduced to nothing by degrees. In the *Critique of Pure Reason,* Kant refutes Mendelssohn's proof of the permanence of the soul, arguing that even if we admit that it is "simple" and that it has no "extensive quality," it possesses nevertheless "intensive quality" and can therefore dwindle to nothingness "by a gradual loss of its powers." Thus "the permanence of the soul, regarded merely as object of inner sense; remains undemonstrated, and indeed indemonstrable." [1] He also criticizes Herder's views which expressed the conviction that "the belief in a future life is . . . necessary, even natural to man" [2] and advanced the doctrine of *Palingenesie.* Here the idea of immortality based on the rationalistically conceived antithesis of spirit and matter is abandoned in favor of belief in spiritual and corporeal rebirth based on a mystically apprehended unity of creation, a perpetual *stirb und werde* (dying and becoming) in which the future state emerges from the present in the same way that higher forms of organic life result from the development of lower organisms.

In his review of Herder's *Ideen zur Philosophie der Geschichte der Menschheit* (Ideas concerning the Philosophy of History of Mankind), [3] Kant points out that there is absolutely no similarity between the elevation of the individual into a more perfect state in the future life and what we observe in nature, which, moreover, shows only the destruction of the individual and the preservation of the species. The claim of knowing that the human individual will survive its destruction can perhaps be made on moral and metaphysical grounds, but never through analogy to natural processes.

Nevertheless, Kant was from the outset committed to the belief in "the infinitely prolonged existence and personality of one and the same rational being," as he defines immortality.

In the *Dreams of a Spirit-seer* (1766) he writes: "I admit that I am very much inclined to assert the existence of immaterial natures in the world, and to put my soul in that class of beings." [4] In view of Hume's critique, such an assertion might indeed be nothing but a dream. We can therefore assume that when Kant undertook his investigation into the problem of knowledge and into the possibility of metaphysics as a science, he expected that the results of such an investigation would be of decisive and positive consequences for the belief in immortality, or, as Kant prefers to call it, "future life."

It is difficult to say when exactly Kant became convinced that human reason has limitations in its ability to provide certainty concerning "the only proper object of metaphysics: God, freedom, immortality" and that proofs were to be sought somewhere else. But he seems to have felt already before he undertook the *Critique of Pure Reason*, which appeared in 1781, that the criterion of certainty for these beliefs is given in moral experience through *practical* reason. The extraordinary achievement that the *Critique of Pure Reason* represents and that has been considered variously as the greatest triumph or the most humiliating defeat of human reason, was primarily intended "to deny knowledge in order to make room for faith." Therefore, the facetiously advanced suggestion that "the postulates of practical reason" have been added by Kant as an afterthought to appease the distress of his manservant Lampe is based on a complete misunderstanding of Kant's position. The declaration of the primacy of practical reason,[5] a possession of all men, was not so much the result of a reluctant admission of the impotence of reason as of the moral injunction that man ought not to know, since knowledge would destroy the possibility of free action and of the faith that moral demand can be met.[6]

Kant argues that it is a mistake to accuse nature of having provided man "in a stepmotherly fashion" when it did not equip pure speculative reason with the ability to solve the ultimate, the most weighty problems. He insists that if pure (speculative) reason were not so limited, the consequence would be that "God and eternity in their awful majesty would stand unceasingly before our eyes. . . . Transgression of the law would indeed be shunned. . . ." But this would mean that "most actions conforming to the law would be done from fear. The moral worth of actions, on which alone the worth of a person and even of the world depends in the eyes of supreme wisdom, would not exist at all." [7] As it is, however, although we have only a dim and ambiguous view of the future, the moral law, without threatening or promising anything, demands a disinterested respect, and when this respect becomes dominant, a view into the "supersensuous" opens. Thus "the inscrutable wisdom through which we exist is not less worthy of veneration in respect to what it denies us than in what it has granted." [8] That an answer to the most weighty problems can be found, even though not through speculative reason, testifies to Kant's optimism; he cannot conceive that "nature should have visited our reason with the restless endeavour whereby it is always searching for such a path" if there were no such "sure road," for "nature cannot lure us on by deceitful promises and in the end betray us." [9]

And even though reason cannot provide certainty with regard to the metaphysical problems, scientific knowledge *is* possible, and Hume's skepticism is unjustified. In the *Critique of Pure Reason* he traces the path out of the dilemma between the unfruitful tautology of a priori analytical judgments and the incompleteness and dependence on sense of the synthetic a posteriori judgments. In other words, he shows how synthetic judgments a priori, that is, judgments about reality which are both universal and instructive, are possible.)

To be sure, in order to do so, nothing less than a revolution in the approach to the problem of knowledge is necessary. "Hitherto it has been assumed that all our knowledge must conform to objects"; but such an assumption does not lead us anywhere. We must therefore see what happens if we reverse the procedure, that is, "if we suppose that objects must conform to our knowledge." [10]

Kant acknowledges having been inspired by Copernicus in this revolutionary approach to the problem. In an attempt to explain the movements of heavenly bodies Copernicus asked himself "whether he might not have better success if he made the spectator to revolve and the stars to remain at rest." Kant decides to imitate the same procedure "so far as the analogy which [mathematics and natural science] as species of rational knowledge may bear to.metaphysics." And he finds that "if intuition must conform to the constitution of the objects, I do not see how we could know anything of the latter a priori; but if the object (as object of the senses) must conform to the constitution of our faculty of intuition, I have no difficulty in conceiving such a possibility." [11]

It is an interesting question whether or not Kant was aware of the profound difference between the actual Copernican revolution and his own. Be that as it may, Copernicus, by making "the spectator revolve" instead of having the universe, the sun, and planets revolve around him, broke with geocentrism and dealt a crushing blow to anthropocentrism. Kant, however, by making nature conform to man's intuition and understanding, by insisting that "the laws of nature are the laws of the experience of nature" (as Alois Riehl puts it), reaffirms anthropocentrism. In this sense it has been correctly said that what he calls his Copernican revolution in philosophy is rather a Ptolemaic counter-revolution.

In short, Kant assumes that objective reality, to be known at all, must conform to the essential structure of the human mind. If this be true, the insight we get into the basic structure of human thought will furnish us with a reliable clue to the discovery of the unvarying structure of knowable reality, and a synthetic a priori knowledge of reality will be in our grasp. Kant asserts "that space and time are only the forms of things as appearances; that, moreover, we have no concepts of understanding, and consequently no elements of knowledge of things, save insofar as intuition can be given corresponding

to these concepts . . . that we can therefore have no knowledge of any object as thing in itself, but only insofar as it is
an object of sensible intuition, that is an appearance." [12]

Without this distinction between "phenomenon" and "thing
in itself," Kant could not, as he himself points out, say "without palpable contradiction" of, for instance, the human soul,
"that its will is free and yet subject to natural necessity, that
is, not free. But if our Critique is not in error in teaching that
the object is to be taken in a twofold sense, namely as appearance and as the thing in itself," and if the principle of causality applies to things only insofar as they are objects of
experience, then "there is no contradiction in supposing that
one and the same will is in the appearance subject to the law
of nature, and so far *not free,* while yet, as belonging to a
thing in itself, is not subject to that law and therefore *free.*"
But "my soul, viewed from the latter standpoint, cannot indeed be known by means of speculative reason." [13]

"Our unavoidable ignorance of things in themselves" applies also to the immortality of the soul: "Even the *assumption* of God, freedom and immortality is not permissible
unless at the same time speculative reason be deprived of its
pretensions to transcendent insight." [14]

Thus, "on speculative principles" there is not the least
ground for the assertion "that the soul after the cessation of
all communion with the corporeal world could still continue
to think. . . . But it is equally impossible for anyone to bring
any valid dogmatic objection against it. . . . Thus all controversy in regard to the nature of the thinking being and its
connection with the corporeal world is merely the result of
filling the gap where knowledge is wholly lacking to us with
paralogisms of reason, treating our thoughts as things and
hypostatizing them." [15] The "necessary limits of our reason"
do not, however, exclude the possibility of other proofs; on
the contrary, the latter "gain in clearness and natural force.
. . . Nothing is hereby lost as regards the right, nay the
necessity, of postulating a future life in accordance with the
principles of the practical employment of reason, which is
closely bound up with its speculative employment. . . ." [16]

Man, Kant is convinced, "feels an inner call to fit himself,

by his conduct in this world, and by the sacrifice of many
of its advantages, for citizenship in a better world upon
which he lays hold in idea. This powerful and incontrovertible
proof is reinforced by our ever increasing knowledge of pur-
posiveness in all that we see around us, and by the contemplation of the immensity of creation, and therefore also by the
consciousness of a certain illimitableness in the possible extension of our knowledge, and of a striving commensurate
therewith." [17]

Even though "we must renounce the hope of comprehend-
ing, from a mere theoretical knowledge of ourselves, the
necessary continuance of our existence," [18] and as Kant insists, "no one, indeed, will be able to boast that he *knows* that
there is a God, and a future life; if he knows this, he is the
very man for whom I have long (and vainly) sought," [19] he
boldly declares: "I inevitably believe in the existence of God
and in a future life, and I am certain that nothing can shake
this belief." [20] Kant acknowledges however that his conviction "is not *logical,* but *moral* certainty; and since it rests on
subjective grounds (of the moral sentiment), I must not even
say, It is morally certain that there is a God, etc., but
I am morally certain, etc. In other words, the belief in God
and in another world is so interwoven with my moral sentiment that as there is little danger of my losing the latter,
there is equally little cause for fear that the former can ever
be taken from me." [21]

Kant concedes that "it may seem questionable to base this
rational belief on the assumption of moral sentiment." Thus,
if "we take a man who is completely indifferent with regard to
moral laws, the question propounded by reason then becomes
merely a problem for speculation, and can, indeed, be supported by strong grounds of analogy, but not such as must
compel the most stubborn skepticism to give way."

He argues, however, that "in these questions no man is free
from all interest . . . enough remains to make him fear the
existence of a God and a future life. Nothing more is required for this than that he at least cannot pretend that there is
any certainty that there is no such being and no such life.
. . ." [22] To understand the power which the moral argument

has for Kant, his philosophy of life and his view of morality is decisive. On both, there are revealing statements in The *Critique of Judgment*.

"The value of life for us, if it is estimated by that which we enjoy (by the natural purpose of the sum of all inclinations, i.e., happiness), is easy to decide. It sinks below zero; for who would be willing to enter life anew under the same conditions? Who would do so even according to a new, self-chosen plan (yet with conformity with the course of nature) if it were merely directed to enjoyment." [23] But there is "the supreme end, the happiness of all mankind" [24] and "morality is not really the theory how we could make ourselves happy, but how we can become deserving of happiness." [25]

In the last resort it is Kant's deep conviction that "in the world we everywhere find clear signs of an order in accordance with a determining purpose, carried out with great wisdom"—which includes the happiness of mankind—that serves as a foundation and criterion of his belief in the existence of a "better world" and justifies man's hope of a future life.

It disturbs Kant very little that the achievements of pure reason "in opening up prospects beyond the limits of experience" do not exceed that which "common understanding could have achieved." And he asks whether one can really require that "a mode of knowledge which concerns all men should transcend common understanding, and should only be revealed to you by philosophers?" [26]

This may explain why he did not avail himself of his own doctrine of the "ideality of time" in order to prove the imperishability of man's "true nature," which later on Schopenhauer considered the best and most conclusive argument for "immortality."

In the *Critique of Pure Reason* Kant has given his first formulation of his doctrine of immortality as a "postulate of practical reason": happiness and virtue do not correspond in this life, though reason demands that they should; for although happiness is attainable in this world, virtue is really attainable only if there is infinite progress, hence there must be another life. But in the *Critique of Practical Reason* the argument is somewhat different, with greater emphasis on morality. We are *required by moral law to be perfect*. And an obligation is, according to Kant, invalid unless it can be fulfilled.

> The achievement of the highest good (*summum bonum*) in the world is the necessary object of a will determinable by the moral law. In such a will, however, the complete fitness of intentions to the moral law is the supreme condition of the highest good. This aptness, therefore, must be just as possible as its object, because it is contained in the command that requires us to promote the latter.[27]

But how can the finite sensuous being fulfill the demand of the moral law? Only if endless progress from lower to higher stages of moral perfection is possible. And infinite progress is possible only if our existence is infinite, that is, if our souls are immortal:

> Thus the Highest Good is practically possible only on the supposition of the immortality of the soul, and the latter, as inseparably bound to the moral law, is a postulate of pure practical reason. . . . By a postulate of pure practical reason I understand a theoretical proposition which is not as such demonstrable, but which is an inseparable corollary of an a priori unconditionally valid practical law.[28]

The reliance on the moral argument for immortality, instead of falling back on religious experience or blind faith, is to be understood as a consequence of Kant's dislike of mysticism, of the impact of the rationalistic temper on his view of religion, and most of all of his view of the primacy of moral experience over religious. It was the "moral law in us" that reveals to him that the world is in the hands of a wise Providence and that man is a being of two worlds, the phenomenal as well as the noumenal.

It is, however, necessary to point out that when Kant speaks of the "two things which fill the mind with ever new and increasing admiration and awe . . . the starry heavens above me and the moral law within me," he is aware of the tension and contradiction of the two views: "the former view of a countless multitude of worlds annihilates, as it were, my importance as an animal creature, which must give back to the planet (a mere speck in the universe) the matter from which it came, the matter which is for a little time provided with vital force, we know not how." But the other view, which comes from the apprehension of the moral law within me "infinitely raises my worth as that of an intelligence in which the moral law reveals a life independent of all animality and even of the whole world of sense—at least so far as may be inferred from the purposive destination assigned to my existence by this law, —a destination which is not restricted to the conditions and limits of this life but reaches into the infinite." [29]

The phrase, "at least so far as may be inferred," is crucial. It indicates that we are not yet at the end of the road, only at the beginning. The problem is how the intimations of immortality and purpose could become as "clear and henceforth unchangeable" an insight into the structure of the world as that which natural science has "finally brought through patient examination." Kant is hopeful that in following the same path in dealing with the moral capacities of our nature we shall arrive at a "similarly good issue." [30]

In the meantime, what does Kant tell us about the "future state"? Precious little, for his general attitude to this question is that "we can know nothing of the future, and we ought not to seek to know more than what is rationally bound up with the incentives of morality and their end." [31]

He expects, however, that it would not be radically different from the present existence. "At least, man has no ground for believing that a sudden change will take place. Rather, experience of his state on earth and the ordering of nature in general gives him clear proofs that his moral deterioration, with its inevitable punishments, as well as his moral improvement and the well-being resulting therefrom, will continue endlessly, i.e. eternally." [32] Such continued existence is that of the conscious soul, which survives the death of the body. Kant does not seem to believe in resurrection of the body, nor to attach any importance to it: (for who is so fond of his body that he would wish to drag it about with him through all eternity if he could get on without it)" [33]

But the idea of a future state in which virtue is still sought after, in pursuit of moral perfection, implies that in it man will be susceptible to pain and eager for happiness. One has to be constantly aware, however, that for Kant immortality of the soul is a side-issue, and its importance for him does not reside in its ability to satisfy our desire to outlast death, but in its function of making morality efficient in our present existence. It does not serve as an inducement for moral conduct, which will be rewarded by "good" immortality; obedience to moral law is a duty. Immortality provides merely a counter-argument, as it were, against the view that it may be irrelevant how we conduct ourselves here and now, since death seems to annihilate equally the wrongdoer and the saint.

In the famous article, "The End of All Things," [34] Kant deals with the topic of future life and the last judgment. Speaking of eternal life, he points out the difficulties inherent in this concept. Eternity cannot be merely infinite continuation of time, but must be rather a transcending of time. We can think of our present life, however, only as existing under the form of time, and it cannot be conceived as persisting outside of time, in eternity. Moreover, becoming eternal involves a change, which contradicts what Kant said of immortality as the endless continuation of a previous state. He partially resolves the difficulty by pointing out that the change from time to eternity does not affect the moral disposition, which is already an "eternal thing" in the phenomenal world, belonging to the noumenal man whose "life is in heaven." Thus eternity is already present in us as moral beings. Nevertheless, Kant admits that this is a transcendental idea that belongs rather to the other fancies regarding the future life to which religious thinkers and seers of all times are especially addicted, but which has no claim upon reason.

Some of Kant's contemporaries were quick to point out the contradictions inherent in the "thing in itself." For instance, it is supposed to underlie our world of phenomena as their cause, and should thus fall under the category of causality; yet, on the other hand, according to Kant, causality may only be applied to phenomena, and never to "things" that lie beyond our experience. Friedrich Heinrich Jacobi insisted that we cannot enter into the Kantian system "without the assumption that things make impression on the senses, and we cannot remain there with this assumption."

Another of Kant's contemporaries, Salomon Maimon, remarked that if we say that the thing in itself is inconceivable, we cannot possibly talk of it; and if we say it is conceivable, it ceases to be a "thing-in-itself." It is an impossible idea, an *Unding*, a "no-thing." It is not an *x*, as Kant thought, but $\sqrt{-a}$.

One of the consequences of these criticisms was the view that the defeat of reason has been too hastily asserted by Kant and that the belief that there can be anything unknowable in the universe is mistaken. Undeterred by Kant's warning, philosophers again took up the pursuit or omniscience. Fichte and Hegel started with the rejection of the "thing in itself," and Schopenhauer declared that not only can it be known, but that he knew what it was.

For those who feel that Kant's moral argument for immortality is not overly strong, Fichte's "absolute idealism" seems to promise a more solid basis for the belief in immortality. As we shall see, such is not the case.

Kant's position on immortality rests ultimately on the belief that the universe is ruled by Divine Providence, which is mindful of human values. Fichte (1762-1814) seems at first to follow in Kant's footsteps, at least insofar as he too is convinced of the moral order of the universe: "It is not at all doubtful, but the greatest certainty, actually the basis of all other certainties, that there is a moral order in the universe; that each rational being is assigned its definite place in that order; that the destiny of the individual, insofar as it is not caused by his own conduct, results from this plan so that not a single hair falls from his head without it." [35]

And he follows Kant in grounding the assertion of immortality in moral considerations: "Death is but the mask which conceals a deeper, a more meaningful activity" and "what mortals call death is the visible appearance of my higher life." This higher life is the moral life. And "what is called death cannot break up my work; because my work must be accomplished, because I have to fulfill my vocation, there is no limit to my life. I am eternal."

But there is a significant difference. While Fichte is "absolutely certain" about the moral order of the universe, he is not at all without doubt about God's existence, in any case as far as a personal God who cares is concerned. Whatever such doubt does to belief in the moral order of the universe and the assertion of immortality, Fichte, in addition to the moral argument, bases his assertion of immortality on the primacy of the ego. His "subjective idealism" in transforming the thinking subject into the free volitional ego provides the assurance of the imperishability of the *I*: "Even my body may decay and become dust; this body is not I. . . . Long after the youngest among the millions of suns which shine over my head has sent forth its last rays of light, I shall still remain, unaltered and intact, the same as I am today." [36] There is, however, a much greater difficulty in Fichte's arguments for immortality than the primacy of the ego, which must appear, psychologically speaking, as the hypertrophy of the "experience of self," and this is the confusion surrounding the meaning of the ego in Fichte. He speaks as if he meant the individual ego and as if he asserts personal immortality. But gradually it becomes clear that even if he thought in these terms in the beginning, what he means is the "pure," the "absolute" Ego. Under these circumstances what he says about the indestructibility of the ego cannot be interpreted in the sense of personal immortality, which Kant means when he speaks of the immortality of the soul.

And indeed, in the later period of Fichte's philosophizing, when he came to identify the pure Ego with God, all possible ambiguity about Fichte's answer to death vanishes. There is not even a soul. "The existence of the soul is absolutely denied, and the whole concept is a bad invention." [37] The individual is merely a passing stage, something that ought not to be. The ghost of Anaximander reappears and Schopenhauer is anticipated. But individuality should not be overcome by a Buddhistic denial of the will, but by active work for eternal goals. These are knowledge of God (of the absolute Ego) and the love of God, which is the true aim of life. [38] To the mystic Fichte has become, death is good, for it leads back to God.

Chapter 18

Hegel (1770-1831)

Death Is the Reconciliation of the Spirit with Itself

THOSE WHO TURN to Hegel in the expectation of finding in his philosophy of "absolute idealism" new arguments for personal immortality will be disappointed. Nowhere does he deal with this topic exhaustively or clearly.

Some interpreters even hold that Hegel regarded immortality as something that stands for "the infinitude of spirit and the absolute value of spiritual individuality." For him, "immortality is a present quality of the spirit, not a future fact or event."[1]

This view seems to follow from Hegel's conception of history. Loewith writes of it that "history is a history of the spirit; and, though it is self-consuming, it does not merely return to the same form but comes forth, 'exalted, glorified,' with each successive phase becoming, in turn, a material on which the spiritual history of man proceeds to a new level of fulfillment. Thus the conception of mere change gives place to one of spiritual perfection, though involved with the conditions of nature." [2]

As for the individual, after having played his insignificant part on the world stage, he disappears completely to make room for a new "self-alienation" of the Idea, "which alone is eternal."

It is, however, of the utmost importance for the correct understanding of Hegel that, contrary to what has often been said, Hegel was not insensible to the tragic aspects of the historical process, and he did not disregard completely the suffering of the individual and his despair at his mortality.

As for the first point, it suffices to read what he says in his *Lectures on the Philosophy of History:*

We can scarce avoid being filled with sorrow at this universal taint of corruption. . . . Without rhetorical exaggeration, a simply truthful combination of the miseries that have overwhelmed the noblest of nations and politics, and the finest exemplars of private virtues, forms a picture of most fearful aspect, and excites emotions of the profoundest and most hopeless sadness, counter-balanced by no consolatory result. We endure in beholding it a mental torture. . . . The question necessarily arises: to what final aim these enormous sacrifices have been offered? [3]

He was keenly and painfully aware of death. In the "Jena Aphorisms" of the young Hegel we read: "The highest that ought to be transcended is death." As a thirteen-year-old he was deeply affected by the death of his mother, and in later life he could never become reconciled to the death of his firstborn, his only daughter. But be it the death of someone we love or our own inevitable end, Hegel wanted to be courageous about it. This courage was for him a necessary endowment of the true philosopher: "Not the life that shuns death and keeps itself clean of desolation," he writes in the Preface of the *Phenomenology of the Spirit*, "but which bears death and abides in it, is the life of the Spirit. It wins its truth only when it finds itself in absolute despair (*in der absoluter Zerrissenheit*)."

These quotations clearly indicate that even if Hegel's position was that of pure and simple denial of personal immortality, he was seeking a justification for death. His conception of history aims at supplying it. And as we shall see, it sometimes appears as if "the absolute despair" of which he speaks in connection with death at times brings him close to the Christian answer to death.

In his youth Hegel discovered Heraclitus. The Greek words *One and All* as the symbol of Heraclitian thought were written into the young Hegel's notebook, presumably, by the poet Hoelderlin, the closest friend of his youth. And Hegel's philosophy may be seen as a systematization of what Hoelderlin expresses poetically at the end of *Hyperion* when he writes: "*Wie der Zwist der Liebenden sind die Dissonanzen der Welt.*

Versoehnung ist mitten im Streit und alles Getrennte findet sich wieder" (The dissonances of the world are like a lovers' quarrel. Reconciliation is in the midst of strife and all that is divided becomes united again).

It is in this that Hegel's opposition to the dominant tendency of German thought, his denial of the unbridgeable gap between spirit and matter, reason and faith, individual and society, men and universe, is rooted. Also due to the influence of Hoelderlin and the Romantics is the tendency toward the glorification of death, which appears on and off in Hegel.

But once Hegel came to formulate his philosophy of the Spirit—"everything is Spirit, and Spirit is everything"—a significant change in his view of death takes place.

In his *Introduction to the Reading of Hegel,* Alexandre Kojève insists on "the momentous role which the idea of death plays in the philosophy of Hegel." He even goes so far as to say that "Hegel's dialectical or anthropological philosophy is, in the last analysis, a philosophy of death (or, what is the same thing, of atheism)." [4]

He points out that "the man Hegel analyses is not what the Greeks and subsequent philosophy believed to have perceived —a purely natural being—but man as he appears in the pre-philosophical judeo-christian tradition . . . the free historical individual ('person')." But Kojève finds that an important difference separates Hegel's position from this tradition. For Hegel to describe man as the free historical individual is to describe him as finite on the ontological plane, as "worldly," or spatial and temporal on the metaphysical, and as "mortal" on the phenomenological planes. On this latter plane man appears as a being always conscious of his death, who often accepts it freely and sometimes even inflicts it upon himself voluntarily.

Kojève further refers to the recurrence in Hegel of the essential difference between human death and death—"corruption"—of a creature that is merely alive. He quotes Hegel: "The animal dies. But the death of the animal is the becoming of human consciousness." The crucial point is that man could not transcend himself were he not finite and mortal, and Kojève concludes that for Hegel "man is the mortal sickness of nature." And he adds: "Man is not only mortal, he is death incarnate; he is his own death." As opposed to natural, the purely biological death, the death that man himself is, is a "violent" death, conscious of itself and voluntary. "Man's death and consequently true human existence are in a manner of speaking, a suicide." [5]

Whether one accepts this interpretation or not, it is decisive for the understanding of Hegel's position that he is convinced that the philosopher is "privy to the World-spirit" (*Mitwisser des Weltgeistes*) and that as such he knows that in the unfathomable depth of Being—even though the process of world history with its misery, suffering, sacrifice, decay, and death of uncounted millions, seems to spell out the meaninglessness of human existence—there is no absurdity nor injustice, but "whatever is, is right." To demonstrate this is the task of philosophy, and he believes that philosophy is able to accomplish this seemingly impossible task. "Philosophy then is not a consolation; it is more, it reconciles, it transfigures reality,which appears unjust, into the reasonable, reveals it as something rooted in the Idea itself (God), and something whereby reason shall become satisfied." [6]

At first Hegel tried to justify human death by the "dialectics of love," the love which calls for a "going beyond itself" in the child. Later on he gave up this idea—which anyhow fails to take into account sterility—when he began to think more and more in terms of subordinating the individual to the state instead of to the species. It is then that death became for Hegel *ein Aufheben*—with its threefold meaning in German: to annul (abrogate), to preserve, and to "elevate"—of "the natural finitude." "Such a death, the suffering and pain of death, is the element of the reconciliation of the Spirit with itself." [7]

Discussing Hegel's threefold justification of death, Morin finds that Hegel's original contribution was the idea of the absolute necessity of the risk of death "for every consciousness which desires to be free and universal." He says that the metaphysical justification of death—the necessity of negation—is based on an improper assimilation of death and negation. The biological justification is based, according to him, on an "animal truth" that "it is proper for man to reject." As for the third justification—the absolute necessity of the risk of death for the progress of humanity—his objection is that the risk of death "makes sense only to those who do not die." [8]

Morin wonders how this "cultural" justification of death can be reconciled with a culture which is committed to the liquidation of the danger of death and in which death seems more and more "absurd." But he seems to overlook that, according to Hegel, when individuals pursue their own goals, "something entirely different comes to pass in world history through the actions of men from what they themselves aim at and attain, from what they directly know and desire. They fulfill their interests; but something more is being thereby accomplished which was already contained there, but that was not present in their consciousness of their intention." [9]

In *Lectures on the Philosophy of History* Hegel spells out that this something that is being accomplished is essentially God's plan. And he concludes the *Lectures* by saying that "only this insight can reconcile the spirit with world history and reality, that what has happened and happens every day, not only comes from God and with God's consent, but is essentially the work of God Himself."

In his *Lectures on the Philosophy of Religion* Hegel repeatedly explains death as the dying of God, and this death is the highest act of love:

> Love is precisely this identity of the divine and the human, and this reduction of consciousness to finitude is pushed to its extreme, namely death; thus here the intuition of unity in its absolute stage is the highest intuition of love. For love consists in relinquishing one's personality, property and so forth.[10]

> Death is love itself; in death absolute love is being revealed. It is the identity of the Divine and the human, that God is at one with Himself in man, in the finite. . . . Through death God has reconciled the world and reconciles Himself eternally with Himself.[11]

The above makes it understandable that, as a former student of Hegel reports, when Mrs. Hegel asked her husband what he thought of immortality and whether he believed in it, he silently pointed to the Bible.[12]

Chapter 19

The Glorification of Death

WHILE KANT AND FICHTE were endeavoring to reassert the belief in immortality and the French materialists urged the Stoic attitude to death, which they held to be total annihilation, the Romantic poet-philosophers of the early nineteenth century give a radically new answer to death. It differs in its strong emotionalism from the idealization of death in Plato. And what distinguishes it from the praises of death of a Theognis of Megara and those who repeated after him that the best thing is not to be born at all, and the second best is to escape this miserable existence as soon as possible, is that these sprang from a pessimistic view of life,[1] where death was seen as the lesser of two evils. The early Romantics, however, were not pessimists in the strict meaning of the word. Life for them was not necessarily bad, nor a "wrong," it was merely too narrow and empty compared with their vision of a truer and higher existence.[2]

The death for which the Romantics long is rarely total annihilation. For some it means absorption into the *Whole,* a view very similar to Bruno's, and stimulated by the philosophy of Schelling; for others it is the beginning of life eternal of the Christian religion, and then the attitude to it is similar to that of Christian mystics or martyrs.[3]

Thus Heinrich von Kleist, the tortured poetic genius who committed suicide at the grave of his mistress at the age of thirty-four, dreamed of the heavenly meadows where in the company of his beloved he will enjoy a blissful existence.[4] For Novalis (1772-1801), the greatest and profoundest of the Romantics, death is not the return into the Whole, although his philosophy, as far as it can be pieced together from hundreds of *Fragments,* shows certain similarity with that of Schelling. But from the outset there is a stronger emphasis on the spirit of man and its untapped possibilities, which gives it a certain affinity to the position of Fichte. All knowledge is in the last resort mystic and the spirit of man has to turn inward in order to recreate a new world. "The world is not a dream, but should, and perhaps will become one." What is meant is that we should "penetrate into the objects" and give them another—their true—aspect.[5] This is the goal of Novalis' philosophy of *magic idealism*, which, when achieved, will enable man to "turn things into thoughts and thoughts into things," and make him so far emancipated from nature that he may be capable of restoring lost limbs and even die simply by willing his own death. Then, perhaps, he may achieve real insights into the true nature of death and of the spiritual world. The tool to be used for this purpose is what Novalis calls the *romanticizing principle;* "romanticize" means for Novalis a certain operation of thought of his own invention, which consists in "elevating the lower into a higher quality" through which the original and deeper meaning is reached.[6] And death is the "romanticizing principle of our life . . . through death life is strengthened" [7] because it opens the doors to eternity and to the Supernatural. Death is essentially not the reverse of life, but rather the completion of life. "Life is the beginning of death. Life exists for the sake of death. Death is at the same time the ending and the beginning." [8]

This magic idealism gradually becomes fused in Novalis' mind with Christianity. It was as the founder of a new religion, of an inspired version of Christianity, that he appeared to some of his friends.[9]

In the *Fragments* we already find the significant aphorisms: "What reason is to the philosopher, faith, in the narrower sense, is to the poets." "Out of the power of faith the whole world originated. . . . In the Will is the Ground of creation . . . Faith is the action of the will on intelligence." [10]

The Christian view of death clearly emerges in the *Hymns to the Night: "Im Tod wird euch das ewige Leben kund."* It is the death of the Savior that is opening the doors of eternity to mankind. Here Christianity is a religion of death,[11] but of a death that is vanquished by the sacrifice of the Savior.

Schelling (1775-1854) speaks of his system as that of *objective idealism* in order to emphasize its opposition to Fichte's *subjective idealism*. Nature is not dead matter, an interplay of mechanical forces, but is ensouled, spiritual, and living. He consequently dismisses the materialistic, mechanistic approach of natural science as totally mistaken. The essence of reality is irrational; therefore it is not accessible to logical thought and can be grasped only through intuition and understood only symbolically. Nature is "the Odyssey of the spirit," of which man represents the highest form, and which strives to return to itself. Matter itself is nothing but dormant spirit,[12] and duality, contradiction, polarity pervade the whole of Nature, as can be seen in the phenomena of magnetism and electricity, in the mutually neutralizing acids and alkalis, in the opposite relation of plants and of animals to oxygen, as well as in the conscious and unconscious spheres of the individual psyche.

It is to this living Whole in its incomprehensible and immeasurable splendor, greatness, and holiness that the Romantic longs to return.[13] "How wonderful," writes Creuzer, "will it be in death, or rather in the great All, wherein the individuality will become absorbed." Shelley, who is similarly enthusiastic about death—"how wonderful is death"—says, speaking of the death of Keats,

> He is made one with Nature; there is heard
> His voice in all her music, from the moan
> Of thunder to the song of night's sweet bird.
> *Adonais*

Similarly, Hoelderlin proclaims in *Hyperion* that "to be one with everything that lives, in blissful forgetfulness to return into the Whole of Nature, this is the epitome of thoughts and joys, this is the sacred mountaintop, the abode of eternal rest . . . From the union of Beings death disappears" (*"aus dem Bunde der Wesen schwindet der Tod"*).[14] This thought is also used as consolation in the face of death by Schleiermacher, who writes to a friend that

personal existence is not essential to spiritual life, it is only
an appearance. How it repeats itself we do not and we can
not know, we can only use our poetic imagination. But do
not, in your holy pain, oppose your loving and pious
imagination, and let it roam freely in all directions. And
when your fantasy will show you your merging into the great
All-One, dear child, do not permit bitterness to take hold
of you. Just do not think of it as dead, but as living and as
the highest life! It is, actually, what we all aspire to in this
life but can never attain—to live only in the All-One and
to free ourselves from the deception that we are—or could
be—something unique.[15]

Madame de Staël, however, remarks rather sarcastically:

That the individual in us disappears, that the inner qualities
which we possess, return to the great Whole of eternal creation, this kind of immortality has a frightening similarity
to death; because physical death is nothing else than the
universal nature taking back from the individual the gifts
which it lent to him.

And indeed, this romantic "love of death," particularly when
death is conceived as total loss of one's conscious personality,
stands in such a flagrant contradiction to the usual attitude to
death that it was considered by many as merely a pose.

Thus Stendhal speaks scornfully of "these young men who
. . . well fed and well sheltered, do not cease to proclaim the
miseries of life and the joys of death." However, there can
be little doubt about the sincerity of the Romantics, although
they are clearly victims of what one of the leading Romantics,
Clemens Brentano, called "the hypertrophy of the poetic
organ." We have to consider that most of the Romantics lived
in close proximity to death. Most of them died young. Novalis
was consumptive and died at the age of twenty-nine. We read in
his diary: "I shall not achieve anything here, I shall take leave
from everything in my bloom." An early death carried off his
beloved brother Erasmus; his great love, Sophie von Kuehn,

died at the age of fifteen and "with her the whole world died for me." [16]

Schelling, as a consequence of the sudden death of his beloved Caroline, came for a short time close to the glorification of death. The loss of his wife, twelve years his senior, made the thirty-four-year-old Schelling turn to the glories of the spiritual world. At the same time, as his thoughts turned to immortality, his melancholy disposition asserted itself and he bewailed the horrors of existence "of which we are usually not aware because God in His goodness hides them from us." To a friend he writes that "those who are liberated from earthly existence ought to be congratulated."

This phase was not of long duration. Very soon Schelling asserts that he is "far removed from any sentimental nostalgia for death, and firmly resolved to live and work as long as it will be granted me." Three years after Caroline's death he married a twenty-year-old girl, the friend of a friend of his wife, and lived to the ripe old age of seventy-nine thoroughly enjoying his large progeny and the many honors that came his way.

At no time, however, does Schelling look forward to the merging with the Whole, but to personal immortality; and not merely to the reunion of the souls but to bodily immortality, for "it is not enough to think of the continuation of our dear departed ones, but of their whole personality." And this is vouchsafed for him through the conviction "of the real unity of God and Nature which became revealed through Christ." The certainty that Christ "went through death, has re-established the connection between Nature and the spiritual realm, transforms for us death into a triumph toward which we advance like warriors toward certain victory." [17]

Even though Schelling's answer to death is that of Christianity, his philosophical insights intimate other possibilities. We think in particular of his famous question, "Why is there at all something and not nothing?" [18]

We are not concerned here with his various answers to this question,[19] but with his remark that no one has really begun to philosophize who was not stunned and awed by the fact that there is something rather than nothing. And when this question is asked and one's reason, as Schelling puts it, is "made dizzy by the abyss of eternity," one becomes aware of the mysteriousness and miraculousness that something exists at all.[20] To awaken this awareness and to extend it to one's own existence— to make one feel the mystery of life and death—may well be the main service philosophy can render to those who turn to it in search of an answer to death.

If the glorification of death is unusual, the lure of death in a less extreme form is nevertheless found in most of the subsequent answers to death which deny personal immortality.

Chapter 20

Schopenhauer (1788-1860)

Death Is the True Aim of Life

ARTHUR SCHOPENHAUER was the first modern philosopher who investigated the problem of death in a systematic and comprehensive manner. His views are of particular interest because in spite of his profoundly pessimistic view of life, which makes him say that "the brevity of life, which is so constantly lamented, may be the best quality it possesses," [1] he seeks to prove that "our true nature is indestructible." And he attempts this with the help of a philosophical system which, as he himself says, "could not have arisen before the rays of the Upanishads, of Plato and Kant had converged in my mind."

Before we turn to Schopenhauer's answer to death, it is important to consider the intimate connection which according to him exists between death and the philosophical enterprise.

Death is the true inspiring genius, or the muse of philosophy. Socrates has defined the latter as θανατον μελετη. Indeed without death men could scarcely philosophize. The brute lives without a proper knowledge of death. . . . In the case of man the *terrifying certainty of death* necessarily entered with reason. But as everywhere in nature with every evil a means of cure, or at least some compensation, is given, the same reflection which introduces the knowledge of death also assists us to metaphysical points of view, which comforts us concerning it, and of which the brute has no need and is incapable. All religious and philosophical systems are principally directed to this end, and are thus primarily the antidote to the certainty of death, which the *reflective reason produces out of its own means*. Yet the degree in which they attain this end is very different, and certainly one religion or philosophy will, far more than the others, enable man to look death in the face with a quiet glance. [2]

162

Two assertions made by Schopenhauer merit special attention: He takes for granted that the certainty of death is terrifying. And he holds that Nature always provides a cure or compensation for every evil: "Reflective reason" produces, as it were, an antitoxin against the fear of death, in the form of religious or philosophical systems, and these systems are not fancies, for there is some grain of truth in all of them. The first contention is debatable, the second surprisingly optimistic for a pessimist.

The main thesis is that death is the muse of philosophy, and it is undoubtedly true in the case of Schopenhauer himself. But he is not only concerned with his own death. He cannot accept the idea that all that lives and breathes simply disappears after a brief span of time.

> That while what is most imperfect, the lowest, the unorganized, continues to exist unassailed . . . the most perfect beings, the living creatures, with their infinitely complicated and inconceivable organizations . . . absolutely pass into nothingness, to make room for other new ones like them coming into existence out of nothing—*this is something so obviously absurd that it can never be the true order of things,* but rather a mere veil which conceals this, or, more accurately, a phenomenon conditioned by the nature of our intellect. Nay, the whole being and not-being itself of these individuals, in relation to which death and life are opposites, can only be relative. Thus the language of Nature, in which it is given as an absolute, cannot be the true and ultimate expression of the nature of things and of the order of the world, but indeed only a *patois du pays,* i.e., something merely relatively true—something to be understood *cum grano salis,* or to speak properly, something conditioned by our intellect.[3]

What is this other, the true nature of things, according to Schopenhauer?

The World as Will and Idea

The title of Schopenhauer's main work contains in a nutshell his basic thought: [4]"that the world is my idea is a truth that holds good for everything that lives and knows." Obviously, it requires some effort to realize that what one knows is not the sun, but only an eye that sees the sun, that the world that surrounds him is there only as a "representation," only in relation to consciousness. But once this is done, man has attained philosophical wisdom and no truth appears more self-evident, more certain than that "this whole world is only object in relation to subject, perception of a perceiver, in a word 'representation,' 'idea.' [5] "The world is my idea" does not mean, however, that the world is a dream, even though "on one side at least [it] must be recognized as akin to dreams." For "the function of the brain which, during sleep, conjures up before us a completely objective, perceptible, and even palpable world, must have just as large a share in the presentation of the objective world of waking life." [6]

But Schopenhauer does not deny the *empirical* reality of the external world. For "it presents itself as that which it is, and performs directly what it promises." The scientists, from their point of view, are quite right, he holds, "to assume the objective world as something absolutely given," for "the empirical point of view of science is quite enough for the practical purposes of life." But from the point of view of the philosopher who "has to go back to what is first and original," the "empirical point of view" is "by no means sufficient to afford us any conclusion as to the existence and real nature, or rather as to the intelligible substratum of the phenomena which in this way arise for us." "The inner nature of things," which alone concerns philosophy, is "absolutely impossible to attain upon the path of mere knowledge and perception." And "as long as we are concerned . . . with objective comprehension, that is, with *knowledge,* the world is, and remains for us, a mere idea. . . ." [7]

Schopenhauer calls his position "transcendental" idealism. It "leaves the empirical reality of the world untouched, but holds fast to the fact that every *object,* thus the empirically real in general, is conditioned in a twofold manner by the subject: in the first place *materially* or as *object* generally, because an objective existence is only conceivable as opposed to a subject, and as its idea; in the second place formally, because the mode of existence of an object, i.e. its being perceived (space, time, causality), proceeds from the subject, is prearranged in the subject."

Thus "the whole material world, with its bodies, which are extended in space and, by means of time, have causal relations to each other . . . is not something which is there *independently* from our head, but essentially presupposes the functions of our brain *by means of which* and *in* which alone *such* an objective arrangement of things is possible. . . ." [8]

To conclude from this position that there exists nothing but myself, no world independent of me, but only my own ideas, and no other perceiving minds besides my own, in short, to assert solipsism, would be to misunderstand Schopenhauer completely. Even when he says that "with the entire abolition of knowledge, the rest of the world would of itself vanish into nothing; for without a subject there is no object," [9] he never intends to deny the existence of other perceiving minds; and the world that would vanish into nothing with the abolition of knowledge is only the world as my idea, which is only *one* "aspect" of the world. As a matter of fact, Schopenhauer takes a very strong stand against solipsism, which he calls "theoretical egoism." [10] Although theoretical egoism can never be refuted, yet

in philosophy it has never been used otherwise than as a sceptical sophism, i.e., a pretence. As a serious conviction, on the other hand, it could only be found in a madhouse, and as such it stands in need of a cure rather than a refutation. We do not therefore combat it any further in this regard, but treat it as merely the last stronghold of scepticism, which is always polemical. Thus our knowledge, which is always bound to individuality, and is limited by this circumstance, brings with it the necessity that each of us can only *be one,* while, on the other hand, each of us can *know all;* and it is this limitation which creates the need for philosophy. [11]

As we have seen, Schopenhauer considers the proposition, "The World is my Idea," the first step to philosophical wisdom. He is aware, however, of the inward reluctance to accept it, and this reluctance serves as a warning that this truth must be one-sided and incomplete.

To discover the complete truth requires, in Schopenhauer's words, "a deeper research and more severe abstraction." It seems clear to him that "we can never arrive at the real nature of things from without." As a matter of fact, we would never be able to find it, if we were merely a knowing subject. But man is more than "pure knowing subject." He is "rooted in the world; he finds himself in it as an individual, that is to say, his knowledge . . . is yet always given through the medium of a body . . . [which] for the pure knowing subject is an idea like every other idea, an object among objects." But the body "is given in two entirely different ways . . . as an idea in intelligent perception . . . subject to the laws of objects . . . and as that which is immediately known to everyone, and signified by the word 'will.' " Thus "in a certain sense we may also say that will is the knowledge a priori of the body, and the body is the knowledge a posteriori of the will." [12] Now Schopenhauer applies this knowledge, which everyone has of the nature and activity of his body, as "a key to the nature of every phenomenon of nature" and considers all objects, which are given to our consciousness only as our *idea* (or *representation*) also to be, in their inner natures, *will*. It is an open question whether it is justified to assume such an analogy with our body, and even if we could, whether *will* is what is immediately known to us and whether it is the ultimate reality. In asserting the latter, Schopenhauer intentionally goes beyond Kant, who declared that the thing in itself cannot be known. Schopenhauer says that it can be known and that it is *will*. As the thing in itself, the will is outside of time and space and, according to Schopenhauer, totally blind—that is, without any ability to know.

This universal will, which is the thing in itself, is present "entire and undivided in every object of nature and in every living being." [13] The world is indeed the manifestation of the will that "objectifies" itself in different degrees; and the grades of the objectification of will [14] which are manifested in innumerable individuals, and exist as their unattained types or as the eternal forms of things, not entering themselves into time and space, which are the medium of individual things, but remaining fixed, subject to no change, always being, never becoming, while the particular things arise and pass away, always become and never are—are . . . simply Plato's Ideas.[15]

These grades or levels are related to individual things as their eternal forms or prototypes.

The lowest grades of the objectification of the will are to be found in those most universal forces of nature which partly appear in all matter without exception as gravity and impenetrability, and partly have shared the given matter among them, so that certain of them reign in one species of matter and others in another species, constituting its specific difference as rigidity, fluidity, elasticity, electricity, magnetism, chemical properties and qualities of every kind. They are in themselves immediate manifestations of will, just like human action; and as such they are groundless, like human character.[16]

Man is the highest grade of objectification and "every man is to be regarded as a specially determined and characterized phenomenon of will, and indeed to a certain extent as a special Idea." [17]

A higher Idea or objectification of will can, according to Schopenhauer, appear only through the conquest of a lower; it has to endure their opposition, since they, "although brought into subjection, still constantly strive to obtain an independent and complete expression of their being." Thus, the subdued forces of nature strive to win back from the organism the matter it took from them. "Hence also in general the burden of physical life, the *necessity* of sleep, and finally, of *death*." Each level of the objectification of will fights for the matter, the space, and the time of the others; and "thus everywhere in nature we see strife, conflict. . . ." [18]

But, with the ever-increasing multiplicity of the individual phenomena, the struggle and competition has become so great that the *chances of survival* of the individual "that is moved merely by stimuli and must wait for its food" has become greatly reduced. It is here, then, that *"consciousness becomes necessary;* and consequently it appears as an agent, called in at this stage of objectification of will for the *conservation of the individual* and the propagation of the species." [19] With consciousness "the world as idea" comes into existence "at a stroke, with all its forms, object and subject, time, space, multiplicity, and causality. The world now shows its second side. Till now mere 'will,' it becomes also idea (representation), object of a knowing subject. The will, which up to this point followed its tendency in the dark with unerring certainty has at this level kindled for itself a light as a means which became necessary for getting rid of the disadvantage which arose from the throng and the complicated nature of its manifestations . . ." [20]

The will itself, as thing-in-itself, is exempt from multiplicity and change. All this does not concern it. "As the magic lantern shows many different pictures, which are all made visible by one and the same light, so in all the multifarious phenomena which fill the world together or throng after each other as events, only one will manifest itself, of which everything is the visibility, the objectivity, and which remains unmoved in the midst of this change." [21]

Some believe to have discovered in Schopenhauer's philosophy a vicious circle, since it is presumed to state that on the one hand consciousness presupposes matter and on the other matter presupposes consciousness, or that the world is in the brain and at the same time the brain is part of the world. Such criticism is based on a superficial acquaintance with Schopenhauer's views. Even though Schopenhauer starts his exposition with the statement that "the world is my idea," the title of the work, *The World as Will and Idea,* clearly indicates that the world as *idea* is *secondary,* for the world is *primarily Will.* It is the prearranging in the subject of the *"mode* of existence of the objects" in time, space and causality by the brain, or by what Kant called "the faculty of knowledge," that makes the world "my idea," and brings about that empirical reality, the world of phenomena, our everyday world. Schopenhauer clearly says that

> the origin of the world is not to be sought in either of the two, matter or intelligence. . . . Intelligence and Matter are correlates, i.e., the one exists only for the other, both stand and fall together. . . . Matter is the idea of the intelligence; the intelligence is that in whose idea alone matter exists. The two together constitute the world as idea, which is just Kant's phenomenon, and consequently something secondary. What is primary is that which manifests itself, the thing in itself . . . the will.[22] And previously, he said that it is evident, that the existence which is conditioned through a knowing subject is only the existence in space, and therefore that of an extended and active being. This alone is always something *known,* and consequently an *existence for another.* On the other hand, every being that exists in this way (that is as an object for a knowing subject) may yet have an *existence for itself* . . . for which it requires no subject. Yet this existence for itself . . . is necessarily a being *of another kind,* that of thing in itself, which as such can never be an *object.*[23]

What is idea? A very complicated *physiological* process in the brain of an animal, the result of which is the consciousness of a picture there. Clearly the relation between such a picture and something entirely different from the animal in whose brain it exists can only be a very indirect one.[24]

Consciousness is conditioned by the intellect, and the intellect is a mere accident of our being; for it is a *function of the brain,* which . . . is a mere fruit, a product, nay (so far) a parasite of the rest of the organism . . . The organism itself, on the other hand, is the visibility, the objectivity, of the individual will, the image of it as it presents itself in that very brain (which . . . we learned to recognize as the condition of the objective world in general), therefore also brought about by its forms of knowledge, space, time and causality. . . . According to this one may say: The intellect is the secondary phenomenon; the organ-

ism the primary phenomenon, that is, the immediate manifestation of the will; the will is metaphysical, the intellect
physical . . .[25]

The separation in subject and object is misleading: they
are both "poles of the world as idea, the objective world. . . .
Both are completely unknowable; the subject because it is that
which knows, matter because without form and quality it
cannot be perceived. Yet both are fundamental conditions of
all empirical perception." [26] And they are inseparably joined
together as necessary parts of one whole, which includes both
and exists through them. And that which includes both is "the
world as idea, or the world of phenomenon. When this is
taken away there remains only what is purely metaphysical,
the thing in itself . . . the will." [27]

Thus if we interpret the title of Schopenhauer's magnum
opus to mean "The (Transcendental) World as Will and the
(phenomenal, objective, empirical) World as Idea," [28] we
would correctly reflect the main proposition of his philosophy.

A particular feature of this philosophy is that it is in *will*
that the cause of man's unhappiness resides. Because the will
"of which human life, like every phenomenon is the objectification, is a striving without aim and end," the consequence
is "the impossibility of attaining lasting satisfaction and the
negative nature of all happiness." [29]

> Now the nature of man consists in this, that his will strives,
> is satisfied and strives anew, and so on forever. Indeed, his
> happiness and well-being consist simply in the quick transi-
> tion from wish to satisfaction, and from satisfaction to a
> new wish. For the absence of satisfaction is suffering, the
> empty longing for a new wish, languor, ennui. . . .[30]

The life of the great majority is only a constant struggle for
this existence itself, with the certainty of losing it at last.

> The basis of all willing is need, deficiency and thus
> pain. Consequently, the nature of brutes and man is sub-
> ject to pain originally and through its very being. If, on the
> other hand, it lacks objects of desire, because it is at once

deprived of them by a too easy satisfaction, a terrible void and ennui comes over it, i.e., its being and existence itself becomes an unbearable burden to it.[31]

Life swings like a pendulum backwards and forwards between pain and ennui. But what enables us to endure this wearisome battle is not so much the love of life as the fear of death, which yet stands in the background as inevitable, and may come upon us at any moment.

The Fear of Death

Why does man fear death when even the simplest reflection plainly shows that life is "want, wretchedness, affliction, and misery"? Why is death considered "the greatest evil; the worst punishment that can be threatened"? And why is the fear of death the "greatest fear"? [32] Moreover, "man fears death not only for himself but for his loved ones, and bitterly bewails their passing not so much because of his own loss, as out of pity for the great misfortune that has befallen them."

Schopenhauer argues that it cannot be the painfulness of death that makes us fear it, since pain belongs to sickness and old age, that is, to life. "What we fear in death is not pain, for it lies clearly on this side of death, moreover we often take refuge in death from pain, just as we endure the most fearful suffering merely to escape death. Pain and death are two entirely distinct evils." [33] Moreover, for the dying person death is merely the split second when his consciousness ceases —a sensation like fainting, which is anything but disagreeable.[34] Nor is it so much the thought of non-being, for in such a case, Schopenhauer argues, we would also think with terror of the times when we did not as yet exist.[35]

"What we fear in death is the *end of the individual,* which it openly professes itself to be, and since the individual is a particular objectification of the will to live itself, its whole nature struggles against death." [36] It is then in the Will that the fear of death resides.

There seems to be a paradox in Schopenhauer's assertion that consciousness, which knows of death and which is destroyed by it, does not fear it.

And there is indeed a real contradiction. On the one hand he says, "In fact, the fear of death is independent of all knowledge; for the brute has it, although it does not know death. Everything that is born brings it with it into the world. But this fear of death is a priori only the reverse side of the will to live, which indeed we all have. Therefore in *every brute the fear of its destruction is inborn.*" [37] But two pages earlier he said, "The brute lives without a proper knowledge of death; therefore the individual brute enjoys directly the absolute imperishableness of the species, for it is *only conscious of itself as endless.* In the case of man the terrifying certainty of death *necessarily* entered with reason." [38]

Perhaps the difficulty arises from the failure to distinguish clearly enough between the conscious fear of death that derives from knowledge of the certainty of death, which man alone possesses, and the fear of annihilation, the awareness of the fragility of life, which every living being may be presumed to have.[39] It is also possible that the contradiction may have something to do with the circumstance that, according to Schopenhauer, the fear of death is due to a "mistake" of the will. The will mirrors itself in the world of phenomena that issues from its drive for manifestation, and comes to know itself through it and in it. But this knowledge of its essential nature is given to the will in the individual appearance; it thus comes unavoidably to the erroneous conclusion that it perishes with the individual, an error similar to mistaking one's reflection in a mirror for one's real self, and then when the mirror is broken and the image in it disappears, concluding that oneself is destroyed.

The truth is, according to Schopenhauer, however, that just as the person seeing himself in the mirror does not perish when the mirror is broken, so the will is not affected when the individual perishes. That which is really affected and destroyed by death—consciousness and intellect—feels no fear, for it is incapable of having any desire or emotion and is therefore indifferent to being. In other words, whatever the contradictions as far as the sources of the fear of death are concerned, the important thing is that this fear is, according to Schopenhauer, groundless even if one does not share the pessimistic view of life and does not want to escape life. For we do not perish completely.

It is, then, the will that on the one hand causes unhappiness and on the other puts a formidable obstacle in the way of escape from the misery of existence in the fear of death.

But does suicide not present a way out of this dilemma? In this connection Schopenhauer's view of suicide is of particular interest. He holds that the "always open door" of Epictetus does not lead anywhere, because the all-pervading and all-powerful will to live is not suspended or denied through the death of the individual.

> Whoever is oppressed with the burden of life, whoever desires life and affirms it, but abhors its torments, such a man has no deliverance to hope from death, and cannot right himself by suicide.[40]

"The suicide denies only the individual not the species . . ." and therefore "the willful destruction of the single phenomenal existence is a vain and foolish act; for the *thing-in-itself* remains unaffected by it, even as the rainbow endures however fast the drops which support it for the moment may change." [41]

It is here that his metaphysics of the will seems to come into conflict with the obvious conclusions one might expect in view of his pessimism. The pessimism demands an escape from the misery of existence, but such an escape in the usual and only logical manner, through self-inflicted (or even natural) death, is made impossible by the indestructibility of our true nature. Perhaps Schopenhauer was so afraid of death that he could not envisage the obvious solution and wanted an excuse for not committing suicide by showing that it would be of no avail anyway.

Be that as it may, Schopenhauer asserts, that which constitutes man's true nature—will—is unaffected by death. And this "indestructibility of our true nature" is one of the pillars on which Schopenhauer's complex answer to death rests.

> Since man is Nature itself, and indeed Nature at the highest grade of its self-consciousness, but Nature is only the ob-

jectified will to live, the man who has comprehended this point of view may well console himself, when contemplating his own death and that of his friends, by turning his eyes to the immortal life of Nature, which he himself is.[42]

The Indestructibility of Our "True Nature"

The doctrine of indestructibility of our "true nature" seems to be a concession to Schopenhauer's own desire for at least partial immortality. In any event, it is quite in tune with his conception of will.

Schopenhauer begins his argument by pointing out that there is in all of us an intimation of our imperishability. No one truly believes in his own death, or as Schopenhauer puts it, "Man does not really receive death in his living consciousness." [43] And he considers insufficient the purely psychological explanation that this peculiarity is the result of habit or of acquiescence in the inevitable.

The explanation lies deeper: this feeling that we are imperishable (and, according to Schopenhauer, the existence of dogmas at all times and in all peoples relating to continuous existence of the individual after death confirms the universality of this feeling) reflects correctly the indestructibility of our true nature. And this "inward and merely felt consciousness of that which we have raised to distinct knowledge is sufficient to prevent the thought of death from poisoning the life of the rational being." But it does not protect the individual from "being seized by fear of death, and trying in every way to escape from it, when it presents itself to him in some particular real case, or only in his imagination.[44]

In such a case more solid proofs become necessary, and Schopenhauer proceeds to present them. But first we have to determine what that indestructible something in us is. According to Schopenhauer, it is not our consciousness or soul. For consciousness is merely the "product and result" of organized life; and there is no reason to conclude that individuality is inherent in the principle that imparts life. On the other hand, "there is as little occasion to conclude that because organized life has ceased, the force which hitherto actuated it has also become nothing," as there is to infer the death of the spinner from the stopping of the spinning wheel.[45]

That it cannot be the individual that in any shape or form survives death, a look at Nature shows with unmistakable clarity. We see there a total disregard for the individual. But would Mother Nature expose her children to a thousand perils, if she did not know that when they fall they nevertheless return into her lap? Death mows relentlessly, and yet "despite death and decay, everything is still there."

Of course, says Schopenhauer, if we think of the individual as originating out of nothing at conception, or beginning at birth, he indeed becomes nothing at death. But to view the individual in this way is a mistake, as can easily be seen from the fact that the features of the parents appear in their progeny. If it be foolish to maintain that the cat playing right now in the yard is the same as the one that played there three hundred years ago, it is even more foolish, in Schopenhauer's opinion, to think that the present cat is essentially and in every way different from the one three hundred years ago. And yet we know that this present cat is perishable. What is indestructible, however, is the idea—in the Platonic meaning—the species, which is the direct objectification of the will, the unchangeable and imperishable.

"The idea, or species, is that in which the will to live is actually rooted." As the waterdrops of a waterfall change, appear and disappear continuously, though the rainbow they support remains standing in majestic repose, untouched by the constant change, so each idea, that is, each species, remains unaffected by the change of its individual members. The lions that are born and die are like the drops of water; but the "leonitas," the idea of the lion is like the rainbow.[46]

"It is Nature's great doctrine of immortality, which seeks to teach us that there is no radical difference between sleep and death, and that the latter endangers our being as little as the former." [47]

"Whether the fly which now buzzes around me goes to sleep in the evening, and buzzes again tomorrow, or dies in the evening, and in the spring another fly buzzes which has sprung from an egg: that is in itself the same thing. . . .

"In agreement with this we find Nature, which is free from that delusion of the individual, as careful for the maintenance of the species as it is indifferent to the destruction of the individuals. . . ."

The crux of his argument is that there is no creation out of nothing, and that if we affirm it, we must also agree that death is the absolute end, nothing.

"Really the most solid ground for our immortality is the old principle: ex nihilo nihil fit, et in nihilum nihil potest reverti. . . .

"The assumption that man is made out of nothing leads necessarily to the assumption that death is his absolute end." For to assume that man originated out of nothing, "yet has an individual, endless existence, and indeed a conscious existence, while the dog, the ape, the elephant are annihilated by death, is really something against which the healthy mind revolts and which it must regard as absurd." [48]

In addition to the indestructibility of the species Schopenhauer falls back on the conservation of matter. However, he attributes to the "dust" into which we return at death characteristics not usually associated with it. "Matter," he writes, "through its absolute indestructibility guarantees us our indestructibility. 'But what?' people would say, 'the conservation of raw matter, of mere dust should be considered as the continuation of our essence?' But, do you know this dust? Do you know what it can do? Get to know it before you despise it." [49]

So far Schopenhauer was speaking merely "from the empirical point of view." He therefore turns to the "genuine philosophical consideration of the world" [50] and looks at death in the light of "philosophical knowledge," especially of Kant's great philosophical achievement—the distinction between the thing in itself and the phenomenon, and his theory that time is merely the form of our perceiving of phenomena.[51] It is especially in the latter that Schopenhauer believes to have found the most powerful support for his view that death cannot be total annihilation: "the most thorough answer to the question as to the continued existence of the individual after death lies in Kant's great Doctrine of the ideality of time." [52]

Kant states in the part of the *Critique of Pure Reason* called "Transcendental Aesthetic" that "time is not an empirical concept that has been derived from any experience." It is given a priori and is a purely subjective condition of our human intuition. "Time is the formal *a priori* condition of all appearances whatsoever." [53]

What Kant maintains is therefore the *"empirical reality of time,* that is, its objective validity in respect of all objects which allow of ever being given to our senses" as well as "the transcendental ideality of time," which means "that if we abstract from the subjective conditions of sensible intuition, time is nothing, and cannot be ascribed to the objects in themselves. . . ."

Put in the simplest terms, time is in us, even though in order to say this one may have to overlook the necessity of distinguishing between time as the necessary form of all intuitions and time as the form of activity that brings together all representations, time as form of receptivity and time as form of spontaneity, as form of the contents of consciousness and as condition of consciousness. If Kant is not very clear in his demonstration, he is very clear as to what he wants to demonstrate: the human mind "produces" or "brings forth" time.

The inference to be drawn from this doctrine seems obvious to Schopenhauer: our existence in time is merely an image of our essential being. Death is merely the end in time of a time-enclosed phenomenon. Man, as thing in itself, is outside of time, timeless, eternal, since for the thing in itself there is no end in time and the word time loses its meaning. Of course,

the end of the person is just as real as was its beginning, and in the same sense in which before birth, we were not, after death we shall be no more. Yet no more can be destroyed by death than was produced by birth. . . . But now the whole of empirical knowledge affords us merely phenomena; therefore only phenomena are involved in the temporal processes of coming into being and passing away, and not that which manifests itself in the phenomenon—the thing in itself. For this, the opposition of coming into being, does not exist at all, but has here lost meaning and significance.[54]

The concepts of cessation and continuation can be applied only to *phenomena*. Therefore we can say about our true essence that it continues after death, because it is misleading to say that it perishes; but we can also say that it perishes, because it is false to assert that it continues. One proposition is as true as the other.

If, however, one denies both predicates, not together but singly, it seems as if the opposite of the predicate, which is being denied in each case, were being affirmed. This is so, says Schopenhauer, merely because two incommensurable quantities are compared, for the problem removes us to a scene where time is abolished, and yet asks about temporal properties, which it is consequently "equally false to attribute to, or to deny of, the subject. This just means: the problem is transcendent. In this sense death remains a mystery." [55]

What we can do, however, is adhere to the distinction between the phenomenon and the thing in itself and maintain that man is perishable as a phenomenon, but that his true nature is not affected by this; in other words, that man's essence, which because of the non-applicability to it of the concept of time cannot be spoken of as continuing, is indestructible; to will "life is certain and to life the *present* is certain." We thus arrive at a concept of *indestructibility without continuation*. But such a concept is a mere abstraction; it cannot be visualized.[56] Schopenhauer reminds us, however, that he does not follow Kant when the latter denies the possibility of knowing what the thing in itself may be; for the thing in itself is *will;* so also is man. As such he remains unaffected by the end of time. The concept of cessation is applicable to him only as far as his phenomenal aspect is concerned, and man's true essence remains and maintains an existence to which the concepts of beginning and continuation cannot be applied.[57]

The doctrine of the indestructibility of our true being teaches that each of us is "something more than merely a thing created out of nothing by someone else, some time ago;

from this springs the assurance that if death puts an end to his life, it still does not end man's existence." [58] This is, according to Schopenhauer, what Spinoza meant when he said that we feel and know that we are eternal. However, only if we can think of ourselves as without a beginning, as outside time, can we conceive of ourselves as indestructible. Still, there is the disturbing feeling that we perish, but that the world continues. Here too the realization that we are one with the world, that its inner essence is *will,* helps to quell our apprehension. The terrors of death, which are rooted in the false assumption that the *I* disappears, are completely unfounded; the inner kernel of the *I,* the bearer of the subject in whose representation alone the world exists (and perishes), remains.[59]

The word *I* is "the great equivocum," for, "according to how I understand this word I can say, 'Death is my complete end.' But I can also say, 'This my personal phenomenal existence is just as infinitely small a part of my true nature as I am of the world.' " [60]

Therefore, when we experience the fear of death, we see a strange, nay "almost comic spectacle, where the master of the world fears to perish, to go under into the abyss of eternal nothingness, whereas in reality everything is full of him and there is no place where he is not . . . for it is not being which carries him, but he who upholds being." [61]

For those, then, who love life, the remedy for their fear of death is the knowledge that time is only "a form of our intuition" and that their "true nature" is indestructible.

A man who has thoroughly assimilated the truth we have already advanced, and does not know from his own experience that constant suffering is essential to life, who finds satisfaction in it and for whom all that he wishes in life is that it may endure forever or repeat itself ever anew and whose love of life is so great that he willingly and gladly accepts all the hardships and miseries . . . such a man would have nothing to fear. Armed with the knowledge we have given him he would await with indifference the death that hastens toward him on the wings of time—he would regard it as an illusion, an impotent spectre, which had no power over him, who knew that he is himself the will of which the whole world is an objectification or copy, and therefore he would be always certain of life, and also of the present, the peculiar and only form of the phenomenon of the will—thus he would no more fear death than the sun fears the night.[62]

The Denial of the Will

What about those who cannot endure life and desire death as deliverance from pain and suffering? For these, as we have seen, death is not an escape and suicide is no solution. For since our true nature is indestructible, man can terminate his life, but not the will to live.

> Suicide is a phenomenon of strong assertion of will; for the essence of negation lies in this, that the joys of life are shunned, not its sorrows. The suicide wills life, and is only dissatisfied with the conditions under which it has presented itself to him. He therefore by no means surrenders the will to live, but only life. . . .[63]

The will to live is responsible for the fact that "every individual . . . has regard for his own existence and well-being before everything else; indeed, from the natural standpoint, is ready to sacrifice everything else for this—is ready to annihilate the world in order to maintain its own self . . . a little longer. This disposition is *egoism,* which is essential to everything in Nature." [64]

In man egoism reaches its highest degree and brings about the conflict between individuals "in its most terrible form." But, at the same time, on the human level, egoism is endowed with reason and seeks escape from its own evil consequences, which turn against itself, and now each promotes the well-being of all because he sees that his own well-being is involved in it. Moreover, "every man has from birth on besides his natural egoism a sympathy for the suffering of others, which actually contradicts the natural order of things." [65]

Once man comes to *know* that his existence (as an individual) is "a constant passing away, vain striving, inward conflict, and continual suffering," once "he sees wherever he looks suffering humanity, the suffering brute creation, and a world that passes away . . . why should he now, with such knowledge of the world, assert this very life through constant acts of will, and thereby bind himself ever more closely to it?" Thus the combined effect of the knowledge that life and the world are full of suffering and of "the knowledge of the nature of the thing in itself . . . becomes a *quieter* of all and every volition. The will now turns away from life; it now shudders at the pleasures in which it recognizes the assertion of life. Man now attains to the state of voluntary renunciation, resignation, true indifference, and perfect will-lessness." [66] Thus it is intelligence that "imparts to the will that knowledge in consequence of which it denies and abolishes itself." [67] In this way "the momentary cessation of all volition, which takes place whenever we give ourselves up to *aesthetic contemplation,* as pure will-less subject of knowledge . . ." [68] may become permanent.

However, "the denial of the will . . . cannot be forcibly attained by intention and design, but proceeds from the inmost relation of knowing and volition in the man, and therefore comes suddenly, as if spontaneously, from without. This is why the Christians called it the work of grace." [69]

Once the denial of the will is achieved, asceticism—"the intentional breaking of the will by the refusal of what is agreeable and the selection of what is disagreeable"—is "practiced by him who has attained to the denial of the will in order to be able to persist in it." [70] And it is in asceticism that Schopenhauer also finds the definitive solution to the problem of mastering the fear of death.

If at last death comes, which puts an end to this manifestation of that will, whose existence here has long perished through free denial of itself, with the exception of the weak residue of it which appears as the life of the body; it is *most welcome,* and is gladly received as a longed-for deliverance. Here it is not, as in the case of others, merely the manifestation which ends with death; but the *inner nature* itself is abolished, which here existed only in the manifestation, and that in a very weak degree; this slight bond is now broken. For him who thus ends, the world has ended also.[71]

At this point the question arises how the denial of the will whose essential trait consists in "assertion" is at all possible? Schopenhauer realizes himself that "denial of the will is irreconcilable with the earlier explanation of necessity." His answer is that "will" is free: "Assertion and denial are opposite acts of the same will whose capacity for both is the only true freedom." [72] That the will as such is free "follows from the fact that, according to our view, it is the thing in itself." [73] But "in truth real freedom . . . belongs to the will only as thing in itself, not to its manifestations, whose essential form is everywhere the . . . sphere of necessity." [74] But since will itself is "beyond causality" it is impossible for us even to ask for the cause for this change from assertion to denial. Thus a veil of mystery surrounds this problem of why the will either asserts or denies itself, and no human hand will ever be able to lift it. And Schopenhauer approvingly quotes Malebranche, who said that "la liberté est un mystère,"— freedom is a mystery—and he himself says that "the freedom of the will is precisely what the Christian mystics call the *work of grace* and *the new birth*." [75]

Death itself is "the moment of liberation from the onesidedness of individuality, which is not the innermost kernel of our being, but has to be conceived as a kind of aberration of it. The true, original freedom comes back to us in this moment which can be considered as a restitutio in integram." [76] In death we return to our original condition, the condition of the thing in itself. When our consciousness and our intellect perish in death, we are merely put into an unknowing condition. But this does not mean that it will be a totally unconscious one, but rather a superior condition, since in it the dichotomy of subject and object disappears.

Schopenhauer's philosophy shows certain similarities with

the philosophies of Bruno and Spinoza. Schopenhauer was aware of this. "The philosophy of Bruno and that of Spinoza might also lead anyone to this point of view whose conviction was not shaken and weakened by their errors and imperfections." [77] Schopenhauer especially emphasizes his closeness to Spinoza's pantheism and says that his philosophy stands in the same relation to Spinozism as the New Testament stands to the Old. "What the Old Testament has in common with the New is the same God-Creator. Analogous to this, the world exists, with me as with Spinoza, by its inner power and through itself. But with Spinoza his *substantia aeterna,* the inner nature of the world, which he himself calls God, is also, as regards its moral character and worth, Jehovah, the God-Creator, who applauds His own creation, and finds that all is very good. . . . Spinoza has deprived Him of nothing but personality. Thus, according to him also, the world and all in it is wholly excellent and as it ought to be: therefore man has nothing more to do than *vivire, agere, suum esse conservare* . . . he is even to rejoice in his life as long as it lasts . . . in short it is optimism. . . . With me, on the other hand, the will, or the inner nature of the world, is by no means Jehovah, it is rather, as it were, the crucified Savior, or the crucified thief." [78]

He also acknowledges his great indebtedness to Buddhism: "The great truth which is expressed here," e.g., in Schopenhauer's philosophy, "has never been entirely unacknowledged . . . and (is) coming nearest to the truth . . . in Buddhism." [79]

He reports that already as a youth of seventeen he was "as possessed by the sorrows of the world as was Buddha in his youth at the sight of illness, old age, pain and death." [80] And when he became acquainted with Hindu philosophy he found that "the Hindus have long ago learned the lesson of Nature which shows that death is the great reprimand which the will to live, or more especially egoism, which is essential to this, receives through the course of nature; and it may be conceived as a punishment for our existence. . . . We are at bottom something that ought not to be: therefore we cease to be." [81] But disappearing as individuals we remain in the great All: "In spite of time, death and decay, we are still all together." [82]

Is this the kind of immortality most people crave? Schopenhauer knows that such is not the case:

> The imperishable nature of our true being can be proved with certainty. But it is true this will not satisfy the claims which are wont to be made upon proofs of our continued existence after death, nor insure the consolation which is expected from such proofs. However, it is always something; and whoever fears death as an absolute annihilation cannot afford to despise the perfect certainty that the inmost principle of his life remains untouched by it.[83]

He reminds those who are not satisfied with such an immortality, that

> to desire that individuality should be immortal really means to wish to perpetuate an error infinitely. For at bottom every individual is really only a special error, a false step, something that had better not be; nay, something which it is the real end of life to bring us back from.[84]

And once it is understood that man does not exist in order to be happy but that "suffering is clearly man's true destiny" [85] and that "dying is certainly to be regarded as the real aim of life" [86] death can be accepted not only with equanimity, but with joy. Dying is the true aim of life because "in the moment of death all that is decided for which the whole course of life was only a preparation and introduction" and "the whole striving whose manifestation in life was a vain, idle and self-contradictory effort, to have returned from which is a deliverance." [87] It is important to realize, however, that "The nothing which remains [?!] after the entire abolition of will," when "our world which is so real, with all its suns and milky ways has become nothing," [88] is for Schopenhauer not really nothing. He says that the world is the manifestation of the will that asserts itself, but that we do not know the manifestation of the will that *denies itself*. This implies that there is such a manifestation. And, although "the nature of things before and beyond the world and consequently beyond the will, is open to no investigation," he adds that "the world does not fill the whole possibility of all being, but in this there still remains much room for that which we denote only negatively as the denial of the will to live." [89]

As Schopenhauer points out, the main object of his philosophical writing was to "impart that one thought," [90] namely, that the world of suffering and death is "something merely relatively true and not the true and ultimate expression of the nature of things." [91] For those who have been convinced by his arguments, his philosophy brings consolation to those who suffer from what is mislabelled "the tragic sense of life"—the terrible feeling that death proclaims the futility of life.

Chapter 21

Feuerbach (1804-1872)

Life Must Be Lived
Fully in Spite of Death

THE INJUNCTION not to let our enthusiasm for life be dampened
by the fact that "there is no cure for death" is in Feuerbach's
case not simply a matter of overflowing vitality which con-
veniently ignores our mortality. Feuerbach was all his life
concerned with death and the problem of immortality and his
first and last writings deal with these issues.[1] To investigate in
detail how he was able to combine the joy of living with the
awareness of death, to affirm life and at the same time joyfully
acquiesce to death, and whether others can follow in his path
is the more pertinent today, since the horror of ceasing to
exist poisons the lives of not a few and the need to come to
terms with death as total annihilation is deeply felt by many.

In his first work, the *Thoughts on Death,* he is still
very much under the influence of Hegel, much more so than
he himself wants to admit. Characteristically, he begins with
the ethical significance of death. All human action can be
derived from love. "Man loves, must love," and man becomes
truly man, that is a truly moral being, when he relinquishes
his natural egoism, overcomes his self-seeking existence, and
surrenders to the existence of others. The further one moves
in this direction, the more human one becomes. The highest
life, the life in religion, thought, and morality, is one in which
man completely surrenders his false *selfhood.* But, "with the
very same will with which thou willest love and truth, thou
causest death." Love would not be complete if there were no
death. Death is the last sacrifice, the last proof of love. Only
once is man his true self and this he is in the moment of
non-being. Death, therefore, precisely because it reveals man's
true self, is at the same time the revelation of love.[2]

But love presupposes freedom. Feuerbach assumes, however, that there is a kind of pre-established harmony, a "secret
and intimate unity" between the true will of man and Nature
—and that a necessity in nature corresponds to the free action
of man, so that the inner negation corresponds to a negation
in the natural realm. Death as a natural phenomenon is also
the last expiatory sacrifice, the last vindication of love. Those
who look deeper know that "death does not begin with natural
death, but concludes and ends with it." Natural death is
nothing but "an exhalation of the inner and hidden death,"
and in the "outward" death, death as it is perceived by our
senses, this captive and hidden death is released, since this
death of self is love.[3]

But why, then, do animals and plants die? Only because
men die. Human death is the reason for the death of other
living beings, as the death of the truly loving and truly moral
beings is the reason for the death of those whose love is
limited. For the highest is always the cause of the lower: "Out
of the highest man takes down death and pours it into
creation." [4]

According to Feuerbach, death has a metaphysical, a psychological, and a physical reason, cause, and origin.

The first, the undetermined, infinite reason of death is the
Infinite—God. The determined, finite reasons are Time, Space
and Life; and the determined, infinite cause is mind, spirit,
consciousness.[5] The speculative or metaphysical ground of
death, Feuerbach argues, becomes apparent when we realize
that what is commonly known as death presupposes a supra-
temporal, suprasensible (*ueberzeitlich* and *uebersinnlich*)
death. Even if one has no knowledge of God, one knows at
least that God is unlimited, the Infinite Being. In order to
make God an object of the spirit, one has to negate all limitations and determinations. But this necessity of negating all
that is finite in order to arrive at the idea of the infinite is
rooted not in man but in the object itself. Because the infinite
itself is the negation of the finite, man's abstracting, through
which he succeeds in creating the idea of the infinite, is only
an imitation of that which the infinite itself does.

The real and true nullity of the finite is therefore the infinite itself. That things are actually finite, that they change and pass away, is based solely on the real existence of the infinite. . . . Only through the infinite and in it is the finite finite, and is the nullity, the death of the finite posited: The "sensible" death is, as it were, the sound by which the temporal thing expresses and announces its supernatural death—it is the light that illuminates and reveals the hidden and secret death, and that which does not contain the infinite cannot die.[6]

Therefore, to desire something after death is a profound aberration. For one dies precisely because there is already before death all that one imagines one is able to attain after death. Death does not come out of deficiency and poverty, but out of fullness.

All the things that exist outside of man, all that he distinguishes as different from himself under the general concept of Nature, are the points of limitation and negation (*Grenzund Negationspunkte*) of man. Every collision with a tree, a wall, is a collision with death, with the limit and the end of existence. One does not have to go walking in a cemetery to become aware of one's finiteness—every object outside oneself conveys this message; every push against one's ribs, every pressure from outside is a living *memento mori*. Were there no objects, the subject would be without limits, infinite, and consequently immortal per se. This brings us to the physical ground of death. That which is, in its essence, determined and limited, a definite person, exists only a certain time, and only in this life, limited in time, is one this concrete person, and when this life ceases, one ceases to be oneself. Furthermore, to say *I am this concrete individual* makes sense only when it means *I have sensibility*. Time is inseparable from sensibility; and where time stops, sensibility, and with it individuality, ceases to be.[7]

The individual is thus a definite being in time and space. It is an individual only in the concrete bodily form, and there is nothing beyond this concrete body: "The end of the body is your concrete end." The soul is as little a soul without the body as the master is still master without the slave. The soul relates to the body as fire relates to fuel—the body is the wick, the nourishment of the soul.[8] The separation of body and soul and the latter's existence outside the body can mean but one thing—that the soul is different from the body in the same way as thought and reason, otherwise we would have to visualize the body-soul relation as something spatial, as if the soul itself were taking up space. The belief in immortality, insofar as it consists in the image of the soul really leaving the body, is therefore a "theoretical insanity." [9]

Whatever is the cause and principle of one's life is also the cause and principle of one's death. Space and time are affirmations of one's life and also its negations—man begins in space and time but he also ends in them. But death in space and time is given only by the senses, so that the physical grounds of death are mere consequences, appearances, mediate grounds and not the ultimate ones; and therefore those who are satisfied with these grounds as the last and real ones are mere empiricists, materialists, naturalists. And when idealism affirms against such materialism the truth of immortality, it cannot be refuted by the latter, for both reflect a truth based merely on sensual experience. The true end of the individual goes beyond the death disclosed by the senses—"the true cause of the individual's death is reason." [10]

Reason, consciousness, spirit is the third ground of death. Spirit is the limit of all that which is sensuous, and it can become, in itself and by itself, its own object. Spirit is universal, and what was the unity and universality of Will for Schopenhauer is, at this early stage of Feuerbach's thinking, the unity of the spirit. "You are one with consciousness as conscious, one with thinking, in which everything is one, as thinker. You founder, you are dissolved in the spirit." The true, the innermost self realizes itself as spirit, and "death is the outward realization of this spiritual dissolution." Spirit, consciousness, reason are independent of the concrete person, the concrete individual. As colors change, disappear and pass away, so also concrete persons pass away; for they are not themselves self-conscious, pure subjectivity, but merely its objects. Death is, however, nothing else but the action by which the subjects step out of their "principle"—subjectivity —and become mere objects. And only what becomes can die. To consider death a law of nature is superficial, for where there is no spirit, no freedom, there is no death. Death presupposes spirit.[11]

Man dies only because he is a free, thinking, and conscious being. Feuerbach is here still completely immersed in the idealistic tradition, which he relinquishes shortly after. As Schopenhauer did before him, he starts with man—who distinguishes himself from all other living beings in that he can become his own object; he is subject and object, a knowing and an existing. And the more man is spirit, the more freedom he has and the higher he elevates himself above his physical being.

The conclusion Feuerbach arrives at is that neither death nor immortality, as they are usually understood, are real: "Only before death and not in death is death really death and painful; death is such a spectral being [*gespentisches Wesen*] that it only is, when it is not, and is not, when it is." This is obviously a variant of the famous statement of Epicurus. Feuerbach goes on to say that "death is nothing in itself, nothing positive and absolute, and has no reality except in man's imagination, and only if one compares the dead with the once living being." Through this comparison, however, we mistakenly attribute to death an independent existence and think of death with fear and trembling as a cruel destruction that, we further assume, is painfully experienced by the dead. But death is

death only for the living, it is not absolute annihilation, but only a self-annihilating annihilation [*eine sich selbst vernichtende Vernichtung*], an annihilation which is itself nothing; death is actually the death of death—in ending life it ends itself. . . . A real, positive annihilation is one that is within reality itself. . . . Death is, however, not a positive limit of life. Were it this, then it would have to be a higher reality, more life than life itself. Death, however, is a limit of life which has no reality . . . life is therefore infinite, since its limit is Nothingness.[12]

If death is merely a "negation of a negation," as Feuerbach, using this Hegelian term, considers it to be, then immortality in the usual sense of personal immortality, as merely the opposite of nothingness, is an unreal and indeterminate affirmation of the individual, of life, and of existence. And if we say of a man that he is a living, sentient, feeling, and loving being, then we say infinitely more about him, something infinitely more definite, real, and true, than when we say that he is immortal. The essence of a man is far above his mortality or immortality: "And as death and transitoriness do not deprive him of anything, so immortality does not add anything to him." [13]

Since death as negation is merely a fiction, immortality as an affirmation is equally fictitious.

> Immortal life is the life which exists for its own sake, and contains its own aim and purpose in itself—immortal life is the full life, rich in contents. . . .
>
> Every moment of life is of infinite importance and significance, for its own sake, posited by itself and fulfilled in itself, an unlimited affirmation of its own self; every moment of life is like a draught which empties completely the cup of infinity, which like the cup of Oberon miraculously fills itself again and again . . . Life is music, and every moment is a melody, or a sound full of deep feeling . . . the sounds of music pass away, but each sound has meaning as a sound, and before this inner significance, the "soul" of the sound, transitoriness recedes as something unimportant and inconsequential.[14]

The sound can be short or long, but is it nothing but short or long? To be sure, the whole sonata ends, but those who make transitoriness the chief predicate of life, who believe that they pass a correct judgment on life in emphasizing its finitude, whether they call themselves Christians, rationalists, or even philosophers, are, in Feuerbach's eyes, simple fools against whom he affirms, even with his last breath, the truth of this life.[15]

In spite of the very obvious influence of Hegel, the

Thoughts on Death already foreshadow the later, the real Feuerbach.[16] No sooner did he finish his *Todesgedanken,* than he realized that, although it was directed against the belief in "personal" immortality, it was inadequate for the purpose, since its arguments were still based on speculative philosophy, a philosophy that Feuerbach now came to consider misanthropic and ascetic, and whose dualism of spirit and flesh, natural and supernatural, eternal and temporal, was repugnant to him. He felt that, in the frame of reference of speculative philosophy, immortality is of necessity considered an abstract problem without a true relation to the concrete human being, and therefore a refutation of immortality based on such a philosophy cannot give full satisfaction. Since something always remains that speaks against the belief in immortality when it is asserted, there also remains something that speaks for this belief when its denial is based on the tenets of speculative philosophy. A truly effective denial of immortality, one that could be wholeheartedly accepted, must be based on a genetic explanation, where this denial appears as a by-product of the explanation of origins and of a determination of what real immortality is. Such an exhaustive and satisfying solution of the riddle of immortality is possible only from the point of view of anthropology.[17]

Anthropology starts from the fact of the existence of belief in immortality. And it concedes that it would never be able to conceive of such a belief if it did not encounter it.[18] Once it has found that people believe in immortality it asks why they believe, and gives an explanation of the origin of the belief. The root of this belief is not man's tendency toward continual *perfection.* As a rule, man cannot undertake anything of importance without attaching the idea of duration (*Dauer*) to it, and although the object may be destroyed overnight, the assumption is that it will endure indefinitely. The same approach applies to human life itself—and the desire for immortality is not for eternal life, which religion promises, but for this life prolonged indefinitely.

The fundamental conclusion of Feuerbach's anthropological investigation is that the idea of immortality stems from the instinct of self-preservation and from the unconscious transformation of man's idea of the future into objective existence. The concrete idea of a celestial future arises when man begins to become conscious of the limitations of space and time. And conversely, when he realizes, as Feuerbach wants to make him realize, his practically infinite possibilities in this world, he puts in place of the future life in heaven the concrete life here and now—"in place of the other world all the rest of the real world until then ignored by him—the world of civilization which causes the limits imposed by time and space to disappear, elevates us into times far removed . . . and permits us to know, by analogy, and in advance, future centuries in which we shall no longer exist." [19]

Thus the question of immortality is answered by Feuerbach in a manner reminiscent of that of Condorcet. There is nothing after death. To be sure, this is only true

if one is All. If, however, you are not All, it remains after death all that which you were not. If you are humanity, spirit, consciousness themselves, then, naturally, all is ended with you. If however, as I believe, you are no God, but a man among other men, and as experience shows man does not exist alone, his existence is inseparable from that of others.[20] There is nothing, as far as the individual is concerned, but the world, and the individual's traces in it remain.

It is this position that permits Feuerbach to assert that "death is only death for the living," as if the Epicurean argument takes care once and for all of every possible fear of death, and as if the anxiety and frustration of non-being were merely due to false reasoning.

Another, perhaps no less important, characteristic that supports Feuerbach's philosophy of death is his glorification of it. In this glorification two elements come together, his conviction that "nature is not avid for life" (the instinct of self-preservation is at the same time the instinct of destruction: the birth of a creature is at the same time death for another [21]), and the very noticeable and clearly stated attraction to death that already appears in the *Thoughts on Death:*

194 / Death and Western Thought

O Death, I cannot tear myself away from the sweet contemplation of thy gentle nature, so intimately bound up with my own. Mirror of my spirit, reflection of my own being! Out of the separation of the simple unity of Nature from itself arose the conscious spirit, emerged this self-contemplating light and, as the moon shines in the reflected glory of the sun, so you too mirror in your mild glow only the burning flame of consciousness. You are the evening star of Nature and the morning star of the spirit. Only fools think that these are two distinct stars and that only after death they attain the realm of the spirit, that the spiritual life begins only after death, as if only a sensuous negation [*sinnliche Negation*] could be the ground and condition of the spirit. . . .[22]

This attraction to death is, however, not predicated as might appear from this particular passage, on the identity of death with the spirit, which was Feuerbach's original view. In a long poem, written in doggerel rhyme soon after the publication of *Thoughts,* in which Feuerbach expresses what he will say many years later in *The Immortality Problem from the Point of View of Anthropology,* we find from the outset an expression of this attraction to death, entirely divorced from the original idealistic and speculative position.

> I am drawn away from this life
> So that I surrender to Nothingness.

begins this poem, *Reimverse auf den Tod* (1830),[23] and the theme recurs again:

> I am drawn toward Nothingness
> As the kindler of new life.

The particular interest and significance of this poem is not only that it shows that Feuerbach abandoned his Hegelian position almost as soon as he wrote the *Thoughts on Death,* but that it brings out the highlights of his considered views on death even more clearly than his much later prose exposition.[24] These are the unity of body and soul; the reality and finality of death; the denial of personal immortality in a hereafter; [25] and finally, the view that the only immortality is biological immortality in our offspring, and that the true heaven is to live for, and abide in the memory of, future generations.

Perhaps still more interesting is the fact that we find there the formulation of the two ideas about death that have become so prominent in later thought: death not as a sudden catastrophe but bound up with life from the very first; and the anticipation of death as the instrument of the knowledge of Being, as well as of authentic existence, in Heidegger's meaning of the term. But Feuerbach, as we shall see, thinks that the shock of the acute awareness of death will produce a healing catharsis that will result, automatically as it were, in peace of mind and reconciliation with the fact of having to die.

The following are the most telling passages of the *Rhymed Poem on Death*.[26]

[Unity of body and soul]

> *Of undivided nature I,*
> *One Being, one I, one totality.*
> *Nought that I am I do disown,*
> *Can't add to nor subtract from it.*
> *Man cannot be carved up in parts*
> *Nor be excerpted as you please.*

[The finality of death]

> *For death is not a silly joke*
> *And nature plays no merry tricks,*
> *It truly seals all life with death.*
> *Being indeed wastes by itself,*
> *And joins the ranks of Nothingness.*

[The fairytale of after-life]

> *Though we are taught by fables old,*
> *That of the angels I shall be,*
> *The theologians' folly this,*

They, who have lied to us for ages.
My empty selfsameness rots in
The sepulchral shrine,
Thus terminates identity . . . .

I, though, shall never rise again,
Death puts an end to my career
I must perish into Nothingness
If a new "I" should grow out of me.

[The only immortality is to live on in our offspring]

New mankind's better "I"
For which to nothingness I fled
This is the Heaven true
To which I rise after my death.

To all those am I driven
Who are not yet, and have not been . . .
You, dear infants,
Who shall enter instead of us,
Who draw your breath of life
From the cold depth of our tomb.

[Death is immanent in life from the very first]

As in the pulp of yellow lemons
The acid juice makes its abode
So sits as if in its wrapper
Death in your very marrow.

[Death as instrument of knowledge of Being]

Death does disclose the ground of being
On nature it alone throws light.
Being is but in death revealed,
And is, therefore, in death fulfilled.

[How to come to terms with death]

. . . Hence take this good advice from me,
Though right away no pleasure it may be:

Confront death on your knees, in prayer,
Almighty is the pain of dying!
At first, permit death to shake you up.
And let yourself be filled with its horror;
Then comes by itself into your bowels
The gentle warmth of peace of mind.
First cleanse yourself, through death, from Self,
Reconciliation will be sure to follow.

A survey of Feuerbach's philosophy of death would be incomplete without mention of his view of history.

History, as the self-expression of self-conscious, thinking, rational beings, of the spirit, is however not a simple flow, like the flow of water, but a purposeful, reasonable course. The historical existence of the individual is therefore a purposeful existence; it is a definite link in the historical whole. . . . Every human being has his vocation, a purposeful and reasonable destiny, and it reveals itself in the individual as drive, desire, talent, inclination. The vocation of the individual man is his sacred and invulnerable essence. . . . You ought to be, you should be, it says; but this ought is a tender and mild one, it is not coercive. . . . Man's inner goal is also the goal of his existence . . . only if history is nothing, only if the naked individual, stripped of all historical determination and all goals (that is, the vain, empty individual, which is "nothing"), is something . . . only then is there indeed nothing after death.[27]

It is in the combination of this confidence in the purposefulness of the historical process with the romantic attraction to death that Feuerbach brings about his coming to terms with death, emotionally and intellectually.

Death in itself is not terrible, no! The natural, the healthy death which occurs in old age, which occurs when man has enough of life, as the Old Testament tells us of the patriarchs and the other blessed ones, is the last will and desire of man, at least insofar as he remains in his wishes and ideas true to Nature. Terrible is only the violent, the cruel, the unnatural death. Only such death appears to mankind as a divine retribution.[28]

As far as the meaning of life is concerned, it is, as we have seen, to be found in a full, active, and creative life, which permits us to achieve the only immortality open to us: to live on in the memory of future generations, whose endless stream is assured by history and by Nature, where man is at home: "Fear not death! For you remain always in your native country, on the familiar ground, which lovingly receives you." [29] But this requires humility:

Don't be snobbish, condescend to the stone,
Get the feeling of that which is deprived of feeling,
Share your life with that which eternally lives only death,
O, then death will be gentle for you, like love.[30]

And Feuerbach admonishes those who cry out for personal immortality to seek rather the perpetuation of their good name:

Leben begehrst Du vom Tod?
O, strebe doch lieber darnach,
Dass die Menschheit dereinst
Dein noch mit Liebe gedenkt.

(You crave life from death?
O, rather strive toward the goal
That mankind in the future
Remembers you with love.)

Chapter 22

Nietzsche (1844-1900)

The Doctrine of the
"Eternal Recurrence of the Same"

AMONG NIETZSCHE'S PHILOSOPHICAL ANCESTORS Schopenhauer looms larger than anyone else.[1] As a student he read
The World as Will and Idea and immediately experienced not
only the impact of but a deep affinity with Schopenhauer's
thought; he felt, he reports, as if this book were written especially for him.

Later on he describes Schopenhauer in the image of Dürer's
Knight with Death and Devil, "Who bravely travels along his
path of horror, unperturbed by his terrible companions, and
yet without hope." [2] Whether this is the real Schopenhauer
or that of Nietzsche's imagination is beside the point here. But
this is clearly also Nietzsche's own ideal: he himself wants to
be such a Knight. The admiration for Schopenhauer does not,
however, prevent him from gradually parting company with
the great pessimist on several crucial issues.

While Schopenhauer was, as Nietzsche says of him, "as a philosopher, the first self-confessed and uncompromising atheist
which we Germans had," [3] he did not show any signs of
distress about it. Nietzsche, however, was profoundly affected
by the terrible truth that *God is dead.* For him it was not
merely the most terrible and world-shaking event. The unbearable loneliness and the collapse of all supports that, as he
saw it, must follow this discovery, were aggravated by
the sense of an unredeemable guilt, since "We have killed
him—you and I." [4]

At the same time, however, he feels that although existence is pain, the answer does not lie, as with Schopenhauer, in the denial of the will to live, but in life's ecstatic
affirmation, in spite of its suffering and pain.[5] In a letter to

a friend he says: "The terrible and all but incessant torture of my life makes me thirst for the end. . . . As far as agony and renunciation are concerned, my life during these last years is a match for that of any ascetic at any time. . . . *Yet no pain has been able or shall be able to tempt me into giving false testimony about life as I recognize it.*" [6]

"Suffering is no argument against life." [7] To accept and affirm life while being keenly aware of the terrible burden of existence and to overcome pessimism—this is the task Nietzsche considers particularly his own: "To have paced out the whole circumference of modern consciousness . . . this is my ambition, my torture, and my bliss. Really to overcome pessimism. . . ." [8]

Nietzsche experienced in his own person, to an unusual degree, that life was suffering and pain. Torturing headaches, recurring blindness, loneliness, plagued him incessantly. He confesses in one of his letters: "My existence is a terrible burden; I would have thrown it away long ago, if I had not made the most enlightening tests and experiments in the spiritual and moral domain precisely in this state of suffering." [9] In addition to physical pain and mental suffering there is the torture of nihilistic despair brought on by the death of God, and the realization that if God is dead nothing can be true and everything is permissible. He is Ivan Karamazov come alive. But, unlike the Russian, Nietzsche is not even for a moment complacent or cynical about it.

Although feeling "with every shred of his being that the weight of all things must be defined anew," [10] he stands alone and with a bleeding heart scans the horizon for a guiding star. At first the answer to his search for the meaning of life—in the face of the abyss of absolute Nothingness—seemed to lie in what he discovered in his classical studies. In the Greek tragedies he sees the reconciliation of the two opposed attitudes, the Dionysian and the Apollonian. The feeling of being one with the unconscious forces of Nature in a state of exaltation is combined with the artistic gift to clothe the unbearable reality with the veil of a beautiful illusion. Art is that which allows us to forget the dreadful emptiness of existence.

"Man is a living dissonance," writes Nietzsche in the *Birth of Tragedy,* and in order to live needs a consoling illusion. The artist of genius is alone able to maintain contact with the dark sources of life and at the same time make life endurable with the help of beautiful dreams *(der schöne Schein),* and he alone is able to give meaning to life. Very soon such a solution appeared unsatisfactory to Nietzsche. The enthusiastic attitude gives way to the detached, critical one, and the ideal of artistic creation yields to the new ideal of the free spirit, the enlightened man who follows without fear his will to know, no matter what the consequences may be. Whoever lives in this clear and purified atmosphere of knowledge and truth is impervious to the misery of existence. This knowledge, Nietzsche was well aware, is not objective, absolute knowledge. The *interesting* illusion of science replaces the *beautiful* illusion of art.

After a time, however, Nietzsche began to feel that the exalted heights of knowledge were "ice-covered regions" in which he could not breathe. And the problem of the meaning of human existence presented itself with new force. The idea of superman, of a new species of man, not, however, in the Darwinian sense, but as a *great, truly human* being, takes possession of him. The *Uebermensch* is the Dionysian man, who overcomes his animal nature, "disciplines himself into wholeness," and masters his passions and impulses so that he is able to accept life with its pain and suffering and at the same time live it fully and creatively.

Thus the superman is not only an ideal, he is also a necessity. Only the superman can bear the truth, and find life bearable. For, as Nietzsche writes in 1888, shortly before darkness will descend upon him, "It is impossible to live with Truth . . ." [11] And in *The Will to Power* he says: "Truth is ugly. . . . We have art in order not to perish of Truth." [12] Yet the task of Art is not seen any more as the creation of the beautiful illusion, although Nietzsche realizes that the will to illusion . . . is profounder, more metaphysical "than the will to truth, reality and being." [13] The purpose of art now is to "create perfection and the fullness of life, to affirm, bless and deify existence." [14]

Life's meaning is not outside it, but life is its own aim and goal (*Ziel und Zweck*). And this life, whatever suffering and pain it may bring, must be affirmed. "The highest stage a philosopher can attain is that of taking a Dionysiac attitude toward life: my formula for it is—*amor fati*." And it is partly in order to test the sincerity and firmness of the resolve to love fate that Nietzsche formulates the doctrine of *Eternal Recurrence of the Same.*

The vision of superman goes hand in hand with this doctrine. "The doctrine of the superman is the basis for the doctrine of eternal recurrence, since only the man who has overcome himself can want the eternal recurrence of all that is," writes Loewith.[15]

It is a mistake to assume that Nietzsche considered himself the discoverer of *eternal recurrence.* He notes that Heraclitus might have taught it, and that the Stoics show traces of it; what he did not realize, however, is that it had been advanced so often by others and that all through the nineteenth century there were numerous references to this doctrine, and speculations about it.[16] One finds it in Heine, in Hoelderlin, in Louis Blanqui, in Guyau, and (however vaguely mentioned) in Spencer and Byron.[17] Nevertheless, Nietzsche was the first to consider this idea not as a possibility but as a certainty, as a law of the universe; he even tried to establish it scientifically and studied mathematics, astronomy, physics, and biology for this purpose. The scientific proof failed; in spite of this, the doctrine of eternal recurrence became his *idée maîtresse*—it took complete possession of him and became the cornerstone of his philosophy.

> Everything goes, everything returns; eternally rolls the wheel of existence. Everything dies, everything blossoms forth again; eternally runs the year of existence. . . . All things return eternally and we ourselves have already been numberless times, and all things with us.[18]

There is no contradiction between the doctrine of eternal recurrence and the principle of the will to power. In the last paragraph of *The Will to Power* Nietzsche writes:

And do you also know what "The World" is to me? An enormity of force, without beginning or end . . . that does not become depleted, only transforms itself . . . a household without expense and loss, but equally without additions, without receipts, circumscribed by "Nothing" as its frontier . . . as an interplay of forces and waves of forces, at the same time one and many, here piling up, there diminishing, a sea . . . eternally transforming itself, eternally flowing back, with enormous years of recurrence . . . affirming itself . . . blessing itself as that which has to return eternally, as a Becoming, that knows no saturation, no weariness and no fatigue. This my Dionysian world of the Eternal-self-creation, the Eternal-self-destruction, this mysterious world of the twofold lusts, this my "Beyond good and evil," without goal, if the goal is not in the bliss of the circle, without will, if a ring does not have the good will toward itself. . . .

We know through Nietzsche's intimate friend, Lou Andreas-Salomé, that the thought of the eternal repetition of existence struck terror in his heart. In a book that is still today one of the best introductions to Nietzsche, she relates that he spoke of his "great discovery" of eternal recurrence

. . . only in a subdued tone of voice and with all the marks of a profound horror. And indeed his life was so full of suffering, that the certainty of eternal return of existence must have appeared to him as something unspeakably horrible. The Quintessence of the doctrine of eternal recurrence, the luminous apotheosis of life, which Nietzsche subsequently proclaimed, represents such a profound contrast to his own painful feelings of existence, that it appears to us as an uncanny mask.[19]

It becomes obvious, then, that this doctrine fulfilled still another function besides that of a supreme test of the wholehearted acceptance and affirmation of life that must be all but unendurable in its misery and meaninglessness. It is also an attempt to give, within the framework of the naturalistic world-view, a consoling answer to death, which appears as total annihilation.[21] Thus eternal recurrence was for Nietzsche at once terrifying and soothing. So terrifying indeed, that *amor fati,* which expresses the acceptance of the horror of living, becomes a superhuman achievement. But it also gave him consolation in the face of ceaseless change and all-destroying death.

There can be no doubt that Nietzsche's attitude to death was ambivalent. At first death did appear to him to be a liberation from an unbearable existence. Three times he attempted suicide and we find in his writings a glorification of death that rivals that of the earlier romantics. "Dying is not a slander against man and the earth . . . all that became perfect, all that is ripe wants to die. . . . Death has been made into bitter medicine by narrow pharmacist minds," whereas "one should make a feast out of one's death."

On the other hand, death often appeared to him to be an enemy. There are utterances showing an attempt toward reconciliation with the necessity of dying: "One is certain to die, why should one not be gay? . . . Death belongs to the conditions of true progress . . . the act of dying is not so important after all." But then there is open resentment— "Hateful to the fighter is the sneering death"—and there is open revolt—"Let's break the tablets of the preachers of death!"

That the doctrine of eternal recurrence was for Nietzsche also a defense against death and annihilation becomes clear when we consider that he gave special attention to the workings of eternal recurrence as far as death is concerned:

> Between your last moment of consciousness and the first ray of the dawn of your new life no time will elapse—as a flash of lightning will space go by, even though living creatures think it a billion of years and are not even able to reckon it. Timelessness and immediate rebirth are compatible, once the intellect is eliminated.[20]

Nietzsche desired to eternalize the fleeting existence of the finite man,[21] and the belief in "eternal recurrence of the same" appears to fulfill for him the same function that the belief in the immortality of the soul does for others.

There is a similarity between the doctrine of eternal recurrence and that of reincarnation. In both the identity of the personal self is preserved. But in the doctrine of recurrence the whole world returns; in reincarnation only the soul comes back and participates in the further progress of the same world—and if life is felt to be a burden, there is always hope that in the next incarnation the soul will have a better life; whereas in the eternal return the exact same life repeats itself to the smallest detail. Can eternal recurrence be a consolation in the face of the only possible alternative—the total annihilation in death? How desperate must one be about death in order to wish the return of the same existence? As Loewith points out, there is an inner contradiction in Nietzsche's thought. His doctrine fails because the will to eternalize the modern ego, "thrown" into the world, does not fit in with the vision of eternal rotation (*Kreislauf*) of the natural world.[22]

Nietzsche's answer does not suffer from this contradiction only. The doctrine of eternal recurrence is totally alien to the western mind, for it requires the abandonment of the concept of lineal time. That the man who was possibly the most sincere thinker of modern times was reduced to the necessity of going back to the world view of primitive man to find a solution for the tormenting problem of death is symptomatic. It is in line with the general tendency in modern philosophical thought to seek in the myths the higher truths of poetry and religion, or to rediscover the wisdom of the East.

That it will be possible for the seeds of oriental wisdom to be transplanted, to take root and to blossom in the totally unsuitable asphalt pavement of western industrial civilization, appears at present unthinkable. This impossibility is what makes the search for the *lux ex oriente* so tragic. For if Nietzsche's answer is unacceptable, his problem nevertheless remains.

Nihilism has become the heritage of modern man and the torment and despair of the lonely soul of the "assassin of God" is known to multitudes. In the innermost recesses of their hearts they know or at least suspect what Zarathustra openly confessed: "Human life is frightful and still without meaning."

From what source will the superhuman strength to carry the weight of estrangement and emptiness of human existence come? It may be easier for the average man to say yes to life than it was to the long-suffering Nietzsche. But affirmation of life poses the problem of acceptance of death. To do so was never easy, and it becomes much more difficult once man has become god and life itself the highest value.

Chapter 23

Bergson, Klages, Simmel

Death and "Philosophies of Life"

IN MANY RESPECTS Nietzsche belongs to that group of thinkers who fit into the loose designation of "philosophers of life," whose common bond is their revolt against Cartesian rationalism and their attempts to explain all reality in terms of life. Their answers to death, however, and their concern with it, vary greatly. The most influential representative of this movement, Bergson (1859-1941), makes in *Creative Evolution* (1907), his major work, only a passing reference to death. He expects it to yield to the all-embracing *élan vital* and sees "the whole of humanity in space and time as one immense army galloping beside and before and behind each of us in an overwhelming charge able to crush the most formidable obstacles, perhaps even death." [1] But in his later writings he devotes considerable space to the problem of survival after death. In *The Two Sources of Morality and Religion* (1932) he militates against the view that man is but a minute speck on the face of the earth, the earth a speck in the universe. "For if our body as the matter to which our consciousness applies itself is co-extensive with our consciousness, it comprises all we perceive, it reaches to the stars." [2] As far as survival is concerned he argues that

if, as I have tried to show, the mental life overflows the cerebral life, if the brain does but translate into movements a small part of what takes place in consciousness, then survival becomes so probable that the burden of proof comes to lie on him who denies it, rather than on him who affirms it: for the only reason we can have for believing in the extinction of consciousness at death is that we can see the body become disorganized, that this is a fact of experience. But this reason loses its force if the independence of almost the

209

whole consciousness with regard to the body has been shown to be also a fact of experience.[3]

Ludwig Klages (1872-1955), on the other hand, takes up Schopenhauer's theme that individual existence is a mistake. The desire for personal immortality appears to him to be "the extreme outrage and a criminal encroachment on the right of Nature." [4] Klages considers the conscious and reflecting ego— *den Geist*—the archenemy of life. Its emergence is the original sin: "The expulsion from Eden is identical with the emergence of the ego." But if spirit is the enemy of life, what about death? Although Klages sees the apparent inexhaustibility of life, he realizes not only that individual existence is a constant dying, and after a short reprieve dissolves into eternal silence, but that all life is doomed to annihilation. "The universe itself is only of limited duration. In the back of everything waits, assured of final victory, the Night of death." [5] The philosophy of life becomes with Klages a philosophy of death.

Simmel (1858-1910) in his "Metaphysics of Death," [6] occupies a middle position between these two views. He suggests that in order to understand what death is we have first of all to discard the idea of it as something threatening life from the outside, as a power independent of life and opposed to it.

As long as this erroneous notion exists and finds its symbolic expression in a veiled mysterious figure or a grinning skeleton hovering over his victim, so long death will be associated with horror, fright, and sadness. We have to get rid of the image of death as the "cut of the Parcae" (*Parzenschnitt*), as if at a particular moment the thread of life is suddenly cut. In this symbolic representation death hangs like a dark shadow over each man's life. Actually, however, death is bound up with life from the very beginning. Death is immanent in life. The hour of death is merely the last phase of a continuous process that began with birth.

(We already encountered a similar idea in antiquity, in Manilius' *Nascentes morimur*—In being born, we die—and in Seneca, *Prima, que vitam dedit, hora capsit*—the first hour infringes on life, while it gives it. Montaigne says that "the continuous task of your life is to build death," and Sir Thomas Browne that "we live with death, and die not in a moment.") Because man does not realize that death is his destiny, he does not accept it, and flees before it, a flight that Simmel compares to the behavior of a person on a boat who walks on deck in a direction opposite to that of the vessel, and which is as illusory.

The idea that death permeates life at all times should replace the image of death as sudden catastrophe. Life and death belong together. Simmel suggests that this relationship is that of Hegel's thesis and antithesis. He says that the Hegelian formula shows its depth perhaps nowhere so clearly as in the relation between life and death. The two move toward a synthesis, where their apparent opposition is eliminated, and something "more than life" emerges. The phenomenon of death is in no way a refutation of the idea that life points beyond itself. On the "level of the spirit," the creation of meaningful content is as characteristic of life as the creation of new beings is on the biological level. And out of the fact of the transcendence of life springs the feeling of the eternity of the soul. This feeling is at odds with the fact of mortality, and the deep desire to outlast the death of the body points to the plausibility of the doctrine of immortality.

As we saw, Schopenhauer thought that man has an unperishable kernel, the blind unconscious will, which is, as it were, a chip from the cosmic will. Simmel points out that although we perceive ourselves as constantly changing—physically, mentally, emotionally—we are still the same selves: "Something in us remains unchanged while we are wise or foolish, animals and then again saints, happy or despairing." But this mysterious something that remains unchanged is neither something real, concrete, nor an illusion. It is the point of reference for all that life experiences, and it is essential to all living activity and suffering of the individual. This point of reference, which we detect in us, is what may be expected to continue and transfer to another being. Simmel feels that the doctrine of metempsychosis may contain a grain of truth, however crudely and materialistically it was expressed in materialistic terms by primitive people.

Chapter 24

Survival after Death
Is Plausible and Probable

WITH KANT'S MORAL ARGUMENT for immortality we outlined the third major attempt to prove the immortality of the soul. We have seen the metaphysical-rationalist constructions of Descartes and Leibniz, which are based on the supposed nature of the soul—for instance its simplicity—and which follow in principle the road opened up by Plato. This approach is often tied in with the particular philosopher's religious views, no matter what he may proclaim or imagine. It must nevertheless be clearly distinguished from the assertion of the immortality of the soul derived from religious doctrines, which in turn are based on revelation or mystical experience. Such is the case with Pascal.

In addition to these three ways of attempting to demonstrate survival upon death, Max Scheler, in a short but characteristically penetrating study of the problem, *Death and Survival*,[1] cites two more: the endeavour to demonstrate empirically the existence and activity of the souls of the dead —Spiritism (or Spiritualism)—and one that consists of making more or less daring analogies in which the basic conditions of our experience are extended to the sphere of being that lies outside of experience. Scheler has in mind here Fechner's "inductive metaphysics," where death is assumed to be a second birth.[2]

In answer to Kant's attempt to justify the belief in immortality on moral grounds, Scheler points out that there is no reason to believe that reality will yield to the moral demand, and that to expect it is nothing more than an empty wish. Nor can the high moral order of such a demand make the granting and fulfillment of it any more probable. It is merely a subjective fact, and neither the universe nor the "ground of being" did contract to fulfill it. It is possible that insight into one's survival is not independent from heeding and becoming aware of the call of infinite duty. But then only the fact of this awareness, but not its contents, and certainly not its reality, is morally conditioned.[3]

With regard to spiritism, which is based on the presumed commerce with the souls of the dead, Scheler concedes that it would be the best conceivable, even the perfect, method, if only it would lead to sure results. As far as he is concerned, this road is closed to him, since he does not have such experiences and does not dare to judge the available materials. Moreover, these materials can be interpreted in an infinite number of ways, and the assumption that here we have the manifestations of "the spirits of the dead" is but one of many.[4]

It is with Fechner's approach that Scheler feels the most sympathy. It is based not on rational constructions or on empirical "facts" of the manifestations of the souls of the deceased, but starts from the experiences of our inner life and extends them, in accordance with their immanent laws, rules, and forms, and through a mixture of creative imagination and rational analogies, beyond experience. According to Scheler, Fechner possessed the feeling for the basic insight that is decisive for the existence and meaning of metaphysics— namely that the structure and machinery of the accidental and circumscribed existence is applicable to all possible existence. In other words, he says that what is valid for this small corner accessible to us, extends beyond these limitations, permits the knowledge and has validity and meaning for the whole of existence.

Scheler does not ask how immortality can be proved, for it cannot be proved. "To be immortal" is a negative "fact" (*Sachverhalt*), and as such is incapable of proof. Therefore, he speaks of the "survival of the person," not of its so-called immortality. But if we had empirical evidence of survival, then we could with some justification infer the possibility of what is usually called immortality.

Scheler takes quite seriously the possibility of survival. He says "that the assumption that survival after death is merely a human 'wish fulfillment' is refuted by ten thousand historical facts." Thus, for instance, one can definitely raise the question "whether in the Christian centuries the fear of Hell and purgatory was not much stronger than the hope of Heaven."

But how can we demonstrate that there is survival of the human person?[5] Making a sharp distinction between the direct experience (*Erleben*) on the one hand, and concrete existence, including life as it is being lived (*gelebtes Leben*) on the other, Scheler says that the spiritual person in each and every one of its acts—perceiving, remembering, willing, expecting, being able to (*koennen*), feeling—passes beyond, overflows, as it were, that which is given to it as a limit set by the body that always accompanies this experience.[6]

Moreover, he insists that the quantity of the contents of these acts is always larger than the quantity of the contents of the bodily states. If it belongs to the essence of the personal spirit to go beyond the limits of the bodily frame in its acts, it is permissible to ask: What belongs to the essence of the person, when in the act of dying the body ceases to be? And Scheler answers that it is nothing new, but precisely what belonged to the person while it was alive, namely the concrete, actual unity of all its acts. Precisely as during life its acts "swung out" beyond the bodily states, so will the spiritual person itself "swing out" when its body has deteriorated.[7]

This is, however, all that can be said. "More than this 'swinging out' beyond the borders of life I do not know anything." Thus we do not know whether the spiritual person exists after death, and certainly not how it exists, for it is quite possible for the person to cease to be with this last swinging out. But although we shall never know whether the spiritual person survives, we cannot be sure that it does not. As far as he himself is concerned, Scheler not only believes that it *does* survive, since he does not see any reason to assume that it does not, inasmuch as the essential conditions for its survival are fulfilled, but he goes even further and attempts to show that it survives as a body.

The fact that a body belongs to a person is an "essential insight."[8] Therefore, we know that if this person continues after death, then it is certain that a body will belong to it. A spiritualistic doctrine of the immortality of a bodiless psychic point (*Puenktchen*) is certainly false, and as Leibniz already saw, the Christian view of the resurrection of the flesh is far more profound and meaningful than the modern doctrines of an immaterial soul-substance and its so-called proofs.[9]

In sum, the evidence for survival is derived from an inner experience. "The person experiences for himself, for his own existence what he has already experienced during his life for his acts and their contents: the independence of his being from his body. . . . [But] we have to be clear that man can doubt and still possess in the inner experience the complete evidence for that which he doubts."

Scheler seems to have forgotten that he spoke earlier of the inner certainty man has of the inevitability of death. Now he speaks of the experience of "swinging out beyond death," from which the probability of survival is deduced. But how are we to reconcile these two contradictory experiences and decide which one we should trust?

Scheler takes the same position as Bergson on the question of immortality, namely that the burden of proof—*onus probandi*—rests with those who deny it. He is, however, much more subtle in regard to what has actually to be proved. If the person that is supposed to survive is considered merely a collectivum of its single acts, it must obviously cease with the cessation of these acts. If it is, however, not a collectivum, but something whose essence cannot be exhausted in these single acts, then discontinuance of an act or any number of acts does not have to mean the discontinuance of the person itself, but merely of our knowledge of it. If we do not perceive any further act of the person in question, then it may be that the existence of the person has ceased, since there is no possibility of concluding the existence of a thing from its essence.[10] But the burden of proof falls upon those who maintain its non-existence.

However, even when Scheler insists that the *onus probandi* falls on the denier of survival (and opts for the independence of the person from its acts and from the spiritual and biological laws), he never maintains more than that the fear of death is not a sufficient reason to assume the cessation of the person. Under no circumstances is its survival proved by the fact that its deniers fail to prove non-survival. Moreover, survival is always dependent on the attitude to it of the person itself, on its free acts independent from biological laws. Its continuance would be, as it were, still totally open.

That the person, after death, is no more visible and perceivable (*spuerbar*) does not prove anything against its existence. For even during its lifetime it was neither visible nor perceivable. What was visible was its head, its legs, its muscles; and even these, which interest us merely as anatomists or physicians, were visible only because of an "artificial looking away" from its totality. Is it the abolition of the expression of this body (*Fortfall der Ausdrucks-Erscheinungen*) that led us to the assumption that the person does not experience anything any more? Certainly not. For even as long as it was alive the acknowledgment of its expressions and the understanding of its actions were not based on the perception and the qualities of its bodily organs.

Therefore, only this can be asserted: that the "arena of its expressions," the manner in which the person's body manifests itself in a part of the world of things, has changed at death. And only this can be concluded: that at death the expression and the actions have become inaccessible to us and therefore incomprehensible. For even in its life the now decomposed body was given merely as an arena of the expression and action, and not disclosed by the nature of that body or through intuition. ("It is given as directly as the existence of the outside world itself.") Again the *onus probandi* reverts to those who regard the change of that part of the outside world that this body is, the change that consists in the transformation of a body into a corpse, as something other than a mere exchange of one domain of domination of the person, or of one arena of manifestations of its inner experiences, for another.[11]

Chapter 25

Whitehead (1861-1947)

Immortality of Realized Value

A RECENT ATTEMPT to assert and argue the truth of immortality that we have to consider is that of Alfred North Whitehead. It is significant because of Professor Whitehead's stature in contemporary philosophical thought, based on his new approach to the task of understanding and describing the world in categories that would be more adequate in dealing with physical fact and experience at large. What these categories are intended to accomplish is "to provide exact expressions to the inexactitudes of concrete happenings and thus not only to remove the vexing maladjustments between thought and fact." Nature is to be interpreted in Whitehead's philosophy in terms of "the pattern of the unit of process" and not any more in terms of "the pattern of pellets of energy which care for nothing." [1]

What are the consequences of this new approach for the problem of immortality? In his Ingersoll Lecture on this topic, delivered in April, 1941,[2] Whitehead deals first with "the general concept of Immortality," and "the reference to mankind will be a deduction from wider considerations." These are based on the presupposition "that all entities and factors in the universe are essentially relevant to each other's existence," and it is this doctrine of essential relevance that Whitehead applies to the interpretation of "those fundamental beliefs concerned with the notion of immortality."

The term *immortality* must be, according to Whitehead, understood through reference to its antithesis, *mortality*. These two words refer to two aspects of the Universe, and these two aspects are presupposed in every experience we have. Whitehead terms these aspects *The Two Worlds*: "They require each other and *together* constitute the concrete Universe," [3] and any adequate description of one World includes characterizations derived from the other.

The World "which emphasized the multiplicity of *mortal things*" Whitehead calls the *World of Activity,* which is the *World of Origination,* the *Creative World.* The *World which emphasizes Persistence* is the *World of Value:* "Value is in its nature timeless and immortal. Its essence is not rooted in any passing circumstance." [4] The value inherent in the Universe is independent of any moment of time, but apart from its necessary reference to the World of passing Fact it loses its meaning: "Value refers to Fact, and Fact refers to Value." [5]

The descriptions of either of the two worlds, since they are abstractions from the Universe, and every abstraction involves reference to the totality of existence, include characteristics borrowed from the other. Thus Value cannot be considered apart from the Activity that is the primary character of the other World, and the essence of Values is their capacity of realization in the World of Action.

On the other hand, "Every Fact in the world of Activity has a positive relevance to the whole range of the World of Value." And there is interconnection between the two Worlds in Evaluation. But "the World of Activity is *modified* by the World of Value" and "the process of evaluation exhibits an immortal world of coordinated value." [6]

Creation aims at Value, whereas Value is saved from futility of abstraction by its impact upon the process of Creation. But in this fusion, Value preserves its Immortality. [7]

Whitehead proceeds now to answer the question: In what sense does creative action derive immortality from Value?

He states that the notion of Effectiveness cannot be divorced from the understanding of Values. To see values purely abstractly is an error. The two Worlds of Value and of Action are bound together in the life of the Universe, so that the immortal factor of Value enters into the active creation of temporal fact: "The essential junction of the two Worlds infuses the unity of the coordinated values into the multiplicity of the finite acts" and "each World is futile except in its function of embodying the other." [8]

This fusion involves the fact that either World can only be

described in terms of factors common to both of them, and these common factors are the "Ideas" "which it is the glory of Greek thought to have explicitly discovered." However, Whitehead stresses his disagreement with Plato in one important point: to have misconceived the status of the Ideas in the Universe. This, he holds, is "the tragedy of Greek thought." This misconception lies, according to Whitehead, in the notion of independent existence. He holds that there is no such mode of existence—every entity is to be understood only in terms of the way in which it is interwoven with the rest of the Universe. Each idea has *two sides*—it is "a shape of value and a shape of fact." And the ultimate character of the Universe has two sides: "one side is the mortal world of transitory fact acquiring the immortality of realized value; and the other side is the timeless world of mere possibility acquiring temporal realization. The bridge between the two is the 'Idea' with its two sides." [9]

The topic of *The Immortality of Man* is seen by Whitehead as a side issue of the wider topic of *The Immortality of Realized Value,* in other words "the temporality of mere fact acquiring the immortality of value." He finds the general character of the World of Fact that "expresses its adjustment for the embodiment of Value" in the "tendency of the transitory occasions of fact to unite themselves in the sequences of Personal Identity. . . . Each such personal sequence involves the capacity of its members to sustain the identity of Value." [10] And in this way Value-experience introduces into the transitory World of Fact an imitation of its own essential immortality.

"The survival of personal identity within the immediacy of a present occasion is a most remarkable character of the World of Fact"—it is a partial negation of its transitory character. Personal Identity is realized in the "emphatic experience of the self-identity of the past in the immediacy of the present." [11]

For Whitehead the problem of personal "identity" in a changing world is the main example for understanding the essential fusion of the World of Activity with the World of Value:

"The immortality of Value has entered into the changefulness which is the essential character of Activity."

Whitehead holds that in naturally simplifying the complexity of the Universe by separating it in two Worlds—that of multiple Activity, whose prime characteristic is change, and that of coordinated Value, the prime characteristic of which is immortality—we neglect the requirement for understanding of the Universe, namely that each World exhibits the impress of the other. But it is precisely for this reason that the World of change "develops Enduring Personal Identity as its effective aspect for the realization of value," and to save it from mere futility of abstract hypothesis the effective realization of value in the World of Change should find its counterpart in the World of Value: "This means that temporal personality in one world involves immortal personality in the other." [12]

Whitehead concedes that all he said was in the form of dogmatic statements. But what is the evidence on which they are founded? He says that "the only answer is the reaction of our own nature to the general aspect of life in the Universe." [13] And this answer involves the break with "a widespread tradition of philosophical thought" that presupposes independent existences and excludes the possibility of an adequate description of a finite fact. Without denying the importance of analysis, he objects to "the absurd trust in the adequacy of our knowledge. . . . We cannot rely upon any adequate explicit analysis. . . . There is not a sentence which adequately states its own meaning. There is always a background of presupposition which defies analysis by reason of its infinitude. . . . Logic, conceived as an adequate analysis of the advance of thought, is a fake. It is a superb instrument, but it requires the background of common sense. . . . The final outlook of Philosophic thought cannot be based upon the exact statements which form the basis of special sciences." [14]

Whitehead's position cannot be divorced from his personal exemplification of the idea he wants to convey. As in *Phaedo* the example of Socrates was the best argument, so, as J. S. Bixler notes in connection with the lecture in which Whitehead expounded his views, "the simplicity of his personal persuasiveness as he spoke out of the maturity of his experience, gave his audience not arguments alone but an impression of the entrance of eternal quality into the fleeting moment." [15] With all due respect to Whitehead, it may be asked not only whether such a comparison with Socrates facing imminent death is appropriate. Without an actual appointment with death the arguments presented above could hardly be expected to be convincing.

Chapter 26

Existential Philosophies and the Problem of Death

IN EXISTENTIALISM, one of whose roots is the "philosophy of life" (*Lebensphilosophie*), the fact of death occupies a central place. Simmel is the connecting link here. Heidegger refers explicitly to Simmel's conception of death, but reproaches him for seeing the problem only biologically and not "existentially." The biological view of death is best exemplified by Goethe when he called it "Nature's stratagem to secure more abundant life." The existential view of death, on the other hand, involves the specific significance death takes on for man, who alone among all living creatures knows that he has to die, and who alone "exists."

The concept of "existence" was put forward by Soeren Kierkegaard (1813-1855). It is he who pointed out that the man who knows that "all men are mortal" knows an abstract, theoretical truth about man in general, but what really counts, also philosophically, is that he realizes the relevance of this truth as far as he himself, this concrete individual human being, is concerned, namely that "I, too, must die."

Existence is understood by the existentialist philosophers in a wider sense than the classical meaning of the term, that a thing exists. It refers to the peculiarly human way of being, and it goes under different names—*Dasein* in Heidegger, *Existenz* in Jaspers, the *pour-soi* in Sartre. It is the factual individual existence that can be known only subjectively by one who exists, and is beyond conceptional analysis or definition.

Existential philosophy differs radically from "philosophical anthropology," which also is principally interested in man. In the latter, man attempts to find out what he is, what makes him, as man, different from other beings, and what his place in the world is. But existentialism is not concerned with man in general, but in his concrete individuality. It is very much aware of the world and other men, but the world as the "universe" does not interest it.[1]

It is in the name of the concrete individual that Kierkegaard mounted his attack on Hegel. In this he was, however, not entirely alone. His contemporary, Max Stirner, also insisted that "man" is but a fiction, a "ghost," and that only the individual is real. But his individual is the aggressive and possessive egoist, the "Unique" (*der Einzige*) who is merely concerned with making the world his property. Stirner knows nothing of Kierkegaard's anguish, of the despair and loneliness of the individual soul in its consciousness of sin, in brief, of the existential experience.[2]

This particular experience underlying the thinking of the existentialist philosophers, regardless of their otherwise very considerable differences, is described by Jaspers as the "awareness of the fragility of Being" (*Gewahrwerden der Bruechigkeit des Seins*), or as the experiencing of the "limit situations"; in Heidegger it appears as "the experience of progressing toward death" (*Erfahrung des Verlaufens zum Tode*), and as the experience of "not being at home in the world" (*Unheimlichkeit*); and in Sartre as the all-pervading disgust with existence, manifesting itself as *nausea*.

In the first two instances we actually find two contradictory experiences: the terrifying possibility of non-being, and the horror of being. The latter is either the feeling of an unbearable burden of one's own existence "suffocating under the weight of tons of existence," as Sartre has it, or the feeling of being lost in a hostile world.[3]

It is of great importance, particularly for our theme, to keep these two contradictory experiences apart, and one could even distinguish existentialist philosophers not only according to national origins, or according to their attitude to religion,[4] but also according to whether the dread of being or the dread of non-being is their dominant emotion. Kierkegaard seems to belong to the former. In his *Journals* he writes that "the whole reality terrifies me, from the smallest fly to the mysteries of Incarnation. Everything in it is inexplicable to me, most of all my own self. The whole of existence is poisoned for me, most of all myself. Great is my suffering." [5] But although he says that "for an individual animal, plant, or man existence (to be or not to be) is of quite decisive importance," [6] his "sickness unto death" is not a despair over life's finiteness but a "despair of not being able to die." [7]

The contemporary existentialists, however, are concerned with death. Glockner gives us a very vivid picture of the role of death in the philosophy of existence. He reports a conversation with a philosopher, possibly even Heidegger himself, who said that "we have arrived at the staggering discovery that man is from the very first a moribundus. This knowledge pervades and fecundates our whole philosophizing." [8] It is well to remember, however, that for them, as Mounier emphasizes, "it is not death which is the philosophical problem, but that *I* do die." [9]

For Kierkegaard who, as a theologian, accepted the Christian answer to death, this obviously could not be the central issue. What concerned him was not the fact of death but the salvation of his immortal soul. This depends on the life one leads as well as the purity of one's faith. Thus the problems facing him were that of leading a Christian life and, even more important, conquering his religious doubts.

According to Kierkegaard, there are three "existence-spheres of life" or "three stages"—the aesthetic, the ethical and the religious—in which man leads respectively a life devoted to enjoyment, to moral and social obligations, and to religious pursuits. In each of these stages, however, he experiences, sooner or later, despair and dread; for man is "neither animal nor disembodied spirit, but a synthesis of time and eternity, of the relative and the absolute." A fatal tension is unavoidable. "No man can take note of God without becoming a sinner." [10] Hence arises religious despair, inherent in all natural religion, for religion is "the outward sign of the hidden disease of human sin," and only the paradoxical biblical revelation of the transcendence of the God of grace can solve this despair. Our reason shows us only the absurdity of such a faith; man is caught between the impossibility of unbelief and the impossibility of faith, and only through "decision"—a "leap into absurdity"—can faith be attained.

The secular heirs of Kierkegaard are, however, little con-

cerned with sin and faith. What they took over was his revolt
against intellectualistic essentialism of post-Cartesian thought
and his discovery of despair and dread as means of apprehending reality, his thesis that "truth is subjectivity." Man as
a thinker is not the same as man as a living being. Kierkegaard reverses the order of procedure of both philosophy and
thought. He does not start from the world given in sense
perception, but from the existing ego of the individual being.
He is very far from epistemological subjectivism, but he opposes the "objectivity" of reality apart from his subjective
being as an existing ego. Thought relationship to reality is no
relationship at all to actual reality. In mere thought subject
and object are artificially separated and existence slips away
from both. Only as a solitary individual man truly exists, and
only in his individual existence, only *existentially* can he
relate himself to reality. This relating occurs through *dread*.

Dread, as the word *Angst* has been rendered in the English
translation of Kierkegaard's writings, and for which the term
anxiety may be more appropriate,[11] is a "means of salvation
in conjunction with faith" and also a means of "understanding" what life is all about, for only by going through it can
true reality be reached. For dread, or anguish, or anxiety,
serves to lift man from the sphere of everyday existence to
true existence. Anxiety is a derangement in normal existence,
but if we realize that normal existence is something superficial
and artificial, anxiety appears as "an expression of the perfection of human nature" and "whoever has learned how to be
truly anxious, has learned the *highest*." [12] For anxiety is an
experience of "awakening." It shows us what we might be,
it is "the possibility of freedom." [13] What is the object of
anxiety according to Kierkegaard? It is "nothing": "anxiety
and nothing always correspond to each other," and "the effect
of nothing is to produce anxiety."

Jaspers (1883-   )

Jaspers discovered Kierkegaard as early as 1914. As a former
medical student and psychiatrist, he saw death more often and
at a closer range than a philosopher usually does. Moreover, as
he reports in his *Philosophical Autobiography*, he suffered

since childhood from a bronchial deficiency with cardiac complications. This disease not only brought on frequent states of utter exhaustion that drove him to despair, but he was also aware of the prognosis by the famous Rudolf Virchow that "those affected with this disease will die in their thirties at the latest." [14]

Under these circumstances it is not surprising that Jaspers shows a keen awareness of the human condition. In the *Psychology of World-Views* (1919), in which he investigates "what fundamental attitudes the soul is able to adopt and by which forces it is moved," he advances the concept of *Grenzsituationen*, that is of *limit*—or even better, *ultimate* situations. Man is always in situations, but whereas most situations change or can be changed by human effort, certain situations, such as guilt and dying, are unalterable and irremediable. In them, we *founder, suffer shipwreck (scheitern)*. Death is such an ultimate situation par excellence.

It is important to realize, Jaspers insists, that it is not sufficient merely to know about death, or even to be concerned with one's own death, but in order to become aware of it as an ultimate situation, one must experience it as *absolute failure*. It is characteristic of Jaspers' position that he demands that the awareness of the ultimate situation should not be evaded or obscured. The reason for it is that only through it we can become *Existenz*. It is mainly from this point of view that in his *Philosophie* (1932), Jaspers subjects the traditional answers to death to a critical review.[15]

Jaspers not only deprecates the Stoic ideal of apathy with regard to death, but he finds the Stoic's reliance on the ascendency of reason over the passions unfounded, since it underestimates the radical character of absolute failure, overestimates the independence of reasoning (which is influenced by what presents itself to it), and discounts the possibility of insanity.

With regard to fear of death, Jaspers points out that it is of little help to argue that this fear is based on an error. Although all the arguments are in themselves correct, none is capable of overcoming the horror at the thought of non-being. These arguments do not take into account that "one is not yet ready," that there are "reparations to be made" before the final curtain goes down, and most of all, they overlook not only "the anxiety of trembling before non-being," but also the anxiety of "existential non-being."

Jaspers is equally critical of the world-negating position that "deceives and consoles" through the fantasies of another life. It is as much a retreat from the awareness of death as *ultimate* situation as the Stoic attitude. It attempts to transform the meaning of death, but merely displaces the *limit*. Similarly, the belief in the immortality of the soul is inadequate because it is dependent on the proofs of immortality. But all these proofs, says Jaspers, are faulty. What actually can be proved is mortality. The soul is bound up with the bodily organs; the experience of dreamless sleep demonstrates in retrospect non-being; the facts from pathology show that memory is dependent on the brain. In disregarding all these facts, death is "conquered" in these instances, at the price of giving up the limit-situation.

Not only these traditional responses to death are rejected by Jaspers. Anxiety and despair, which arise "when the unbounded will to live is faced with the prospect of annihilation," equally prevent us from apprehending death as ultimate situation. "When I am dominated by fear and concern with regard to passing ends . . . when I cling to duration as such, when annihilation appears as the greatest misfortune and nothing has meaning any more, I am losing myself in mere appearance," [16] instead of becoming aware of myself as *Existenz*.

In view of the inadequacy of the traditional responses to death, what remains for those who are seeking an answer to death? Is there an answer that Jaspers did not find wanting, or is there, perhaps, a new answer? As far as Jaspers is concerned, since the ultimate situation should not be obscured or evaded, there is no point in seeking refuge in any kind of religious or philosophical system. Moreover, in Jaspers' philosophy, the main characteristic of which is that it wants to remain detached and "floating" between and above various possibilities, one cannot even speak meaningfully of an answer, for this would imply a definite choice of one doctrine in preference to others. Still, this does not mean that in his philosophy there is no possibility of coming to terms with death.

Before we can discuss how this can be achieved, we must consider another aspect of the problem. Jaspers acknowledged that the highest life desires death, instead of fearing it, as is evidenced in the death of lovers (*Liebestod*). But disagreeing with those who hold that the flight into death gives it depth, Jaspers comes to the conclusion that "there is no one stable attitude to death which can be considered as the only correct one; death transforms itself with me." Therefore, "it is no contradiction when man clings to life with every particle of his being, and still, while loving life with its contradictions and absurdities, desires death; when he seems to despair at the thought of death, and at the same time, contemplating death, becomes aware of his true being; when he sees death as a friend and as a foe, avoids it and at the same time longs for it." [17]

But actually, such an ambivalent attitude toward death is exceptional; and even if one accepts the hypothesis of the existence of a death drive, it remains unconscious. Consciously, in an overwhelming number of instances, we love life and despair at the prospect of death. It would seem that Jaspers had this in mind, for in his *Einfuehrung in die Philosophie* (1953), he speaks of learning to die: "If to philosophize is to learn how to die, then this learning how to die is actually the condition for the good life. To learn to live and to learn how to die are one and the same thing." [18]

But this is in essence what the Stoics and Montaigne have already said. We recall, however, Jaspers' criticism of the Stoic response to death. Did he reverse himself, or does he mean something else, the only point on which he agrees with them being the beneficial effect of being aware of and prepared for death on morality, and similar effect of a moral life on the psychological preparedness for death?

Jaspers says in the Foreword to *Philosophie* that "the meaning of philosophizing lies in a single thought, which as such is inexpressible: The awareness of Being itself." This gives us a pointer for the meaning of learning to die for Jaspers. For him philosophizing as learning to die is obviously connected with the awareness of Being. Thus, learning to die has a totally different meaning for him from the one it has for the Stoics, both in technique involved and the contents of what is to be learned. It is neither a mental discipline based on the power of reason to master our emotions, nor is its goal the resigned acceptance of death as total annihilation.

In order to understand what Jaspers means by learning to die, we must consider what happens in the ultimate situation. There either Nothingness becomes visible, or the individual becomes aware of himself as *Existenz,* which is essentially freedom. As such, it tends to transcend itself. Brought on by the awareness of the ultimate situation, and in a way that defies rational explanation and description, "elevation into transcendence" (*Aufschwung in die Transcendenz*) is achieved. And transcendence is "the source and the goal, both of which lie in God and out of whose depths alone we really become authentically human." [19]

Transcendence, the *Encompassing* (*das Umgreifende*), which, "conceived as pure Being, can be called God," [20] remains something totally unimaginable and outside any emotional contact. And the elevation into transcendence is not mystical experience, not Oneness with the living God. What Jaspers gives us is not religion, but philosophical faith, without dogma or credo. It is merely "an experience of the Encompassing." We have seen that it is in absolute failure, in foundering, when man renounces himself and all his aims, that the reality of God shows itself as the only reality. There is unauthentic foundering, which wants the end of all things. It is authentic foundering that brings the revelation and confirmation of the infinity of God—of the only true being. And since this can happen only in an absolute failure, in total ruin, it is in this sense that, for Jaspers, philosophizing means learning to die. In short, learning to die means for Jaspers learning to keep the awareness of the ultimate situation of death open, to choose freely authentic foundering, in order to attain through it the only true being—God.

A comparison with Spinoza will make Jaspers' position clearer. Spinoza strives for and achieves liberation from the oppressive thought of death through the highest knowledge of

God. For Jaspers, on the contrary, it is by standing in the ultimate situation, by becoming aware of death as the wall, against which all our possibilities suffer shipwreck, and courageously taking upon oneself absolute failure, that the experience of the Encompassing of God is attained.

The leap from foundering into transcendence is the leap from anxiety into calm. It is in this "infinite calm," in which success or foundering become irrelevant, that Jaspers comes to terms with death.

It would be going too far to assume that for Jaspers learning to die also includes the acquisition of the *knowledge* that death is not final annihilation. For only faith can assert and claim that the soul is immortal. Jaspers says that we can merely become "conscious" of our immortality, which is our "eternal presence," and this only in "the high moments which efface time." But even to say this, as long as in our thinking we remain in the world of appearance, looks fraudulent, as if one wants "to explain away mortality in time." Such statements must be taken as "ways of expression arising out of a type of thinking which can be achieved, not in the form of expanded knowing information, but as a transformation of basic consciousness." [21]

But man is, for Jaspers as he is for Kant, a citizen of two worlds. Jaspers says that "Being is not in time on the other side of death, but as eternity in the depth of the empirical being," [22] and that "all *authentic* being, whether God or man, is indefinite and infinite." To many, Jaspers' "existential conquest" of death will appear not only difficult, but also unsatisfactory, as his "philosophical faith" must appear unsatisfactory to those seeking religious certainty. But one must realize that this is perhaps as far as a thinker who must meet the challenge of the existential experience of the "fragility of Being" can go without giving up his integrity as a philosopher.

Heidegger (1899-   )

*The Search for the "Meaning of Being"
and the "being toward Death"*

Heidegger's answer to death appears to be incidental to his main philosophical concern—the question of the meaning of

Being (*der Sinn des Seins*). Although *Being* is a concept of utmost generality and therefore, properly speaking, not definable, this is precisely what constitutes the challenge to ask its meaning. To invoke the self-evidence of *Being* does not suffice, since to question precisely and to clarify the self-evident is, according to Kant, "the business of the philosopher."

Being (*Sein*) we attribute to all that is. We have, therefore, to question all that which is—*being* (*Seiendes*)—about the meaning of *Being*. But there are *beings* (*Seiende*) in very different senses: *being* is all that to which we relate ourselves in this or that way, *being* is also what and how we are ourselves. From which *being* should we try to extract the meaning of *Being*? Heidegger declares that in the *being* that we ourselves are and that he calls *Dasein*, we possess a pre-philosophical, self-evident understanding of *Being*. This understanding of *Being* is the heart of all ontology, of the philosophical theory of *Being*.

It is therefore *Dasein*, the "human way" of *being* of the concrete self-conscious individual, that is to be questioned about the meaning of *Being*. The difficulty of such questioning resides in our inclination to understand our *Being* out of the *being* which, as *world*, constantly belongs to us. Thus we have to take pains that our *existence* should reveal itself only as it is in itself, that is, "in its average everyday-ness." [23]

What are the specific characteristics of *Dasein*? First of all it is "specifically mine" (*je meiniges*); it is *personal*, unique. "But even though the 'essence' of *Dasein* lies in its existence," [24] it is neither *merely there* (*Vorhanden*), nor is it only *specifically mine*. Also, it does not only relate itself *understandingly* to its *Being* but it is also *being in the world*. It would be incorrect, however, to understand this *being* in analogy with what we mean when we say that the coat is *in* the closet. For here one speaks not about existence but about things that are simply there and that in themselves are "worldless." What is meant by *being in the world* of *Dasein* are different modes of *being-in*, namely, "to have something to do with," make something, to undertake something, to carry out something, to announce, to question, to contemplate, to discuss and to decide. [25] All these modes have the character of *taking care* (*Besorgnis*). In Heidegger's view these modes of being have not been properly detected until now because one specific way of *being in the world*, namely *knowing*, has overshadowed them. Moreover, knowing has always been conceived as a relationship between two *beings*, the subject and the object, which have been wrongly and naïvely identified with *existence* and *world* respectively. And it is from here that the perennial and tantalizing problem arose of how knowledge can, as a process in the interior of the subjects, get at the objects on the outside. But for Heidegger the world does not mean Nature. The latter is mainly an *inworldly being* (*ein innerweltliches Seiendes*), discovered by existence as a special mode of its *being in the world* (as is done by the natural sciences). And by *world* he means that which surrounds us—*Umwelt*—"about-world."

Our everyday *being in the world* has, as we have already seen, the character of *handling* and *taking care of*. This practical behavior is not *atheoretical*, but has its own knowledge, which Heidegger calls *circumspection* (*Umsicht*).[26] And the *beings* with which we deal in this commerce of *taking care of* is termed by Heidegger *Zeug*—utensil. The mode of Being of the utensil is *handy-ness* (*Zuhandenheit*), which is more basic than its mere *being there* (*Vorhandenheit*).

In its everyday mode of being, *Dasein* "dissolves" itself, as it were, in the world. No one is an isolated *I* for without the others it is a fiction. *Being in the world* is then also *being together with*—*Mitsein*, and it is characterized not by being different from the others, but precisely by being like the others. What corresponds to "care" (*Besorgen*) of the utensils is the "provision" (*Fuersorge*) for the others, whereby this concept is to be taken as widely as possible to cover also *being at cross-purposes* with the others. The everyday mode of existence is the "unauthentic" existence of the *man* (the German indefinite pronoun) and is marked by gossip (*Gerede*), curiosity (*Neugier*), and ambiguity (*Zweideutigkeit*). The unauthentic existence is "secondhand" and superficial since it relies on hearsay. It is the downfall (*Verfallen*) of *Dasein*: *Dasein* surrenders to the world. It is true that this brings appeasement, but also estrangement (*Entfremdung*).

It would, however, be a mistake to interpret the downfall of *Dasein* as degeneration, as the "Night-aspect" of existence. In Heidegger's view it is precisely a proof of the existentiality of existence, for it is still *being in the world,* however unauthentically.[27] What brings *Dasein* before facticity, that is, "before the 'that' of its 'being there' which stares at it in inexorable mysteriousness," [28] is the "mood" (*Gestimmtsein, Befinlichkeit*). It does not show the whence and whereto of existence but its *being thrown* into the *there* (*Da*).

The fundamental mood is *Angst* (anxiety). The Kierkegaardian *Angst,* which although produced by Nothingness points toward the Highest, reveals for Heidegger "Nothingness, which determines the ground of *Dasein.*" It is closely related to the phenomenon of downfall (*Verfallen*). The dissolution in the world and in the *man* reveals as its source the flight of *Dasein* from itself, from the possibility of being one's proper self. The *what from* we flee is existence itself: as something threatening it must provoke anxiety.[29]

Whereas in common usage anxiety and fear are interchangeable, for Heidegger fear concerns *beings* in the world. The "object of anxiety, however, is the being-in-the-world as such." [30] It is wholly indeterminate, is "neither here nor there," but "is so close that it takes our breath away and is still nowhere." Once anxiety is gone, we say it was really nothing. Fear is unauthentic anxiety that has surrendered to the world and is unknown to itself as anxiety. For Heidegger anxiety concerns the *being in the world* as *being toward death.* It springs from our *Dasein,* nay, it is *Dasein* itself, and therefore anxiety is nothing psychological.[31]

What is the importance of *Dasein* for Heidegger's ontological investigation? "Only as long (human) as *Dasein* is, is there Being." [32] This is not to be understood in the sense of subjectivism or idealism. Heidegger does not deny the reality of the outside world; nor does he want to say that Being is the product of man or that it can be derived from the *being qua Dasein.* But *Sein* and *Dasein, Being* and human *existence* (as this term is understood by Heidegger) need each other. Man is intimately bound up with the "down-falling nullity" of the world,[33] and "man is the deputy of nothingness" (*der*

Platzhalter des Nichts). Being and Nothingness belong together, because Being is in Nothingness, as it were "in its veil" (*in seinem Schleier*). Nothingness, before which anxiety brings us, reveals the nullity of human existence whose essential trait is being "thrown" into death.[34]

"Freedom toward Death"

The interpretation of *Dasein* as *care* (*Sorge*) does not, however, take into consideration *Dasein* in its entirety. This interpretation omits what *Dasein* can be, what it, indeed, becomes, which is the end itself—death. Death belongs to the possibility of Dasein and determines and limits every possible totality of existence. True enough, it is impossible for *Dasein* to experience this *not anymore existing* or to understand it as experienced. The experience of the death of others cannot serve as a substitute for it. Just as *Dasein* is *specifically mine,* so is dying. One can die for someone, but no one can relieve another from his dying.[35] Death is more than negation of *Dasein,* because it permeates it, because "*Dasein* dies in fact insofar as it exists." [36] Death is *impending* (*Bevorstand*)— "*media in vita in morte sumus.*" *Dasein* is neither completed in death—for many die too soon, others too late—nor does it simply vanish with death, as one can say, for instance, that a wind vanishes when it ceases to blow. It also does not become "finished" in death, as for instance a work of art can be finished; and it cannot become completely "available," as an amount of money becomes available when it has finally been paid up. In the same way as *Dasein,* as long as it is, is already its *not-yet,* so it is also always its end. The end meant here is not a "coming to an end of *Dasein*" (*Zu-Ende-sein des Daseins*) but "Being toward the end" (*Sein zum Ende*). Death is a mode of being, which *Dasein* takes upon itself, as soon as it is: "As soon as a human being is alive, he is old enough to die." [37]

In the wider sense, death is a phenomenon of life. The death of animals can be considered simply as ending (*Verenden*). But dying is, for Heidegger, "a mode of being in which *Dasein* is 'toward' its death." [38] Between the two Heidegger places the demise—*Ableben. Dasein* can end without really dying, but on the other hand, as *Dasein* it does not simply end.[39]

What is important in this existential interpretation of death is that it precedes all biology and ontology of life. According to Heidegger, it alone gives a basis to historio-biographical and ethnologico-psychological investigations of death. A typology of dying, as characterization of the states and ways in which the demise is being experienced, already presupposes the concept of death. Moreover, a psychology of dying gives information about the life of those who are about to die rather than about dying itself. This is because *Dasein* does not actually die when experiencing the factual demise. More important still, the ontologic analysis of *being toward death* does not decide anything about whether *after death* another, a higher or lower, existence is possible, whether *Dasein* survives death or whether it is immortal. Heidegger avoids the question about the beyond or its possibility, and holds that one can ask meaningfully "what is after death" only "when the ontological essence of death is understood," and it is even an open question whether such an inquiry is at all possible theoretically.[40] *Dasein* comprises that which awaits it, that which is in the cards (*Bevorstehendes*). This may be a thunderstorm, or building a home, or the visit of a friend. But death is not such *Bevorstehendes*. It distinguishes itself from other kinds of *what awaits us* by three characteristics: (1) it is a most private (*eigenste*) possibility insofar as it is specifically mine; (2) it is an unrelated possibility (*unbezueglich*), insofar as in death the relations to all other *Daseins* are dissolved; (3) it is an unsurpassable (*unueberholbare*) possibility, insofar as it represents the most extreme possibility, "the possibility of absolute impossibility of *Dasein*." [41]

As soon as *Dasein* is, it is already thrown into this possibility. This being thrown into death reveals itself to *Dasein* in the phenomenon of anxiety.

If, however, the *being toward death* belongs essentially and originally to *Dasein*, then it must be found also in everyday-ness—*Alltaeglichkeit*. The self of everyday-ness is, as we have seen, the *man*. How does *man* interpret his *being toward death*? It knows death as a death (*ein Todesfall*), as an everyday occurrence; it knows that one dies some day, but it does not feel concerned or threatened. That one dies signifies in fact "everybody but me." Thus dying is brought down to the level of an event that does not affect "me." This camouflaging of death, this dodging of the thought of death, stubbornly dominates everyday-ness. It goes so far that thinking about death is decried as "cowardly fear and somber flight from the world." [42] Such superior indifference to death, however, alienates *Dasein* from its genuine possibility of Being.

This appeasement, characteristic of the estrangement of *Dasein,* this constant flight from death, is possible only because the certainty of death goes hand in hand with the uncertainty of *when—"mors certa, hora incerta."* But *Dasein* is always already given over to death—it dies constantly. Whereas for the unauthentic existence death is in the highest degree probable but not really certain—strictly speaking it has merely empirical certainty, which is less than the apodictic certainty attainable in some sectors of theoretical knowledge —in the authentic *being toward death* the possibility of death is uncompromisingly understood as the "possibility of the impossibility of existence." As such possibility death is the most specific, extreme possibility in which *Dasein* is "running ahead of itself" (*Vorlaufen*).

In this running ahead of itself (in thought) toward certain death, *Dasein* opens itself to the threat (*Bedrohung*) of this absolute possibility. The revelation of this constant threat takes place through anxiety: "the being toward death is essentially anxiety." In it *Dasein* finds itself before the Nothingness of the possible impossibility of its existence. It "brings Dasein before the possibility . . . to be itself." It is here that we find what can be considered Heidegger's answer to death. The anxiety-filled creature resolutely "takes death upon itself" and attains the "anxiety-ridden freedom to death." [43]

This resolve is not an escape, invented for the purpose of overcoming death, but the illusionless confrontation of death. However, with the sober anxiety goes the "armed joy" at the possibility of impossibility of existence. *Dasein* becomes free from the crutches that the unauthentic *Dasein* draws from the events of the world.[44]

The authentic *being toward death* arouses us and makes for a new life. It is similar to the old precept—in order to live one has to die—in the sense, however, that one has to become aware of the essential finitude of existence. Thus, Heidegger does not actually give an answer to death, but merely summons man to change his life, to live "authentically." It is only in the realization of our existence as essentially and necessarily "being toward death" that man can rise above the petty day-to-day life to become truly himself and truly free.

Heidegger's answer to death appears first of all as the last stage of the trend familiar to us already in Schopenhauer, Feuerbach, and Simmel, to see death not as a sudden break but as immanent in life. It also seems at first to be a pure and simple glorification of death, and Jolivet considers it as such.[45] This glorification is, however, very different from that of Novalis, for whom death was, after all, only a door to another existence. However, Heidegger's refusal to discuss the possibility of the beyond must not be interpreted as a categorical denial of such a possibility. It can be maintained that Heidegger's real position is that of the impossibility of an answer to death, at least in the sense of a comforting belief, and perhaps not even in the sense of coming to terms emotionally with the necessity of having to die, since it is precisely all veiling of death, characteristic of unauthentic existence, that he scorns.

According to Sternberger, Heidegger wants to understand death, to make it transparent, and to give it a loftiness that will permit us to see it in a detached way as an interesting event. But Sternberger himself doubts whether the horror and absurdity of death will yield to this process of intellectual sublimation. Heidegger had already pointed out the radical difference between the death of the other and one's own death. And the question is not so much whether the resolute acceptance of death and a detached attitude to it can give comfort, but whether such an understanding of death is altogether within the psychological powers of man. Sternberger points out that Heidegger's position is reminiscent of Nietzsche's *amor fati.*[46]

One may also see in it a certain similarity to Hegel's

view, when he speaks in the *Phenomenology of Spirit* of the "consciousness of slaves" who do not have the courage to accept death and to renounce life, and of the "consciousness of the masters," of those who accept death and even will it; the dialectical tension between the two is what underlies the historical process: the rôle of the master is to provoke the slave into striving for freedom; the struggle for it is the true content of history.

But, as we have seen, for Hegel history has an ultimate goal toward which it moves. For Heidegger, although death is not any more, as it was for Hegel, the terrible foe attacking from the outside, but belongs to the structural profile of *Dasein*, and although anxiety of death is primarily an instrument for philosophical insight into the meaning of Being, there is no comforting vision of history that can neutralize the meaninglessness of human existence that death, as final annihilation, seems to proclaim.

Since, however, Hegel's philosophy of history, and by the same token other optimistic philosophies of history, have become, to say the least, questionable, such a possibility of imparting a broader meaning to individual existence vanishes.

Heidegger's philosophy, however, opens up entirely different vistas on the problem of death. As Rudolph Berlinger points out, for the thinking that is inextricably enmeshed in time and history, dying is a march toward quiet Nothingness. But Heidegger's thought is unhistorical. And as Berlinger spins out the implications of Heidegger's philosophy, it leaves this Nothingness "behind," for, as Berlinger interprets it, "Death itself is not this dialectic of being in time; it is the end of time and of history, the downfall of *Dasein*, of time and of dying. . . . Death overcomes itself in dying as ascension of eternity"—its ascension, not the beginning of eternity—because death brings out that which was already there eternally. "What death is becomes understandable through dying. For the thinking which remains enslaved to time, death is a riddle. And to the extent as our thinking becomes disengaged from time this riddle approaches solution, and eternity reveals itself in time. . . . Through death we withdraw from all that is temporal and rejoin all that is eternal"—that is, Being itself.[47]

Another critic, Ewald Wasmuth, finds that Heidegger does not see the "gate," which, as Wasmuth believes, opens here toward Being. He is hindered in doing so by his faith in the science of Nature. Heidegger confuses Nothing, which exists as a negation of something, with the Nothing of everything, an important difference that Pascal already noted by distinguishing the "not being a thing" and the "Nothing of a thing." Death is not the Nothing of Being, it is first of all and for everyone, the negation of life.

> . . . The paradox inherent in his [Heidegger's] concept of Being is . . . one well known for a long time and which Goethe puts in the mouth of Mephistopheles, who says that he is "the Darkness, which gave birth to light." In still another respect Goethe knew already this paradox which Heidegger's profundity seems to make unfathomable. When Faust wants to descend to the "mothers," Mephistopheles warns him: "Nothing will you see in the eternally empty distance" . . . and Faust answers that he nevertheless "wants to try and hopes to find the All in your Nothingness." [*In deinam Nichts hoff ich das All zu finden*.] Heidegger went the way of Faust, but not as the adept of magic, of the magic-mystical "understanding" of Nature, but as the follower of Kant, Hegel, Kierkegaard and Nietzsche and without referring to mathematics . . . where it expresses itself, for instance, in the formula $\frac{1}{0} = \infty$
>
> This formula, which seems paradoxical, has been confirmed in modern physics since when finite mass becomes the "nothing" of mass, infinite energy appears.[48]

Wasmuth further contends that, strange as it may be, the statement of the pre-Socratic thinker to whom Heidegger feels committed more than to anyone else—namely Parmenides—does not seem to have impressed him sufficiently. Thus he does not heed the warning that "It is necessary to say and to think: Being is, Non-being is not."

For his part Wasmuth holds, however, that "Death limits life, not Being. . . . No matter how grandiose and consequential, on the whole, Heidegger's attempt to take death seriously is, he did not find access to the interpretation of Being, to the new ontology. He remained committed to the Being in which God is dead and where, therefore, Nothingness could represent itself as the All." [49]

In view of Heidegger's emphasis on the anxiety of death, it is only natural to ask whether he is not himself obsessed by the thought of death and the fear of it. Does not what Guardini says about Rilke, with whose thought and feelings Heidegger shows such deep affinity, apply also to Heidegger, that in spite of his original glorification of death "one can hear how little he believed in his own message and how intensely he was afraid of death"? [50]

Whether or not this is so, a new motif appears in his later writings which may indicate a possible change in his answer to death. He speaks of joy, whose essence is feeling oneself at "home" (*Heimischwerden*) in the proximity of the *ultimate sources,* a joy which is *the holy.*[51] Man, who at first appeared as the deputy of Nothingness, is now the guardian or shepherd of Being. Anxiety now becomes merely wonder (*Verwunderung*) and amazement (*Staunen*), and the homelessness (*Unheimlichkeit*) yields to "the reassuring closeness to Being." (*Heimat der Naehe des Seins.*) The visions of the poet Hoelderlin reveal new perspectives. Perhaps the new answer to death to which Heidegger is being led is the consoling certitude of the harmony between human existence and the ground of Being, which he believes Western man has not known or felt since the Pre-Socratics.

Sartre (1905-   )

Whereas Heidegger's principal search is for the meaning of Being, Sartre is primarily interested in human freedom. This is, of course, by no means the whole story, for Sartre too is dealing with the problem of Being, but his inquiry is dominated by the problem of Nothingness. To speak of Sartre as the French disciple of Heidegger or as distorter of the latter's philosophy is to betray an ignorance of Sartre's work and commit an unjustifiable underestimation of it. Sartre owes much to Heidegger, but he does not misinterpret him—he simply disagrees with him. This disagreement is perhaps nowhere as clear as in their respective analyses of the experience of death.

It is important to realize that, although the fact and event of death does not occupy as significant a place in Sartre's thought as it does in Heidegger's, it is not because Sartre never really encountered it. On the contrary, whereas Heidegger appears merely to think and talk about it, Sartre lived under the shadow of death for a considerable time, especially as a member of the French Resistance. It is precisely this proximity to death that leaves its imprint on Sartre's thought. In the *Republic of Silence* he writes:

> Exile, captivity, and especially death (which we usually shrink from facing at all in happier days) became for us the habitual objects of our concern. We learnt that they were neither inevitable accidents, not even constant and inevitable dangers, but that they must be considered as our lot itself, our destiny, the profound source of our reality as men. At every instant we lived up to the full sense of this commonplace little phrase: "Man is mortal!" And the choice that each of us made face to face with death, because it could always have been expressed in these terms: "Rather death than . . ." . . . Thus the basic question of liberty was posed, and we were brought to the verge of the deepest knowledge that man can have of himself. For the secret of man is not his Oedipus complex or his inferiority complex: it is the limit of his own liberty, his capacity for resisting torture and death.[52]

The major disagreement between Heidegger and Sartre, as far as death is concerned, revolves around Heidegger's *being toward death*. Sartre sees Heidegger's position as a reaction against the customary view of death as inhuman, in the sense that it is outside of human existence as if beyond the wall, and that as such it escapes human experience. Heidegger, however, follows the poets, especially Rilke, who, not satisfied to consider death an absolute cessation of existing, or as an existence in a non-human form, tries, as does Malraux too, to "recuperate" death. Death is seen as the last part of a series, and if the series thus recuperates its *terminus ad quem,* death itself becomes interiorized and humanized. There is no other side of death, it is the ultimate phenomenon of life, but of life nevertheless. Moreover, death is not only being humanized, it becomes *my* death. I become responsible for it, as I am responsible for my life. For Rilke the end of every human being resembles his life, because life is preparation for the end. As Sartre describes it, "not the empirical and contingent phenomenon of my demise, but the finite character of life makes my life as well as my death *mine.*" [53]

According to Sartre, it remained for Heidegger to give a philosophical form to this humanization of death. *Dasein,* the human mode of being, is defined as *being toward death.* And insofar as *Dasein* decides about its projection toward death, it realizes the freedom-toward-dying and constitutes itself as a totality through the free choice of finitude.

"Such a theory," says Sartre, "cannot but seduce us. . . . Nevertheless, neither the comfort of these views, nor the element of truth they contain, ought to mislead us. It is necessary to re-examine the question from the beginning." [54]

Sartre holds that even if death were a passage to a non-human absolute, it cannot be considered a window opening on the absolute. Death tells us only about ourselves, and even this only in human terms. Moreover, the interpretation of death as the concluding chord of a melody must be rejected. We have to realize the absurdity of death. The often-used simile whereby man is compared to a condemned to death among other condemned men who ignores the day of his execution and sees some of his companions being executed every day, is, according to Sartre, not quite correct. Man appears rather like a condemned to death who bravely prepares himself for the end, makes a great effort into making a good show on the gallows, but in the meantime dies of influenza. Christianity has understood this and advises us always to be prepared for death. Thus the purpose of life becomes waiting for death, and death becomes the seal that is affixed to life.

Unfortunately, says Sartre, the advice to be constantly prepared for death, and by the same token Heidegger's *resolve,* are more easily given than followed, and this not so much because of human weakness, but because of death itself, since, Sartre insists, one can wait for a specific death, but not for death as such. He finds that Heidegger performs a sleight of hand when, in asserting that death is "the only thing no one else can do for me," he confers on death incomparable individuality, makes it *my* death and then individualizes *Dasein* itself. Sartre, however, maintains that I can speak of *my* death only after I have placed myself already into the perspective of subjectivity. It is my subjectivity that makes my death *my* death. But it is one of the main premises of Sartre's philosophy, and of his disagreement with Descartes, that man in his consciousness is at once aware of the presence of others and that he is more certain of this than he is of himself. For Sartre, consciousness starts on the pre-reflective level and his world is that of intersubjectivity.

As for waiting for death, the word waiting has two meanings where death is concerned. We can anticipate death in principle (*s'attendre à la mort*) and we can wait for death (*attendre la mort*). The latter is possible only in an instance like condemnation to death when the execution is set for a definite day and hour. Otherwise, death is something we can and may take into account, but it preserves its essential characteristic as the unexpected. Under normal circumstances death cannot be foreseen for a definite date and therefore waited for. There is also a considerable difference in quality between death through old age and premature death. Death that comes with age makes life a *limited* affair, but while waiting for such a death we can set goals in life against the general background of life's finiteness. But to wait for premature death is to expect one's life to be a *failing* enterprise. If there were only deaths from old age on the one hand and death through execution on the other, one could speak of waiting for death in the one or the other of the two meanings mentioned above. But it is precisely the characteristic of most deaths that they surprise those who wait for it. And they can be deceived not only by a death that comes earlier but also by a death that comes later than expected. The point Sartre wants to make is that if we were nothing but this waiting for death, *being toward death,* we would survive ourselves, for we would die either before our task—waiting for death—has been accomplished, or after it, and only very rarely would we die through *resolve.* Chance decides the manner of our death, that is, whether we die prematurely or in old age. And because of this it deprives death of all possibility of being like a harmonious conclusion of a melody; for that it would have to arise from the melody. In short, "death is not my possibility . . . but the always possible nullification (*néantisation*) of what is possible for me, which is outside my possibilities." And if the day and hour of my death are not fixed by me, but are decided by the "sequences of the universe," we cannot say that death confers a meaning, a sense to life, for meaning comes only from subjectivity itself. "Because death is not rooted in our freedom, it cannot but deprive life of all meaning." [55]

Sartre argues that if I am expectation (*attente*) and expectation of expectations and so forth, and if the object of my last expectation and the one who expects are suddenly suppressed, this expecting, this waiting, receives retroactively the character of absurdity. He gives the instance of a young man who aspires to become a great writer and dies just when he prepares to begin his magnum opus. All his life-projects, which consist of preparation for becoming a great writer, lose all meaning; we do not even know whether he would have succeeded in writing a great novel. And Sartre concludes that "death is never that which gives meaning to life: it is, on the contrary, that which actually deprives life of all significance. If we have to die, our life has no sense because our problems do not receive any kind of solution and because the very meaning of the problems remains undetermined." [56]

Sartre extends his view, that death can never give meaning to life, also to death through suicide. It is an act of my life and, as such, *only* the future can give a meaning to it. But being the last act of my life it refuses this future and thus remains totally undetermined. And should I not die as a result of my attempt at suicide, I may consider it later on as a cowardice, since it would become clear to me that other solutions were also possible. But since these solutions cannot be but my own projects, they cannot come about unless I live. Thus suicide too is an absurdity that causes my life to become submerged in the absurd.[57]

Before continuing the exposition of Sartre's views on death, it is necessary to say a few words about the main tenets of his "phenomenological ontology" and the particular terminology he uses. *That which is* (Heidegger calls it *das Seiende*) has no ground for its being, but is radically contingent and unexplainable, and its existence precedes its essence. It is also in itself "full" and "rigid," and Sartre accordingly calls it *en-soi* —*in-itself*. There is no place for freedom in it. How then is it possible that there is in the world the knowing and free man? This is possible because alongside *being* there is yet another type of Being, which Sartre calls *le pour-soi—for-itself—* and which is the specific human way of being. This *pour-soi* is, then, analogous to Heidegger's *Dasein* and Jaspers' *Existenz*.

But since everything *that is* must first of all be *being-in-itself,* Sartre deduces that *being-for-itself* must be non-being, Nothingness (*Le Néant*). Nothing is neither before being, and not outside it, but in the midst of it. The *for-itself,* the *being-man* arises because being naughts itself (*se néantise*). That the *for-itself* is Nothing, Sartre demonstrates by pointing out that there are negative realities (*Négatités*). And since Nothingness cannot come from *in-itself* its origin is in man. Man is the carrier of Nothingness. This does not mean that man is the embodiment of Nothingness, for he is also *en-soi* —his body, his ego, his habits. It is, then, the specifically human in him, the *pour-soi,* that is Nothing and the source of Nothingness. The Nothingness of the *pour-soi* appears in its freedom. Freedom is the indeterminate that is Nothing. And freedom is not an attribute of *for-itself,* but is identical with it. The consequence of this is that man has no "nature." But man *is* not first in order to be free later; there is no difference between the being man and being free. Man's essence is his freedom. He is condemned to be free.

The *for-itself* is characterized by three *ek-stases*—the tendencies toward Nothing, toward the Other and toward Being. The first *ek-stasis* is that of freedom and consciousness, the

latter understood as pre-reflexive. The second is that of being-
for-the-other. Sartre holds that we do not have to prove the
existence of the Other—it is given to us directly, as, for instance, in the phenomenon of shame, and we possess the sexual
drive not because we have sex organs but because, on the
contrary, man is essentially sex—that is, he is being-for-the-
Other—and that is why we possess these organs. The basic
relationship between the different *for-itselfs* is that of trying
to dominate each other's freedom.

We can now proceed with our exposition:

In emphasizing that his remarks are not drawn from the
consideration of death but from that of life, Sartre states that

> it is because the "for-itself" is a being which always demands
> an "after," that there is no place for death in a being which
> is "for-itself" . . . the waiting for death destroys itself, since
> it is a negation of all waiting. My project toward *a* death
> is comprehensible (suicide, martyrdom, heroism), but not
> the project toward *my* death as indetermined possibility of
> not realizing any more presence in the world since this
> project would be the destruction of all projects. Thus death
> could not be my proper possibility; it would not be even
> one of *my* possibilities.

However, death is not only the nullification of my projects
—a project that destroys all other projects. It is also the triumph of the point of view of the "Other." This is what Sartre
thinks Malraux has in mind when he says that "death transforms life into destiny."

When the *for-itself* ceases to live, its past is not abolished, but
my life, instead of becoming a harmonious totality, becomes
"fixed," its meaning is fixed forever by the "open totality" that
is the arrested life.[58]

It is characteristic of a life that is terminated that the
Other becomes its guardian. This does not merely mean that
alone the Other can prevent the "shriveling up" of the life of
the deceased, the total severance of its ties with the present,
but that the relation to the dead is an essential structure of
the (fundamental relation of) "being for the other." In dis-

cussing the attitude toward the dead—even forgetting them is also an attitude—Sartre comes to the conclusion that the difference between life and death is that "life decides about its own meaning, because it is always in 'abeyance.' It possesses the power of auto-criticism and of auto-metamorphosis, which allow it to be defined as a 'not-yet.' The dead life also does not stop changing, but it is 'done.' This signifies that for it the game is over and it will undergo these changes without being any more responsible for them. Nothing can happen to it from the 'inside,' it is completely closed and nothing can enter it any more; but its meaning does not cease being modified, albeit from the outside." [59]

Death does not belong to the ontological structure of the for-itself, and to that extent it is the triumph of the Other over myself, it refers to the other fundamental but totally contingent fact, which is the existence of the Other.

In summing up, Sartre says that "we have to conclude, against Heidegger, that far from being my own possibility death is a contingent fact, which, as such, escapes me by principle . . . I cannot discover my death, nor wait for it, nor take an attitude toward it, for it is that which reveals itself as indiscoverable, that which disarms all expectations. . . . Death is a pure fact, like birth; it comes to us from the outside. Basically it is undistinguishable from birth and it is this identity of birth and death which we call facticity." [60]

It seems to follow from the above that death must radically limit our freedom. This is a crucial issue with Sartre, and he asks whether in renouncing Heidegger's *being toward death* we do not actually renounce forever the possibility of giving freely a meaning to our life for which we ourselves would be responsible. He believes, however, that just the opposite is the case, and that in revealing itself to us as it really is, death liberates us from its alleged constraint.[61]

Sartre insists on the strict separation of the idea of death and the idea of finitude. Usually it is assumed that it is death that constitutes and reveals to us our finitude. Thus death takes on the appearance of an ontological necessity, and Heidegger in particular seems to have based his whole theory of *being toward death* on this identification of death and finitude.

Sartre, however, believes he has discovered, on closer inspection, that such an identification is erroneous, and that death is a contingent fact arising from facticity, and that finitude is an ontological structure of the *for-itself*.

> Human reality will remain finite, even if it were immortal, because it makes itself finite by choosing to be human. Being finite is in fact to choose oneself, that is, to tell oneself what one is, in projecting oneself toward a possible, under the exclusion of other possibilities. The very act of freedom is thus assumption and creation of finitude. If I "make" myself, I make myself finite, and by this my life becomes unique. From then on, even if I were immortal, it is forbidden to me to resume my actions; it is the irreversibility of temporality which forbids it, and this irreversibility is nothing else than the real characteristic of a liberty which "temporalizes" itself. . . . Death is in no way an ontological structure of my being, at least not as far as it is "for-itself"; it is the "other" who is mortal in his being. There is no place for death in the *being-for-itself;* it cannot wait for death, nor make it effective [*réaliser*], nor project itself toward it; it is in no way the basis for its finitude. . . .[62]

> What is death, then? it is nothing but a certain aspect of "facticity" [63] and of the "being for the other," that is nothing but the "given." It is absurd that we should be born, it is absurd that we should die; on the other hand, this absurdity presents itself as a permanent alienation of my "being-as-a-possibility" which is not any more *my* possibility, but that of the "other." . . .[64] Death is not my possibility in the above defined sense; it is my limit situation as the reverse side chosen and fleeing my choice. Death haunts me at the core of each of my projects as their inavoidable obverse.

But precisely as it must be taken upon myself not as *my* possibility, but as the possibility that there are no more possibilities for me, "death *does not 'encroach' upon me*. Freedom, which is *my freedom,* remains total and infinite; not that death does not limit it, but because freedom encounters this limit, death is in no way an obstacle to my projects; it is merely a destiny *somewhere else* in relation to *these projects. I am not free for dying, but I am a free mortal.* . . .[65] Therefore we can neither think death, nor wait for it, nor arm ourselves against it; but, at the same time, our projects, as projects, are independent of it, and this not, as the Christian asserts, through blindness or bad faith, but by principle. And although there are innumerable attitudes possible toward death, they cannot be classified as 'authentic' and 'inauthentic,' for we always die 'into the bargain.' " [66]

Sartre points out that this discussion of death is incomplete, and together with the discussions of *my place, my past, my surroundings,* and *my neighbor* aims primarily at the clarification of the concept of *situation*.[67]

Still, though subordinating the discussion of death to that of *situation,* Sartre tells us some more about his views on death. We must consider, first of all, the three fundamental concepts on which his philosophy is based—negation, liberty and situation.

Negation, and in this Sartre agrees with Heidegger, has as its source Nothingness. And asking for the source of Nothingness, he goes beyond Heidegger, for whom it is transcendent and, as it were, super-worldly, and finds it in the world, in the heart of Being, "as a worm." [68]

As to freedom, Sartre does not recognize the validity of the argument of common sense, which denies freedom by insisting on our impotence. It holds that far from making himself, man seems to be made by climate and the earth, by the race and class, by language, the history of the collectivity of which he is part, heredity, the particular circumstances of his childhood, the acquired habits, and the great and small events of his life.

Sartre, however, holds that the amount of the "adversity of things" cannot serve as an argument against our freedom since it is *through us,* that is, through the previous positing of an end, that this mass of adversity arises. He says that a rock that strongly resists our attempt to move it can become a considerable help to me if I decide to use it as a vantage point in surveying the landscape. What is even more important, common sense does not see that the formula *being free* does not mean "to obtain what one wants," but "to determine oneself to will (in the larger meaning of to choose) through oneself." In other words, "Success is of no consequence for liberty." [69]

Sartre explains that a distinction must be made between the popular, empirical conception of freedom (which is a product of political and historical circumstances) where freedom is identical with "the faculty of obtaining the chosen goals," and the technical, philosophical conception where freedom signifies merely "autonomy of choice." It is only in this latter sense that Sartre uses this term. And this is of the greatest importance, for it eliminates many misunderstandings about Sartre's assertions. He points out, however, that his description of freedom does not make a distinction between intention and action. And choice presupposes a beginning of action, otherwise it would be indistinguishable from a dream or a wish. To insist that the prisoner is always free to leave the prison would be absurd, but we can say that he is always free to seek to escape, or to be freed, which means that, whatever his situation, he can "project" his escape and teach himself the value of his project through the start of an action. Applied to what Sartre says of man as being a free mortal and not "free for dying," this makes clear that he means that man can choose to die, but cannot die at will. And finally there is the paradoxical character of freedom: there is no freedom but "in situation" and there is no situation but through freedom. Human reality encounters everywhere obstacles that it did not create; but these resistances and obstacles have no meaning but in and through the free choice that is human reality.[70]

This freedom of choice entails responsibility. Man, as Sartre sees it, is "condemned to be free." And as such "he carries the weight of the whole world on his shoulders"—that is, he is *responsible* for the world in the ordinary sense of this word as *being the indisputable author of the events or of an object.*[71]

Being responsible, the *for-itself* has to assume, alongside the proud consciousness of being the author of his own situation, all the worst inconveniences and threats. And Sartre says that it is pointless to complain, since nothing outside of us decides what we feel, how we live, and what we are: "there are no accidents in life." And he illustrates it by the example of being called up for military service in war: "it is *my* war, for 'I deserve it,' because I can always escape it either through desertion or even through suicide." This is interesting in two respects. First, Sartre does not seem to stop to reflect that the remedy may be worse than the disease. But he is concerned with proving his point that man is alone responsible for the world, and that it is pointless to ask "what would I have become if the war did not take place?" since, according to him, "I am this war" by virtue of having chosen myself as one of the possible meanings of the times I live in, which imperceptibly led to war.[72]

Secondly, it shows that for Sartre death, at least voluntary death, appears to be the "always open door" of which Epictetus had already spoken. Thus death is for Sartre a means of asserting one's liberty. But what about the instances, and they are the most frequent ones, that do not fall under the formula "Rather death than. . ."? We shall see what Sartre's answer appears to be in this respect when we consider what he says about our birth, which, as we have seen, is for Sartre as absurd as death is.

What he said about war applies also to birth. To say that "I did not ask to be born" is a "naive way to put the accent on our facticity." And I am responsible also for my birth, since I am responsible for everything except my responsibility, and everything happens as if I were forced to be responsible. "I am abandoned in the world" should not be interpreted in the sense of being passive in a hostile universe, but as

I am alone in the world for which I am fully responsible and inescapably bound to this my responsibility, since I am responsible also for my desire to shirk responsibility. To refuse to act, to remain passive is also my choice. I can be ashamed of having been born, and I can be astonished by it, or I can be glad about it, or I can, in trying to get rid of my life, affirm that I find it bad and regret to have been born, but in all this I chose, *in a sense,* to have been born. And this choice is wholly afflicted by facticity, for I cannot not choose. And therefore I cannot ask "why was I born?" or curse the day of my birth or declare that I did not ask to be born, since these different attitudes toward my birth are nothing else but the acceptance of full responsibility for this birth, for making it *mine*.[73]

It would appear that the same argument ought to be applied to my death. But obviously, unless it is voluntary death, there is no possibility of choice. Or rather, there is a choice of *how* to die, and this is what Sartre seems to have in mind when in *The Wall* the protagonist chooses to die "properly." This will not appear to be a satisfactory answer to all those who resent the fact of having to die at all and want consolation. It is clear that for Sartre this whole question of consolation with regard to our mortality, that is, the question a Schopenhauer considered the foremost task of philosophy (and/or religion), is unimportant, and he would regard any attempt at consolation a meddlesome limitation of freedom. He would say that it is useless to complain, senseless to protest, and certainly naïve to ask why we have to die. Sartre's tough-mindedness, however, is easy to understand as a consequence of his experience of the "viscosity" of existence and of his view of man as a failure.

It is existential psychoanalysis, as Sartre understands it,[74] that tells us why man "is a failure, by telling us what he seeks." It shows that the *pour-soi* "wants only one thing—to be." Being Nothingness, it wants Being. But it does not want to be *in-itself*, since the *in-itself* is *viscous* and gives man nausea. Man wants to be both *in-itself* and *for-itself*, which amounts to saying that he wants to be God. This passion is, however, the opposite of that of Christ, for here man loses himself in order to become God. "But the idea of God is contradictory and we lose ourselves in vain; man is a useless passion." [75]

But while he is "a useless passion," he is, at the same time, also everything—the creator of the universe and of himself. He is inextricably in a "situation"—biological, economic, political, cultural—and nevertheless he is "choosing himself in a situation" and therefore choosing the situation itself. By choosing himself man becomes what he himself makes of himself, and as such legislates for himself and for the whole of mankind. "The human being is not only that being through which negativities are revealed in the world, it is also that being which can take negative attitudes toward itself," [76] but in this case the free individual is taken almost as the Absolute, and one can say that for Sartre freedom assumes all the trappings of a religious substitute.

What can the free mortal do face to face with death in a world where God is dead?

He can resort to what could be called integrity. The protagonist in *The Wall*, realizing suddenly that he is mortal, does not want to "die like an animal," but to understand. Unfortunately, we are not told what he wanted to understand. The meaning of death? And since he obviously cannot understand, he wants at least to die "properly, correctly."

Sartre's story, however, shows even the absurdity of integrity. Choosing death rather than betrayal of a friend, the hero unwittingly betrays the friend, brings on his death, and himself remains alive.

Nevertheless, death has for Sartre some positive aspects: Death reveals our freedom and this is its main function. One may even go further and say that death accomplishes not only the revelation of liberty, but actually liberates man from the burden of existence. Maybe Jolivet is right when he reproaches not only Heidegger, but also Sartre, with the glorification of death.[77]

But if one does not share Sartre's existential experience of the viscosity of being and is not accidentally in a situation where one can say "rather death than . . . ," death remains "the great enemy."

To most people death appears to deprive life of all sense, making it meaningless. And it is primarily because of the acuteness of the problem of the meaning of life for modern man that Sartre's views are so widely discussed and of such consequence. A competent and astute philosopher confirms what so many have felt since the day man discovered that he was mortal.

But whether Sartre's philosophy becomes a source of despair or a challenge to refute his verdict of the absurdity of life and

of death, will depend on whether we are willing to use our freedom, whose cause Sartre pleads so eloquently, to search with a
new force for a meaning of life.

Gabriel Marcel (1889-   )

HEIDEGGER'S "DISARMING" of death by taking it into one's
consciousness, Sartre's subordinating it to freedom are essentially attitudes to death. They are clearly insufficient as
answers to death. One is overwhelmed with regrets over
wasted opportunities in life, the sorrow of apparently defini-
tively parting with one's loved ones, and the obvious non-sense
of total destruction of what appeared all along as the highest
good.

This disquietude of death has a greater impact on the
thought of the Christian existentialist, Gabriel Marcel,[78] than
on the other philosophers of existence. Death presents itself
from the very first as a permanent invitation to despair. Marcel's keen consciousness of mortality may be due to the death
of his mother when he was four years of age.[79] But there is
a paradox in his abiding concern with death and immortality,
for Marcel became a Catholic in 1929, and as such could be
expected to have found the desired and definitive answer. He
himself suggests an explanation for his continuing preoccupation with the theme of death, when he says that there is a "part
of him which is not yet evangelized"; and it is to that part that
Marcel addresses himself.[80] It is also characteristic of Marcel
that as a philosopher he is driven by an overriding urge to examine experiences and intuitions in the light of reason. This
desire to justify the reasons of the heart by natural reason does
not imply, however, that he doubts the revelation of Catholic
Christianity. It is merely the conviction that faith does not
provide definitive solutions to the problems of man. Faith
only illuminates them, without being able to resolve them. As
a critic remarked, religion for Marcel does not appease or
suppress the disquiet of the human soul; it keeps it alive and
makes it more acute and profound. Particularly as far as death
is concerned, he says that "theological quibbles are not better
than the vain answers of the scientists."

It is difficult to decide, however, whether it is his own death or that of others that concerns him most. There is in *Etre et Avoir* the significant passage dated March 22, 1931: "(a sad Sunday): time as open toward death—toward my death—toward my doom. Time-abyss; vertigo in the presence of this time at the bottom of which is my death which sucks me in." [81]

On the other hand, when Leon Brunschvicg reproached Marcel with attaching too much importance to his own death,[82] our philosopher replied that "what counts is not my death, nor yours, but the death of those we love." And as we shall see, he envisages the problem of death as essentially the conflict between love and death.

In considering what Marcel has to say about death, it is important to realize that although he possesses, as Heinemann points out, "the greatest adventurous curiosity" and is "among the very few metaphysicians of our time," he is not a systematic thinker. His philosophizing is a somewhat confused and obscure philosophical itinerary.[83]

Thus we cannot expect completely sustained arguments, only *aperçus*. Nevertheless, they often throw a surprising and penetrating light on a hitherto neglected aspect of the problem and reveal possibilities of new and original answers.

Marcel is opposed to both empiricism and rationalism. Analytical thought in particular is the target of his scorn. He insists that the proper function of reflection is to illuminate experience from the inside and not to throw light on it from the outside, as it were, and that experience extends also to the transcendent.[84]

Similarly to Spinoza's distinction between *natura naturans* and *natura naturata,* Marcel speaks of "thinking thought" (*pensée pensante*), which, as against "thought thought" (*pensée pensée*), is not cut off from being and existence, but is concrete and existential. Reason has to become incarnate thought. Incarnation is for Marcel *la donnée centrale de la metaphysique.*[85] But he is not very clear about the meaning of incarnation. The word is intended to express the idea of the experience of one's mind as bound up with the body, which is the "absolute mediator" and "the central criterion to which all judgments about existence must be referred." But of this body

"I cannot say that it is me, nor that it is not me, nor that it is for me (object). Thus, there and then the opposition of subject and object is transcended." [86] If the body is neither subject nor object, what is it? Marcel speaks of it as the "frontier zone" between "being" and "having." And the body is at the root of having, for it is the true condition of all possession. He discovers also that we cannot consider our body exclusively in terms of instrumentality. *I am* my body means that I do not possess it as a utensil: It is also *me*. But whereas my body is unknown to me, for others I am first of all my body. In the course of his philosophical journey to the question, "Am I my body?" is added the question "Am I my life?" [87]

In any case my lifeless body, my corpse, is, essentially, *what I am not,* what I cannot be. And the difficulty consists in understanding how it is possible that it is metaphysically false to affirm that I *am* my life, without it being legitimate to deduct from this that I *have* my life, that I have a life, for *I* am *not* my life, nor do I *have* a life.

The "concrete philosophy" seeks to discover the roots and the structure of a human being by referring to everyday existence. The "existent" is "unquestionable" and is bound up with the realization that *I am*. But as soon as the distinction is made between *my life* and *my being* (my existence), the temptation becomes irresistible to ask in what this being consists.[88] But I am a being that is not transparent to myself: "my being is for me a mystery." [89] "Existence" has its "specific mysteriousness." And reflecting upon myself, I discover that I am a unity that transcends the level of subject-object, and as such, transcendence has a metaphysical reality that cannot be analyzed.

It is on the distinction between *my life* and *my existence* that Marcel's views with regard to the possibility of survival after death are based. He also holds that there are a number of metapsychological facts that we have to take seriously, and that can only with the greatest difficulty be explained without the hypothesis of an entelechy that survives what we call death. And he thinks that it is not excluded that some day we may arrive at some kind of "rudimentary verification" of the truth of these phenomena.

Man is outside the world and in the world. I participate in the world of things and I know with great certainty that I transcend this world. The difficulty is that through lucidity I court despair, existence becomes incomprehensible, and death, annihilation.

As Scheler before him, Marcel distinguishes sharply between survival and immortality.

Marcel approaches the "mystery of death" and the immortality problem from the position of a living faith, not limited by any theology. He asks how correct it is to consider the problem of immortality a simple alternative between being a fact and being a chimera. Is such an opposition between the real and the imaginary, which we apply to the empirical world, applicable here? Can the belief in immortality be compared to a simple mirage? "To assert this one must have, in truth, not have understood anything of the views which have been presented about faith and what it cannot be when it is authentic." [90] Marcel is convinced that with regard to the problem of death *intersubjectivity* is the key, for "the idea of a solitary and narcissistic survival is, for me at least, deprived of all significance."

Immortality is seen by him in the light of what he calls "the existential premises of immortality," that is "in the perspective of the death of the other, of the beloved." Thus what is for some the basis for the experience of death, is for Marcel the basis for the experience of immortality.

Science does not speak of reality other than in the third person, but spiritual reality is different.

When I say that a being is given to me as a presence it means that I cannot treat him as if he were simply put before me; between him and myself a relationship is formed which to some extent surpasses consciousness which I can have of him; he is not only before me, but in me; or, more precisely, these categories are inapplicable, they have no meaning. Even when I cannot touch you or see you, I know that you are with me.

And the question is to know whether destruction can affect that which makes a person a being with which I can establish this particular relationship. And "it is this mysterious quality which is aimed at in my love."

In the materialistic view *cadaverization* of life takes place. In the other view we have a *consecration* of life, and by sacrificing it we do not give it up in order to obtain something in exchange for it. For at the root of absolute sacrifice one finds not only the conviction "I die, but you will not die" but rather this one: "because I die, you will be saved," or "my death will increase your chances for life."

> What I have seen clearly this morning is the fundamental ambiguity of what I call *my life,* whether I consider it as a sequence of moments and events or whether I see it as something which is susceptible of being "given away," sacrificed or lost. Perhaps it is only in this sense that one can attribute a significance to the idea of immortality.[91]

And in one of Marcel's plays we find that "to love a person is to say: you shall not die." [92] The notion of intersubjectivity is crucial here, to be understood as "the fact of being together in the light," and therefore it is most important to overcome the idea of being an island (*moi-territoire*), which is a fictitious idea.

Love must not, however, degenerate into what Marcel calls *narcissisme à deux* and is not limited to the couple. Filial love or friendship also lead beyond the "terrestrial horizon." This *beyond,* in which the "intersubjective destiny" fulfills itself, does not have to be thought literally as supra-terrestrial:

> It is much more reasonable to assume that if the word "beyond" has meaning, as one has to assume that it has, it cannot designate another place to which one accedes when leaving this one. One ought to think of it in conformity with the indications which one finds for instance in the works of Stewart White where what we improperly call the beyond is considered to consist in an assembly of unknown dimensions of, or perspectives toward, a universe of which we apprehend only one aspect accessible to our organo-psychic structure.[93]

The concern with one's own death belongs to *having*—it is *unavailability*. And it is to the extent that I situate myself in the *to have* that I become victim of anxiety that the thought of my death rouses in me; it is unavailability that brings about sadness and pessimism. But it is not necessary to go forth on the road to wisdom and holiness to make death cease to be an object of anxiety. It is sufficient that existence be freed from the appetite for life according to the category of duration.

But the death of the other may still remain unbearable and this because of the rupture in friendship or of love, and because of the concern about the fate of the departed.

It is because one cannot truly love without wishing immortality of the loved one that man cannot accept death. "It is for our communication that I hope for indestructibility; and hope here resists the denials of immortality through the conviction that admission of the possibility of destruction would betray the fidelity which binds this community." [94]

Marcel's position is that "death is the springboard of an absolute hope. A world where death is absent would be a world where hope would exist only in an embryonic state." [95] And when death is envisaged on its true plane, that of mystery, it loses its terrifying aspects and ceases to be seen as an evil. It becomes the threshold to another dimension, another birth: the existential moment coincides with the eternal instant, and death itself appears as an accomplishment.

The importance of the belief in immortality is, for Marcel, beyond any doubt. The view that denial of immortality will make life itself more precious and important is a fallacy. On the contrary, "the earthly life appears more and more as without any value, without any intrinsic significance."

The structure of our world (it is necessary, however, to ask oneself about the meaning of this word) is such that despair is possible there, and it is in this way that the crucial importance of death is being discovered. It presents itself as a permanent invitation to despair . . . and this at least, in the perspective of *my* life and of the affirmation by which I declare myself to be identical with my life.[96]

The world has become a world "given over to death," and this is the more terrible because there exists in the world a basic despair that seems impossible to remedy. Marcel is very much opposed to the superficial and illusory consolation of spiritism and feels that theology does not always meet the demands of contemporary man, who is left to shift for himself in his distress and despair.

"Only through criticism of the notion of 'myself' can I open the doors of a liberating metaphysics." And Marcel sees metaphysics as "exorcising of despair," [97] and metaphysical reflection together with metapsychological experiences give the possibility of arriving at certain indications that, although unverifiable, provide a minimum guarantee that "I am of the world and, at the same time, transcend the world and that death is not annihilation."

However, in connection with the idea of immortality, it is impossible not to find one's way into theology and to "the source of all light which is God and His love for His creatures." Thus at the end of his tortuous philosophical journey Marcel ultimately returns to religion. For those who cannot or do not want to follow Marcel in this last step there remains what is perhaps his most original thought, namely his view of metaphysics as "a reflection pointed toward a mystery," and his distinction between mystery and problem. In opposing the *mystery of being, ontological mystery,* to the *problem of being,* he writes: "The problem is something that one encounters, something that bars the way. It is before me in its entirety. Mystery, on the contrary, is something that I find myself involved in (*engagé*), the essence of which, accordingly, consists precisely in not being before me in its entirety." [98]

Marcel emphasizes that there is mystery already in the thinking process itself where "it thinks in me" is much closer to what really happens than the simple "I think." [99]

There is a tendency to convert mystery into a problem, and philosophers ignore the fact that "every individual is . . . a symbol or expression of the ontological mystery." [100]

"My life is something I can evaluate, but who am I who evaluates it?" [101]

"When I pass from the problem of being to that of 'what am I?' I pass from a problem to a mystery. The problem of the relation of the soul to the body is more than a problem." [102]

Heinemann's criticism that the problems of metaphysics may be mysterious, but that they nevertheless remain problems that allow elucidation and discussion,[103] is justified insofar as it refers to the danger of too hasty a conversion of a problem into mystery. But Marcel himself says that "all confusion between mystery and the unknown must be carefully avoided: the unknown is indeed merely a limit of the problematic which cannot be actualized without contradiction. The recognition of mystery is, on the contrary, essentially a positive act of the spirit. . . . The problem of Being would then be nothing but a translation of a mystery into an inadequate language which can be ascribed only to a being . . . whose central characteristic is perhaps that of not coinciding purely and simply with its life." [104]

This recognition of mystery is similar to Cusanus' *docta ignorantia*—learned ignorance—and not a hasty *non liquet*. One can recognize the problems, and be able to solve some of them, but still remain aware of the basic mysteriousness of being an existence—this concrete individual who knows himself to be in the world as well as outside the world.

And it must be admitted that the awareness of this mystery may in itself be sufficient to resist total despair arising from the encounter with death.

AFTERWORD

Afterword

THE SURVEY of the answers which Western philosophers have given throughout the ages to the problems of the fear of death and the nature of death made it obvious that any answer to death that an individual seeks and finds satisfactory depends, in the last resort, on the individual's attitude to life, the intensity of his fear of death, and the particular kind of his death-fear. It is obvious, too, however, that such an answer cannot be merely speculative, but must actually be accepted, made one's own. And it must be added that an answer to death found satisfactory at one time may not be so at another. Thus there can be no universal answer, least of all a universally valid one. A genuine reconciliation with death may not in fact be possible for some; for others almost any argument may modify their apprehension of death and free them from despair at its inevitability and apparent absurdity.

These are among the immediate conclusions from all that has preceded. And there is another result of this survey which is: to define the place of the "problem of death" and of the rôle of death in Western philosophical thought. It is appropriate, therefore, to consider briefly what the fact of death has contributed to philosophy, the extent to which death is the theme and even "the inspiring genius" of philosophical reflection.

Death as Motif and Motive of Philosophy

The problem of the fear of death and of its nature is traditionally the province of religion. Religion, as a rule, denies the finality of death; it affirms the continuation of the human personality, either in its psycho-physical totality or as a disembodied soul, as its common and characteristic assurance. Therefore, philosophy has not begun to concern itself with death except when the "assurance" of religion becomes doubtful or suspect, or when the assurance appears in inescapable contradiction with the most direct and incontrovertible evidence of our senses. When it is a matter of doubt, the philosopher has sought to bolster the religious answer with rational argument; when it is a matter of contradiction, philosophy has sought to arrive by way of speculation at an affirmative answer similar to the one which religion has offered all along, or philosophy has endeavored to come to terms with death conceived as final annihilation or as impersonal immortality.[1]

Accordingly, in the absence of very definite religious convictions as in the fifth and fourth centuries B.C. in Greece, for example, or in the second and first centuries B.C. in Rome, we find death not only as a motif, but as a motive of philosophy. But, with the advent of Christianity and its promise of resurrection and eternal life in the hereafter, the vital necessity for philosophy to deal with death diminishes, for the problem appeared to be solved.

Moreover, the solving of the problem of death was only one of the problems of Christian life and thought; and philosophy itself, for a number of reasons, became a servant of theology. But it would be a mistake to conclude that preoccupation with death disappeared in the Christian era. As we have seen, the gradual emergence of a definite imagery of the after-life, as developed by theology and rendered visibly real by poetry, painting, and sculpture, and the increasing emphasis on the difficulties of salvation from eternal death, brought on the intensification of the fear of death and dying, which culminated in the fourteenth and fifteenth centuries in a paroxysm of obsession with death. Dying, in addition to the usual fears connected with it, became even more terrible because the moment of death acquired special and sinister meaning, since the moment of the soul's escape from the dying body is the last opportunity for the forces of Hell to take possession of the soul.

With the resumption of independent philosophical thought in the Renaissance, we find that as far as the problem of death is concerned, philosophers tend toward the denial of personal immortality. From the moment when Pietro Pomponazzi sided with the anti-immortalists, the denial of the immortality of the soul may be said to have become gradually the philosophical position par excellence in eighteenth century France and in German philosophy of the nineteenth century. This, however, does not spell the complete disregard of the problems of death in philosophy. Even the French materialists, denying immortality of the soul as a "priestly lie" and as an obstacle to the improvement of economic, social, and political conditions, deal with it, although the problem narrows down to that of an *ars moriendi,* of mastering the fear of death and preventing it from poisoning the enjoyment of life. And there was always a continuous effort on the part of some philosophers to prove the immortality of the soul.

On the whole, however, as philosophy becomes an independent discipline, it evolves and concentrates on its own specifically philosophical problems, and death as a motif of philosophizing becomes an exception. Thus, in addition to the differences between philosophies as to the kind of answer to death which they provide, there is another difference to be noted: namely, whether they deal with the problem of death or disregard it completely.

In the former the relationship between the fact of death and the philosophical enterprise appears under three aspects: (1) Death can be the "muse" of philosophy, the impetus behind philosophizing which aims primarily at mastering the fear of death and coming to terms with the inevitability of death. This is, as we have seen, Schopenhauer's view of this relationship. (2) Death can be the "instrument" of philosophy, purportedly alone suitable to lead to an understanding of Being and of revealing its true nature as penetrated by nonbeing, according to Heidegger. Finally (3), it can be, as in Plato, the "ideal condition" of philosophizing, a "state" in which alone the philosopher's quest of true knowledge can be fulfilled.

Properly speaking in the first two instances it is not so much the fact of death as the fear of death—the "terrifying certainty of death" or "anxiety," in which non-being reveals itself—which are respectively "the muse" or the instrument of philosophy. In the third instance, it is not the human attitude to death but the nature of death which serves as the point of departure, and this nature is arbitrarily assumed to be known as the separation of the divine and immortal soul from

the perishable body. The ancient religious idea of the nature
of death precedes in this instance philosophy, whereas in the
first instance it is the task of philosophy to ascertain the nature of death and either to demonstrate that it is not final
annihilation or to show the reasons why our attitude to death,
even though it is the "end," should be not that of fear but of
indifference, acquiescence or even of joyful acceptance.

The tendency to disregard the subject of death, which some
historians of philosophy claim to have begun under the inspira-
tion of Spinoza,[2] has been increasingly asserting itself and became predominant toward the middle of the nineteenth century.

This elimination of the problems of death from philosophy
was greatly expedited by the radical transformation which
took place in the whole of the philosophical enterprise under
the impact of the spectacular advances of the exact sciences.
The ascendancy of the scientific and "positivist" approach was
helped by the growing surfeit with metaphysical speculation.
As a consequence, philosophers were neither inclined nor expected to answer the "big," the "ultimate" questions about
the purpose of the universe and man's ultimate destiny. Accordingly, death and its problems were left by the roadside.
And what we find, as a rule, when we turn to philosophy of
the second half of the nineteenth century is, as it were, a
conspiracy of silence about the literal and figurative "skeleton
in the closet." Only in exceptional cases is there an attempt to
deal with these problems, or can the indifference to them be
attributed to an already attained philosophical position which
provides also an answer to death.

That this was the result of a genuine and universal reconciliation with the fact of mortality would be too much to expect. To many, however, it appeared as such, partly out of
lack of discernment, partly out of wishful thinking. In any
event, the "dying of death" was enthusiastically proclaimed by
the devotees of scientism, and regretfully acknowledged by
the representatives of traditional religion. "Death as a motive
is moribund. . . . Death has lost its terrors," writes a contemporary observer in an article significantly entitled, "The
Dying of Death." [3] Another writes:

The twentieth century is too busy to occupy itself much with the problems presented by death and what follows it. The man of the world makes his will, insures his life, and dismisses his own death with the scantiest forms of politeness. . . . Death is all but dead as an overshadowing doom and an all-absorbing subject of controversy.[4]

A more acute observer, however, like Arthur Schnitzler, found that, as usual, "there is no decent person (*anstaendiger Mensch*) who, in a quiet hour, does not meditate on death." And while professional philosophers withdrew into specialized research and thought of "nothing less than of death," writers and poets of many nations voiced their awareness of death and their lament over the dark shadow which it throws on all that lives and breathes, and their own existence in particular. There was Tolstoy whom the thought of death pursued incessantly and who kept asking in despair "what truth can there be, if there is death?"[5] There was Unamuno whose insatiable "appetite for immortality" and his doubt about a life after death made him seek a vain escape from the "tragic sense of life" through ceaselessly repeating to himself that one has to have "faith in faith itself." And there was Rilke, afflicted with the "torment of transitoriness" (*Leiden am Vergaenglichen*) and struggling valiantly to transform death from a frightful spectre into the "greatest event" in life. There was Proust who sought to escape from the annihilating passage of time by trying to recapture the past in the vain hope that if he can do this "the word 'death' will have no more meaning" for him.

In philosophy it is only around the turn of the present century that a reaction against the exclusion of death from philosophical reflection sets in. William James and Henri Bergson rebel against the exclusion of all personal and "tychic" elements from philosophy. And Georg Simmel noted regretfully that "so very little of human suffering has found its way into philosophy."[6]

Present-day Philosophers and the Problem of Death

There is a sharp division also among contemporary philosophers with regard to the question whether death is to be considered a proper subject for philosophy. It is mostly part of a wider issue dividing the "analytical" philosophers from those sympathetic to a broader view of the task of philosophy as being concerned also with the questions of man's ultimate destiny. But there are also other variants of this division. Thus when Leon Brunschvicg rebuked Gabriel Marcel for bringing up the issue of death with the remark that the death of Gabriel Marcel may interest Marcel, but that the death of Leon Brunschvicg does not interest the latter in the least,[7] it was not only because he thought that Marcel's concern with death was morbid. Brunschvicg's lack of interest in the problem of death was due to the fact that for him this problem was already "solved" since in his "philosophy of the spirit" human existence acquires a meaning which death cannot destroy. As Morin points out, when speaking of philosophical idealism in general "the thinker who contemplates the universal . . . is engaged in an activity which repels death in a twofold way: every activity (participation) as such pushes back the thought of death; moreover the activity of cognition reaches or believes to reach that which in any case escapes death, that which is stronger and truer than death—the essence of reality, the universal. . . . Considering himself as partaking in the universal, which is spirit, he rejoices to such an extent over his participation in this supreme eternal and immortal 'life' that he is able to accept a death which does not in any way hurt the universal. . . . The rational intelligence is so confident and so enthusiastic about its own power that it disregards this death which escapes all possible knowledge." [8]

Nicolai Hartmann has other reasons. He speaks of "self-tormenting metaphysicians" and denies philosophy's concern with death because self-torment is "immoral." He argues that if death is nothing but annihilation, it cannot be evil, and the trouble with man is that he takes himself too seriously. If he would only keep a sense of proportion and the proper perspective, he would view himself as what he is—a drop in the stream of universal happenings—and cease to make an issue of his having to die.[9]

Scheler, however, scorns the "metaphysical frivolity" (*metaphysischer Leichtsinn*) of philosophers who do not want to deal with ultimate questions, and the problem of death in particular.[10] Russell seeing man as "condemned to lose his dearest, tomorrow to pass himself through the gates of darkness" is keenly aware of the need for "something that appears to the imagination to live in a heaven remote from . . . the devouring jaws of time."[11] And Berdyaev writes: "I am not prone to fear of death, as for instance Tolstoy was, but I have felt intense pain at the thought of death, and a burning desire to restore life to all those who died. The conquest of death appeared to me as the fundamental problem of life. Death is an event more significant and more fundamental to life than birth."[12]

Berdyaev's statement must make us wary of the attempts to explain away all concern with death and the problems arising out of it as the result of death-fear. It makes clear that not "bothering" with the problem of death is equivalent to divorcing philosophy from the profoundest theme which has troubled, mystified and haunted mankind from the beginning of time. As to this negative attitude, the question is simply whether philosophy can afford to indulge in it, particularly when it is determined, as is so often the case, by nothing more than a misguided sense of guilt and inferiority on the part of philosophers for not being able to match the accomplishments of the scientists.

To dispose of the problems arising from the fact of death by invoking Confucius' retort that "we do not know anything about life; what can we know about death?" will not do, for it is a simple evasion and misses the point. What we do not know about life—its ultimate meaning and purpose—is intimately bound up with death, and the trouble with the latter is that we know all too well what it is.

The other excuse for not concerning oneself with death is that the problem of the nature of death belongs to biology and that the problem of the fear of death to psychology and psychopathology. But it does not take too much perspicacity to realize that for instance the crucial issue of the immortality of the unicellular organisms is essentially a matter of interpretation and semantics. And as far as the problem of the fear of death is concerned, even though psychoanalysis has made here important contributions, the whole problem of "anxiety" is still far from clear and it is questionable whether it will ever be possible to decide whether the fear of death is not, after all, the "basic" anxiety. Whether philosophers like it or not we deal here with philosophical issues. Moreover, Epicurus' notion that it is the task of philosophy to heal "the wounds of the heart" is still pertinent when these wounds are caused by death, one's own or the death of our loved ones. In this connection it is well to recall Clemenceau's remark that war is too serious a business to be left entirely to the generals and we should therefore refuse to leave the treatment of these wounds entirely to psychoanalysts and psychotherapists.

It is not the purpose of this discussion to promote the one-sided view that philosophy is in the main a quest for salvation from death. Philosophy is many different things and in the final count it is up to the individual philosopher to pursue problems which he thinks relevant and for which he is best suited. But by completely disregarding the problems of death, philosophy cuts itself off from one of its main wellsprings which stimulates the philosophical enterprise as powerfully as does intellectual curiosity and "wonder."

The argument that concern with death leads to the neglect of the concrete and urgent task of improving the human condition and promoting human welfare overlooks the fact that death too belongs to the "human condition." Investigations carried out in recent years, although limited in scope, are conclusive enough to show that the average person thinks of death much more frequently than has been generally assumed heretofore. And if the significant literature of our time is at all indicative of the modern temper (we have to mention only Hemingway, Faulkner, Malraux, Camus, T. S. Eliot and Dylan Thomas) "death weighs heavily" on an important segment of contemporary humanity. To disregard the emotional and intellectual problems arising from the fact of mortality amounts to shrinking away from what must be considered the philosopher's particular responsibility for a task which he alone can undertake in a time when religious beliefs are on the wane.

It is true that man is capable of leading a morally good life without being certain whether human existence has a meaning which is immune to the destructive power of death. Some find it even possible to live with the conviction that life is absurd and senseless; and a few would not even have it differently. But aside from the question of the possible morbidity behind this latter attitude, someone who has known and reflected upon the fate of the flower of European and American manhood and the military and civilian casualties of the two World Wars cannot close his eyes to the absurd aspect of such deaths, and in good conscience suppress the question of the meaning of life which ends prematurely and horribly.

It can be argued that these instances are quite distinct from the problem of "normal" mortality. But "absurd" deaths will continue even when man should stop causing them. The question of the meaning of life, brought into sharp focus by these premature and senseless deaths, makes the "reasonable" answers which are advanced in connection with natural death[13] appear shallow and suspect as long as they are not applicable also to these other deaths. Voltaire already acknowledged "the right of this pitiful creature to cry out humbly and to endeavor to understand why the universal law does not comprehend the good of every individual."[14] And it is inavoidable that in Western civilization, with its emphasis on the infinite worth of the individual human being, the dilemma which has already haunted Pascal, how to reconcile this basic precept with the individual's apparent total annihilation in death, comes into sharp focus. Malraux gives an eloquent formulation to it when he says that "une vie ne vaut rien, mais rien ne vaut une vie."[15] Bertrand Russell alludes to the same difficulty when he writes that "those who attempt to make a religion of humanism, which recognizes nothing greater than man, do not satisfy my emotions. And yet I am unable to believe that, in the world as known, there is anything that I can value outside human beings."[16] This dilemma is, at least to some degree, responsible for many a conversion to totalitarianism of the left or right among the intellectuals.

In view of all that we have said above, should the quest for the meaning and purpose of life which would be immune to the destroying power of death be derided or avoided,[17] as long as one succeeds in conquering one's reluctance to die?

For even when one is or becomes genuinely indifferent to one's own death there remains the "nihilistic" conclusion of the futility of human existence which inavoidably arises from the encounter with death, one's own as well as that of others. In short, the question is whether it is the proper philosophical attitude to accept "philosophically" these implications of death?

It may be that all that humans can aspire to is to have led the kind of life which will allow them not to feel before the last curtain as Rabelais felt, that "la *farce* est joué." Still even this may not be possible unless one is supported by a vision of the cosmic drama which gives also to the most humble life a meaning which would place it beyond the ravages of time and death. Perhaps its discovery is not forever denied to those who seek it.

NOTES TO CHAPTERS

Notes to Chapters

(English translations from foreign languages are by the author, unless specifically noted otherwise.)

INTRODUCTION

1. Like an eternally gay festival of the children of Heaven and of the inhabitants of the earth, life swept along spring-like through the centuries . . . until a thought, a frightful vision approached the merry company and filled the hearts with wild terror. . . . It was Death that interrupted the revelry with fear and pain and tears.

2. Levy-Bruhl, *Primitive Mentality*, Lillian Clare, trans. (London, Allen & Unwin, 1923), pp. 37-38.

3. Where these myths exist, death is usually acknowledged as inevitable. This, however, does not appear to be a necessary precondition, since death may still be considered accidental, and the explanation has to do with its being at all possible, even though not inevitable.

4. See Sir James Frazer, *Folklore in the Old Testament* (New York, Tudor, 1923), pp. 21-32.

5. Paul Radin, *Gott und Mensch in der Primitiven Welt* (Zürich, Rhein Verlag, 1953), enlarged German edition of *The World of Primitive Man*, trans. Margaritha von Wyss, pp. 417-418.

6. G. Murdock, *Our Primitive Contemporaries* (New York, Macmillan, 1934), p. 501.

7. A. Gesell and F. Ilg, *The Child from Five to Ten* (New York, Harper, 1946), pp. 439-449.

8. For details see Bromberg & Schilder, "Attitudes to Death and Dying," *Psychoanl. Review*, XX, 1933; and Sylvia Anthony, *The Child's Discovery of Death* (London, K. Paul, Trench, Trubner & Co., 1940).

9. Paul L. Landsberg, *L'Expérience de la Mort* (Paris, Desclée de Brouwer, 1933), p. 18.

10. "Der Tod ist ein A priori fuer alle beobachtende, induktive Erfahrung von dem wechselnden Gehalt eines jeden realen Lebensprozesses." Max Scheler, "Tod und Fortleben," *Schriften aus dem Nachlass*, Bd. 10, *Gesammelte Schriften* (Bern, Franke), p. 12.

11. "Mit jedem Stueck Leben das gelebt ist und als gelebt in seiner unmittelbaren Nachwirkung gegeben ist, verengt sich feuhlbar der Spielraum des noch erlebbaren Lebens." *Ibid.*, p. 14.

12. *Ibid.*, p. 16.

13. Landsberg says: "What he describes . . . is merely the experience of aging. According to him, death appears merely as the extreme limit which one can foresee in following the trace of this process of aging." *Op. cit.,* p. 13.

14. "Und selbst unabhängig vom Altern ist uns, wenn nicht der Zeitpunkt und die Art unseres Endes, so doch das Ende selbst gegenwärtig." Scheler, *op. cit.,* p. 17.

15. "Soweit wir allem Lebendigem ueberhaupt eine Bewusstseinsform zuschreiben muessen—soweit muessen wir ihm auch irgend eine Art der intuitiven Todesgewissheit zuschreiben." (Scheler's editor notes that in his later writings Scheler speaks not of consciousness but of *Psychischem.*)

16. "La conscience de la necessité de la mort ne s'éveille que par la participation, que par l'amour personel dans lequel baignait entièrement cette expérience. Nous avons constitué un "nous" avec le mourant. Et c'est dans ce "nous," c'est par la force propre de ce nouvel être d'ordre personel, que nous sommes amenés à la connaissance vécue de notre propre devoir mourir. . . .

Ma communauté avec cette personne semble rompue; mais cette communauté était moi-même dans une certaine mésure, j'éprouve la mort à l'intérieur de ma propre existence." Landsberg, *op. cit.,* pp. 28-29, 31.

17. Alexander Heidel, trans., *The Gilgamesh Epic and the Old Testament Parallels,* Tablet VIII, 13-14, and Tablet IX, col. 1 (Chicago, University of Chicago Press, 1946), pp. 63, 64. The experience of death in Gilgamesh obviously goes beyond the discovery of the inevitability of death, for there is also an intimation of its finality, and it is characterized by the simultaneous feelings of fear of death and futility of life, which we find later on in St. Augustine following the death of his closest friend (*Confessions,* Book IV).

It is interesting to compare Gilgamesh's reaction with Wilhelm Wundt's description of the usual reaction of the primitive man to the death of a fellow human being, where the first impulse is to abandon the corpse and to flee, because the dead becomes a demon who can kill. *Elemente der Voelkerpsychologie* (Leipzig, 1913) p. 81.

18. Heidel, *op. cit.,* p. 139. However, life in the hereafter is pictured as extremely dismal—"Dust is their food and clay their sustenance"—so that to some it may have appeared worse than complete annihilation. Still, there are exceptions that are predicated on the number of one's sons or the manner of one's death: Those with at least four sons get a drink of cold water, and he who died a hero's death can rest on a couch and drink pure water. It must be realized that there is no contradiction between the disbelief in the inevitability of death and the existence of a theory of an after-life; that *some* people die was an undeniable fact that did not, however, mean for the primitive that all men *must* die.

The myth tells us merely what happens to those who do die, or who are killed.

19. It seems that it is rather the disbelief that death is final annihilation and not, as Durkheim thinks, because "being trained to count his own individuality for little and being accustomed to exposing his life constantly, he gives it up easily enough," that explains the indifference of the primitive to death. And when Durkheim states that "it is not true that the need for personal survival was actively felt in the beginning," he does not seem to realize that the reason for this is simply that primitive man did not believe that death is *the* end; if he could not realize what this means, how could he feel the need of personal survival? Emile Durkheim, *The Elementary Forms of the Religious Life,* Joseph W. Swain, trans. (Glencoe, Free Press, 1954), p. 267. See also Radin, *Primitive Religion* (New York, Dover, 1957), p. 270.

20. Sir James Frazer, *The Belief in Immortality* (London, Macmillan, 1913), p. 468.

21. From *Primitive Religion* by Paul Radin, reprinted by permission of Dover Publications, Inc., New York 14, N.Y., ($1.85), pp. 271, 272, 273.

22. *Ibid.,* pp. 28-29.

23. Murdock, *op. cit.,* pp. 11, 77, 183, 215, 346, 496.

24. Ernst Cassirer writes: "While on the level of thought, of metaphysics, the mind must seek proofs for the survival of the soul after death, the contrary relation prevails in the beginning of human culture. It is not immortality but mortality that must here be proved." *Philosophy of Symbolic Forms* (New Haven, Yale University Press, 1955), V. 2, p. 37.

25. We must revise "the impression that the ancient Egyptians were a morbid people, obsessed with the idea of death, gloomily and solemnly bending their times of life in the preparation for the end of life. . . . Nothing can be further from the truth. They did spend an extraordinary amount of time and energy in denying and circumventing death, but the spirit was not one of gloomy foreboding. On the contrary, it was a spirit of hopeful triumph, a vigorous relish of life, and an expectant assertion of continued future life as over against the finality and gloom of death." A. Wilson, *The Culture of Ancient Egypt* (Chicago, University of Chicago Press, 1956), p. 78.

26. *Ibid.,* p. 297.

27. Landsberg seems to hold this view when he says that the emergence of individual consciousness is preceded by an actual change of "singularity" of man: "This individualization does not consist essentially in the acquisition of a more distinct and more subtle consciousness of singularity, but it consists first of all in the fact that man actually gains in singularity. The altered consciousness presupposes a change in being. Thus it is not essentially the consciousness of the individual death which gains in

intensity, but it is at first the very threat of this death. . . . It is only from this moment on [that is, when the ties to the clan are loosened] that an element is formed which is susceptible of being threatened by real annihilation." *Op. cit.*, pp. 18-19.

28. Radin, *op. cit.*, p. 271.

29. Radin, *Gott und Mensch in der Primitiven Welt*, pp. 190-91.

30. "The belief in some form of reincarnation [is] universally present in all simple food-gathering and fishing-hunting civilizations." Radin, *Primitive Religion*, p. 270.

31. F. M. Cornford, *From Religion to Philosophy* (New York, Harper, 1957), p. 161; also Levy-Bruhl, *op. cit.*, p. 356.

32. Cornford, *op. cit.*, p. 109.

33. See Erwin Rohde, *Psyche* (New York, Humanities Press, 1925), Ch. 1.

34. The early Greeks identify the brain liquid (cerebro-spinal fluid) with the seminal fluid; then the psyche appears not only as the living principle but as the life transmitted by procreation. For details see R. B. Onians, *The Origins of European Thought about the Body, the Mind, the Soul, the World, Time and Fate* (Cambridge: Cambridge University Press, 1951).

35. H. Plessner, "Ueber die Beziehung der Zeit zum Tode," *Eranos Jahrbuch*, V. XX (Zürich, Rhein-Verlag, 1951), pp. 349-386.

36. See Landsberg, *op. cit.*, pp. 57-59. Speaking of the same question, he aptly describes this state of being, first of all, one's body—"la prison était aussi un abri" ["the prison was also a refuge"].

37. Eccl. 3:9, 2:16, 3:19-20.

38. Reprinted by permission of The Macmillan Company from *Early Greek Philosophy* by John Burnet, p. 8. Fourth Edition published in 1930 by A. and C. Black.

BOOK I—ANTIQUITY

CHAPTER 1

1. F. M. Cornford, *Greek Religious Thought*, (Boston, Beacon Press, 1950), p. xvi.

2. Burnet, *Early Greek Philosophy*, p. 8.

3. Edith Hamilton, *The Greek Way* (New York, Norton, 1932), p. 17.

4. Odyssey, XI, 488-491.

5. C. M. Bowra, *The Greek Experience* (New York, Mentor Books, 1959), p. 49.

6. It is, however, Pythagoras' alleged teacher Pherekydes of Samos who is traditionally considered the first to teach transmigration of the soul.

7. F. M. Cornford, *From Religion to Philosophy* (New York, Harper, 1957), p. 8. The authenticity of the first part of the fragment is questioned by Burnet, *op. cit.*, p. 52, note 6. Heidegger agrees with Burnet but considers it a correct expression of Anaximander's thought: Heidegger, "Der Spruch des Anaximander," in *Holzwege* (Frankfurt/Main, Vittorio Klostermann, 1957), p. 314.

8. Nietzsche, *Die Philosophie im Tragischen Zeitalter der Griechen* 1873, (Kroener Taschenausgabe, 1955), p. 277.

9. Werner Jaeger, *The Theology of the Early Greek Philosophers* (Oxford, Oxford University Press, 1947), p. 35.

10. Burnet, *op. cit.*, p. 54, note 1.

11. Wilhelm Nestle, *Griechische Geistesgeschichte* (Stuttgart, A. Kröner, 1944), p. 61.

12. Especially Fragments 24, 25, 27, 29, 36, 48, 62, 63 and 88 (according to Diels).

13. See Olof Gigon, *Untersuchungen zu Heraklit* (Leipzig, 1935), p. 94.

14. Fragment 81 (Bywater), in Burnet, *op. cit.*, p. 139.

15. Burnet, *op. cit.*, p. 143.

16. Fragment 22 (Bywater), Burnet, *op. cit.*, p. 135.

17. Burnet, *op. cit.*, p. 138.

18. *Ibid.*

19. G. S. Kirk, *Heraclitus, the Cosmic Fragments* (Cambridge: Cambridge University Press, 1954) p. 145.

20. *Ibid.*, p. 147.

21. As Philip Wheelwright points out, "the unity of all things as Heraclitus understands it is a subtle and hidden sort of unity ... something which cannot be expressed without parables" (*Heraclitus,* Princeton University Press, 1949, p. 105), and he correctly says that "the most characteristic difficulty of Heraclitus' philosophy lies in the demand which it makes on its hearers to transcend the 'either-or' type of thinking and to recognize in each phase of experience that a relationship of 'both-and' may be present in subtle ways which escape a dulled intelligence" (p. 91).

22. This view is supported by the Fragments dealing with the reward of those fallen in battle, which is posthumous fame, not immortality.

23. Fragments 125-129 (Bywater): "The mysteries practiced among men are unholy mysteries" and "they vainly purify themselves by defiling themselves with blood. . . ." Burnet, *op. cit.*, p. 141.

24. Cornford, *op. cit.*, p. 184.

25. *De Anima*, 415a 27–415b 7.

26. Burnet argues that Heraclitus did not teach "general conflagration" because, although he said that "fire in its advance will judge and convict all things," this does not necessarily mean that it will do so all at once, rather than in turn. Burnet, *op. cit.*, p. 161.

27. That the "corpses are more fit to be cast out than dung" does not have to indicate that with death everything is ended, merely that the mortal envelope has become unimportant once the spirit, or Fire, has left it.

28. Burnet points out that "Parmenides does not say a word about 'Being'—das Sein, or l'être. It is 'what is,' das Seiende, ce qui est." (Burnet, *op. cit.*, p. 178; and note 4, p. 178.)

29. *Ibid.*, p. 175.

30. *Ibid.*

31. Fragment 105 (Diels).

32. Erich Frank, "Begriff and Bedeutung des Daemonischen," in *Wissen, Wollen, Glauben* (Zurich, 1955).

33. This Mind, although not as yet totally devoid of materiality in Anaxagoras, is often considered the introduction of the "spiritual" into philosophy and the beginning of philosophical dualism. Plato's regret, expressed in the *Phaedo* (97B), that Anaxagoras in reality did not make use of Mind at all, and Aristotles' praise of him for the very same reason (Metaph. 984b 15), are quite in keeping with their respective basic positions.

34. In the poet Theognis of Megara (6th century B.C.) we already find the assertion that death is total annihilation. He is among the great pessimists in whom the famous and often repeated dictum that "it is best not to be born at all, the next best to die as quickly as possible" appears. And he adds in this connection "to rest closely surrounded by earth." In Euripides, however, the same dictum about not being born must perhaps be understood not as a praise of non-being but in the Orphic frame of reference as fulfilling the soul's original preference of not being bound to the body and abiding with the divine. It would be interesting to investigate the roots of this pessimism of the early Greeks, which made them say that it is better to be dead than alive (Homer, *Iliad*, XVII, 446-7; Herodotus, Solon's meeting with Croesus). It is not only because of the impossibility of achieving happiness, but, paradoxically, also because of the brevity of life.

CHAPTER 2

1. *Iphigenia in Aulis*, V. 1250-51.

2. *Alcestes*, V. 669-73.

3. *Hyppolytus*, V. 189-97.

4. *Antigone*, V. 332, 360.

5. Friederich Schiller expressed this view in his *Braut von Messina:*

> "Life is not the highest good,
>   Guilt, however, is the greatest evil."

6. *Antigone,* in *The Oedipus Plays of Sophocles,* trans. Paul Roche (New York, Mentor, 1958), pp. 180, 181.

7. Plato, *Apology*, 38C.

8. *Ibid.*, 39D.

9. W. Kaufmann, *Critique of Religion and Philosophy* (New York, Harper, 1958), p. 29.

10. It is here that the belief in a provident and benevolent maker and ruler of the universe appears for the first time in Greek philosophical thought. (Cornford, *op. cit.*, p. xxii.)

11. Xenophon, *Socrates' "Defense to the Jury,"* Todd trans., Harvard, Loeb Classical Library.

11a. *Ibid.*

12. It might be relevant that Plato was present at the trial of Socrates, but Xenophon was not.

CHAPTER 3

1. Cornford, *From Religion to Philosophy,* p. xxiv.

2. *Phaedo*, 70a, in *Plato's Dialogues,* Jowett, trans. (New York, Random House, 1937).

3. *Ibid.*, 70c-77a

4. *Ibid.*, 78a-84b. The "knowledge" of "forms" ("ideas") is, however, not mere intellectual knowledge, but "gnosis." See Gilbert Murray, *The Five Stages of Greek Religion* (New York, Doubleday Anchor Books, 1955), p. 154.

5. *Ibid.*, 91c-107b. In this last argument the soul is being identified with the "idea" of life. See Romano Guardini, *Der Tod des Socrates* (Hamburg, Rowohlt, 1960), p. 167. Guardini remarks that we do not have here an (artificially) constructed concept of absolute life, but that the essence of the soul as "vitality" is a direct inner experience which discovers something, in us, namely the soul, as that which is not transitory (p. 168).

6. For a detailed account of Plato's arguments, especially in *Phaedo*, for the immortality of the soul see A. E. Taylor, *Plato, the Man and His Work* (New York, Meridian Books, 1956), pp. 183-208.

7. *Phaedo*, 107b 5.

8. See Taylor, *op. cit.*, p. 206.

9. *Phaedo*, 64a.

10. Taylor, *op. cit.*, p. 179, note.

11. William Barrett, *Irrational Man* (New York, Doubleday Anchor Books, 1958), p. 82.

12. Aristotle, *Metaphysics*, A 6 987a 32.

13. It is significant that the *Republic* opens with an old man's meditation on death and concern over what comes after death, and concludes with the myth of the judgment of the dead.

14. Why is only fear of death and not also "love" of death considered? In Plato's case the phrase about the pursuit of death and dying is rather suggestive. The immortality of the soul and

its desire to escape the prison of the body would explain the attraction of death at least as well as, if not better than, the theory of a death instinct. Taylor, (*op. cit.*, p. 265), points out that the question of how man can attain eternal salvation is the central theme of the Republic.

CHAPTER 4

1. Richard McKeon, ed., *Basic Works of Aristotle* (New York, Random House, 1941).
2. *De Anima,* 407b 22; 412b 5; 413a 1; I, 1, 403a 16, J. A. Smith, trans., in McKeon, *op. cit.*
3. *Ibid.,* 415a 27.
4. *Metaphysics,* 1070a 19, W. D. Ross, trans., in McKeon, *op. cit.*
5. *De Anima,* 430a 14, 23, J. A. Smith, trans., in McKeon, *op. cit.*
6. *Nicomachean Ethics,* X, 7, 1177b 30, W. D. Ross, trans., in McKeon, *op. cit.*
7. *Ethics,* 1115a 11.
8. *Rhetoric,* 1382a 19.
9. *Ethics,* 1116b 20.
10. *De Coelo,* I, 4, 271a, 33, J. L. Stocks, trans., in McKeon, *op. cit.*

CHAPTER 5

1. Diogenes Laertius, *De vitis,* X, 138.
2. Fragments in Whitney J. Oates, *The Stoic and Epicurean Philosophers* (New York, Random, 1940), p. 31.
3. Lucretius, *De Rerum Natura,* H. A. J. Munro, trans., in Oates, *op. cit.,* Book III, opening lines; VI, 22-24; III, 30-34.
4. Diogenes Laertius, *op. cit.,* X 133.
5. Epicurus; *Letter to Menoeceus,* in Oates; *op. cit.,* p. 32.
6. *Ibid.,* pp. 30-31.
7. Epicurus Fragment XLVII, in Oates, *op. cit.,* p. 42.
8. This insistence on the proof of the mortal nature of the mind shows that it was not as self-evident in its day as it appears to be to modern man. *De Rerum Natura,* III, 830-33, Munro, trans., in Oates, *op. cit.*
9. *Ibid.,* 884-887.
10. *Ibid.,* 912.
11. Unless Glockner (Hermann Glockner, *Europaeische Philosophie* [Reclam, 1958], p. 212) is right in holding that Epicurus is not, as yet, imbued with the self-consciousness of being a unique and irreplaceable personality.

12. In view of the fact that the Epicurean argument is being advanced even today, it is interesting that its inapplicability to the most frequent kind of death-fear was clearly perceived almost as soon as it was advanced. In one of the Platonic Apocrypha, the *Axiochus,* the story is told that when Axiochus fell seriously ill he called Socrates in order that he should appease his anxiety. On hearing, among other consolations, that Death matters neither to the living nor to the dead, for while we live Death is not, and when death comes *we* are not and therefore cannot feel death, Axiochus scornfully rejects such "superficial twaddle" which can impress "only little boys."

13. *De Rerum Natura,* Munro, trans., in Oates, *op. cit.*

14. *De Rerum Natura,* Book III, John Dryden, trans., in Oates, *op. cit.,* (italics added).

CHAPTER 6

1. This doctrine was rejected in the Middle Stoa by Planaetius of Rhodos (185-109 B.C.). And it is questionable whether it was identical with the doctrine of "eternal recurrence of the *same,*" which Nietzsche revived more than 2,000 years later.

2. Zeller, *Outlines of the History of Greek Philosophy* (New York, Meridian, 1955), p. 237.

3. According to the Stoic Chrysippus, however, only the souls of the wise are so returned.

4. Ernst Benz, *Das Todesproblem in der Stoischen Philosophie* (Tübinger Beiträge zur Altertumswissenschaft, Stuttgart, Heft 7, 1929), p. 86.

5. From *The Stoic Philosophy of Seneca* by Moses Hadas. Copyright © 1958 by Moses Hadas. Reprinted by permission of Doubleday and Company, Inc. 65th Letter to Lucilius ("How Many 'Causes'?"), p. 196.

6. *Ibid.,* "On the Shortness of Life," 15, p. 67.

7. *Ibid.,* pp. 47-48.

8. Seneca bases himself on the much shorter average life span of his times.

9. We shall see how differently Montaigne attempts to solve this problem once he overcomes the impact of Stoicism on his thinking and strikes out for himself. Seneca, however, is not only living in the general atmosphere of obsession with the thought of death so characteristic of his epoch, but is at the same time surfeited with all the worldly goods and distractions of the wealthy, powerful, and decadent Roman man of the world. "Is there some new kind of pleasure that an hour may bring? All are familiar, all have been experienced to the full." ("On the Shortness of Life," 7.)

10. Hadas, *op. cit.,* "On Tranquility," 11. It is in this dialogue that the curious assertion occurs that "the fear of death is often the cause of death."

11. *Ibid.,* 90th and 70th Letters to Luc.

12. *Ibid.,* Dialogue, "On the Happy Life," I, 10.

13. "Tu autem mortem ut nunquam times semper cogitat" (ep. ad Luc., Letter 30). However, Francis Bacon remarked that "the stoics bestowed too much cost upon death and by their great preparations made it appear more fearful" ("On Death").

14. Hadas, *op. cit.,* 65th Letter to Luc.

15. *Ibid.,* 102nd Letter to Luc.

16. *Ibid.,* 65th Letter to Luc.

17. *Ibid.,* 102nd Letter to Luc.

18. *Ibid.,* "To Marcia," 24, 4. We have seen already that Seneca speaks of the body as the prison of the soul and in general follows Plato so far as his view of death is concerned. He departs from the basic Stoic doctrine in other respects, too. For instance, he sometimes speaks of God as "the father."

19. *Ibid.,* 102nd Letter to Luc., "Immortality."

20. It can be assumed with considerable plausibility that Seneca's attitude to death was ambivalent. Alongside the fear of death there seems to have existed a *libido moriendi* (Seneca's term) and his view on the "eagerness of the soul to return whence it came" may well be not merely a consequence of his adherence to Platonic doctrine but also a rationalization of his "longing to die." Suicide, however, is a cowardly act and is justified only if circumstances prevent the exercise of virtue. Then, as a means of avoiding doing evil it is good. Under all other circumstances the wise man knows that he is "bound, as if by a military oath, and regards his life span as his term of enlistment." (65th Letter to Lucilius.)

21. Epictetus, *Manual,* sec. 27, P. E. Matheson, trans., (Oxford, Oxford University Press).

22. Epictetus, *Discourses,* Book III, 20, P. E. Matheson, trans. (Oxford, Oxford University Press).

23. Fragments quoted from W. J. Oates, *The Stoic and Epicurean Philosophers* (New York, Random House, 1940), p. 458.

24. *Discourses,* Book II, chap. i, Matheson, trans.

25. *Ibid.,* Book I, chap. xxvii.

26. Marcus Aurelius, *Meditations,* George Long, trans. (Mt. Vernon, N.Y., Peter Pauper Press, 1942), IV, 41.

27. *Ibid.,* II, 2.

28. *Ibid.,* XII, 3.

29. *Ibid.,* VI, 13.

30. *Ibid.,* II, 17.

31. *Ibid.,* VI, 46.

32. *Ibid.,* II, 5.

33. *Ibid.,* II, 11.

34. *Ibid.,* XII, 31.

35. *Ibid.,* XII, 32, 33, 34.

36. *Ibid.,* II, 17.
37. *Ibid.,* XII, 36.
38. St. Augustine, *Confessions,* Book 4.
39. *Enneads,* IV, 8, 1, Stephen McKenna, trans. (London, Faber, 1957).

BOOK II—THE CHRISTIAN ANSWER TO DEATH

CHAPTER 7

1. The King James version reads "But I know that my redeemer liveth, and that he shall stand up at the last day upon the earth: and after my skin hath been thus destroyed, yet from my flesh shall I see God." But the American Standard version differs: "But as for me I know that my redeemer liveth. And at last he will stand up upon the earth: And after my skin, even this body is destroyed; then *without* my flesh shall I see God." It gives, however, also the above variant: "and after my skin hath been thus destroyed, yet from my flesh shall I see God."
2. Ecclesiastes 9:7, 10.
3. See Sir James Frazer, *Folklore in the Old Testament,* abr. ed. (New York, Tudor, 1923), pp. 15-19.
4. Herbert J. Muller, *The Uses of the Past* (New York, Oxford University Press, 1952), p. 85.
5. Mica 6:8.
6. Job 1:21.
7. Isaiah 25:8.

CHAPTER 8

1. "Behold, I shew you a mystery; We shall not all sleep, but we shall all be changed. In a moment, in the twinkling of an eye, at the last trump: for the trumpet shall sound, and the dead shall be raised incorruptible, and we shall all be changed.
"For this corruptible must put on incorruption, and this mortal must put on immortality. So when this corruptible shall have put on incorruption, and this mortal shall have put on immortality, then shall be brought to pass the saying that is written, Death is swallowed up in victory.
"O death, where is thy sting? O grave, where is thy victory?...
"But thanks be to God, which giveth us the victory through our Lord Jesus Christ." (I Corinthians 15:51-57.)
2. Gilbert Murray, *Stoic, Christian and Humanist* (Boston, Beacon, 1950), p. 32.
3. Acts 26:24.
4. Murray, *op. cit.,* p. 33.

5. Whereas in Greek thought immortality is an inherent quality of the soul, in the Christian view God alone can confer a new life upon the individual man as a gift which he, because of his sinful nature, does not deserve.

6. The difficulty that the doctrine of resurrection presents is frankly admitted by some contemporary theologians. So, for instance, James A. Pike tries to overcome this difficulty by giving it the following interpretation:

"Obviously this does not mean that the particular body that I now have will continue into eternity—its elements hardly last seven years, in fact. But it does mean that there will be a continuity of my personality and that a means of expression and relationship, at least as suitable as my body is now for present purposes, will be provided into all eternity by a God who values human personality and individuality even higher than we do at our best." (*Beyond Anxiety,* New York, Scribner, 1953, p. 126.) But Jaroslav Pelikan in his excellent little book *The Shape of Death: Life, Death and Immortality in the Early Fathers* (New York, Abingdon Press, 1961) writes: "The death of man cannot be understood apart from the death of Adam and the death of Christ. . . . The figure which can say all this is the cross. . . . The cross leaves many questions unanswered, much of death uncharted. . . . The Christian view of death is not intended to supplement [the] clinical information about death. . . . It is intended to give men the faith to live in courage and to die in dignity, knowing very little about the undiscovered country, except that, by the grace of his cross, Our Lord Jesus Christ has changed the shape of death." (pp. 122-123.)

7. Justice William O. Douglas quotes these words of his father in *This I Believe,* V. I, Edward R. Murrow, ed. (New York, Simon & Schuster, 1952-54).

BOOK III—THE RENAISSANCE

CHAPTER 9

1. First appeared in the famous Latin Antiphon (a piece of devotional verse responsively sung) by the monk Notker Balbulus of St. Gallen, 830-912 A.D.

2. J. Huizinga, *The Waning of the Middle Ages* (London, Arnold, 1952), pp. 124-25.

3. "Towards the fifteenth century, a new means of inculcating the aweful thought into all minds was added to the words of the preacher, namely the popular woodcut. Now these two means of expressions, sermons and woodcuts, both addressing themselves to the multitude . . . could only represent death in a simple and striking form." *Ibid.*

4. As for the dance of death, it was not clear for a long time whether in the *Totentanz,* the *danse macabre,* it was death that danced, or the dead. Wolfgang Stammler is probably right in suggesting that the dance of death was both: a dance of the dead, of which it was assumed that they performed in the cemetery, and that the mere sight of it entices the living to join them; and the dance of death, expressing symbolically the bitter truth that death is king, and that everything that lives has to perish. Stammler, *Der Totentanz* (München, C. Hanser, 1948).

5. It is interesting that in our time the preference is markedly in favor of sudden death. Not to know that one is dying, or to die in one's sleep is an often heard wish.

6. Walter Rehm, *Der Todesgedanke in deutscher Dichtung vom Mittelalter bis zur Romantik* (Halle, M. Niemeyer, 1928).

7. Francesco Petrarca, "The Ascent of Mount Ventoux," Hans Nackod, trans., in *The Renaissance Philosophy of Man,* ed. by E. Cassirer, P. O. Kristeller, and T. H. Randall (Chicago, University of Chicago Press, 1950), p. 36.

8. Horace M. Kallen, *Art and Freedom* (New York, Duell, Sloane and Pearce, 1942), v. I, p. 119.

9. Or, rather, eternal life. It must be remembered that even though the concept of immortality is frequently used in popular Christian thought as a convenient synonym for everlasting life or eternal life, it is out of place when dealing with the Christian view of death.

10. Petrarca, *op. cit.*

11. The Renaissance spirit expresses itself in a striking manner also in the *Ackermann aus Boehmen* by Johannes von Saaz (also known as Johannes von Tepl), which appeared in the year 1400. Considered by some as "the profoundest creation of German Humanism" [Alois Bernt, *Der Ackermann,* Leipzig, 1934], it is noteworthy not only in that man dares to argue with death, but also in that the arguments used by the author are based on the authority of the pagan philosophers of antiquity, rather than on that of the church fathers.

The Ackermann of the dialogue is not a husbandman but an intellectual, who tills with his pen. He is a widower who summons Death before the highest judge—God—accusing him of the murder of his young and accomplished wife, the mother of his small children.

In trying to refute the charges, Death speaks like the Stoic philosophers: "Don't you know that all earthly creatures no matter how wise, full of life and strength they may be have to face annihilation? . . . One should not lament the dying of mortals . . . life has been created for the sake of death; if there were no life our [death's] office would have no sense . . . but without death there would be no world. . . .

"You ask for advice on how you can eradicate your grief from your heart? Aristotle has long ago taught that joy, sadness, fear and hope bring trouble: joy and fear shorten time, suffering and hope make it unduly long. . . . The earth and all it contains is built on changeableness. In these times everything has become even more so. . . . The masses have turned right into wrong, all men are more inclined to do evil than good, and if someone does good it is only because he is afraid of Us."

And the Supreme Judge seems to decide for Death: "The plaintiff bewails his loss as if it were something belonging to him; he does not realize that it has been granted by us." It is the God of the Old Testament who speaks here, and the whole work seems to be inspired by the book of Job. But the problem of death appears only in a limited aspect, that of the death of a beloved person. It is in Michel de Montaigne that the attempt at reconciliation with one's own death occupies the central place.

12. It is, however, necessary to realize that as far as Pomponazzi himself was concerned his strict Aristotelianism in philosophy is not his final answer to the problem of death and survival. At the conclusion of his essay *On Immortality* he declares that the immortality of the soul is a neutral problem like that of the eternity of the world, and that neither its affirmation nor denial can be demonstrated by natural reason. And in his *Apologia* he defends himself against the accusation of heresy, and it turns out that the whole argument of *On Immortality* was directed against natural theology. He merely wanted to ridicule it, and by demonstrating that by nature the soul was mortal, he wanted to defend orthodoxy, both against Platonists and liberals. Orthodox religion alone holds the truth—the resurrection of the body through supernatural grace and redemption—for, he argues, if the soul were by nature immortal, how would grace be a merit? In his defense of the Aristotelian position, Pomponazzi was not completely victorious in asserting that the soul was individually united to the body in its existence. He was stunted by the question of why intellect did not have a localized organ. Of lesser importance here is the question whether his acceptance of the Christian answer to death was dictated by expediency and fear of persecution, or whether he sincerely believed in it. If the latter is correct, who would not prefer resurrection to the immortality of the disembodied soul?

13. *Convivio.*

14. *"On the Immortality of Man,"* William Henry Hay, II, trans., rev. by John H. Randall, Jr., in *The Renaissance Philosophy of Man,* (Chicago, University of Chicago Press), p. 375.

15. Montaigne, *Essays,* book II, ch. XII, "The Apology of Raimond Sebond" (Paris, Pleiàde édition, 1946), p. 425.

CHAPTER 10

1. This is the title of Chapter 20 of the First Book of the *Essays*.

2. "Votre mort est une pièce de l'ordre de l'univers. . . . C'est la condition de votre création, c'est une partie de vous." Book I, Chap. 20.

3. Book I, 20.

4. Book III, 12.

5. Three hundred years later Tolstoy (*My Confession*) similarly discovered and exalted the attitude of the common people to life and death: "We only see a cruel jest in suffering and death, whereas these people live, suffer and die with tranquillity, and oftener than not with joy."

6. Book III, 12.

7. Book I, 20.

8. "Pour moy donc, j'ayme la vie et la cultive telle qu'il a pleu à Dieu nous l'octroier." (Book III, 13).

9. Quoted in *Montaigne par Lui-même*, by Francis Jeanson, Paris 1951, Editions du Seuil, p. 45.

10. Ignorance and lack of curiosity are two pillows on which a solid head (*une tête bien faite*) can find rest." (Book III, 13.)

11. He says that the clergy's *opinions supercélestes* are too often tied up with their *moeurs souterraines*.

12. In the words of André Maurois: *"Il ne révolte pas, il s'adapte."*

CHAPTER 11

1. During the two years Bruno spent in London (1583-85) he was on friendly terms with John Florio, the translator of Montaigne's *Essays*.

2. *Essays*, Book I, 25.

3. Dorothea W. Singer, *G. Bruno, His Life and Thought* (New York, Henry Schuman, 1950), p. vi.

4. Copernicus, *De Revolutionibus Orbium Celestium*, Lib. I, Chap. X, W. C. D. & M. D. Whetham, trans., as quoted in Dampier-Whetham, *A History of Science* (New York, Macmillan, 1932) p. 121.

5. *L'Infinito Universo e Mondi*.

6. *Ibid.*

7. *Ibid.*

8. Sidney Greenburg, *The Infinite in G. Bruno* (New York, King's Crown Press, Columbia University, 1950).

9. "De la Causa, Principio et Uno" (Concerning the Cause, Principle and One), Sidney Greenberg, trans., *op. cit.*, p. 161.

10. The innumerable worlds, as D. Singer points out, move in relation to other worlds, although all estimates of direction, position, etc., within the universe must be relative. Singer, *op. cit.*, p. 60.

11. "De la Causa," in Greenberg, *op. cit.*, p. 161.

12. *Ibid.*, argument to the 5th dialogue.

13. *Ibid.*

14. *Ibid.*, pp. 162-165.

15. *Ibid.*

16. Singer, *op. cit.*, p. 71.

17. "De L'Infinito," in Singer, *op. cit.*, pp. 243, 244. (Introductory Epistle to "De L'Infinito," Argument of the 5th dialogue.)

18. "De la Causa," in Greenberg, *op. cit.*, pp. 161-163.

19. Singer, *op. cit.*, p. 245.

20. Sonnet, *On Time*, appended to the dedication of "De la Causa," in Greenberg, *op. cit.*

CHAPTER 12

1. Leon Roth, *Descartes' Discourse on Method* (Oxford, Clarendon Press, 1937), p. 7.

2. Samuel S. DeSacy, *Descartes par lui-même* (Paris, Editions du Seuil, 1956), p. 126.

3. Descartes, "Les Passions de l'Ame," in Norman Kemp Smith, sel. and trans., *Descartes' Philosophical Writings* (London, Macmillan, 1952).

4. *Ibid.*

5. *Ibid.*

6. *Ibid.*

7. *Ibid.* In Article 32 Descartes gives the reason that persuades him that "the soul cannot have anywhere in the body any other location for the immediate exercise of its functions" than the pineal gland: "I observe all the other parts of the brain to be double, just as we have two eyes, two hands, two ears, and indeed, all the organs of our external senses double; and that since of any one thing at any one time we have only one and simple thought, there must be some place where the two images which come from the two eyes, and where the two impressions which come from one single object by way of the double organs of the other senses, can unite before reaching the soul."

CHAPTER 13

1. It can be safely assumed that philosophy for Pascal meant essentially the same as for Descartes—the search for truth with the help of natural reason. This remark is necessary to forestall the objection that Pascal, in rejecting philosophy, had a different

idea of the business of philosophy. And it is the failure to bolster the hope of immortality by means of natural reason that makes the rejection of philosophy the precondition of the belief in survival upon death.

2. Blaise Pascal, *Pensées et Opuscules,* Léon Brunschvicg edition, 12th ed. (Paris, Hachette), Numbers 183, 194, 210.

3. One has good reasons to doubt that this whole discussion is merely rhetorical and used by Pascal, who himself was certain of resurrection, only in order to convince the free-thinkers, the *esprits-forts* of his day, by showing what death is like for the unbeliever. If we consider his well-known anxieties, it seems improbable that he was not speaking also *pro domo suo,* and that the above thoughts on death did not come out of the depth of his own suffering soul. Similarly, his famous words about the terror that the "silence of the infinite spaces" (of the universe) calls forth is clearly the expression of his own feelings, since he plainly says: "le silence de ces espaces infinie *m'effraie.*" (The silence of these infinite spaces *frightens me.*")

4. *Pensées,* 194.

5. *Pensées,* 218.

6. *Ibid.,* 67. We find a similar position in Kierkegaard, who wrote some two hundred years later that it makes no difference for man's moral and religious decisions whether the moon is made of blue cheese or something else.

7. *Ibid.,* 194.

8. ". . . infiniment incompréhensible . . . nous ne sommes pas capable de connaître ne ce qu'il est, ni s'il est."

9. For a detailed exposition see Jacques Chevalier, *Pascal* (Paris, Plon, 1948). For criticism, see Dorothy M. Eastwood, *The Revival of Pascal* (Oxford, Clarendon Press, 1936).

10. E. T. Bell, *Men of Mathematics,* V. I (Pelican Books), p. 96. Bell obviously refers to No. 908: "But is it probable that probability gives assurance?" But Pascal adds: "Nothing gives assurance except truth; nothing gives peace except the search for truth."

11. This momentous event in Pascal's life took place, as he the scientist was careful to note, between 10:30 P.M. and 12:30 A.M. on the night of November 23, 1654. The description of this mystic experience was found after Pascal's death, written on a piece of parchment and sewn into the lining of his jacket. "Feu," that is, fire, or better, "flames," is written on the top of the sheet in capital letters. "The God of Abraham, Isaac and Jacob, not the God of scientists and philosophers. Certainty, certainty, certainty, joy, peace. God of Jesus Christ. . . . Oblivion of the world and of everything except God." And it ends with the words: "Total submission to Jesus Christ and to my confessor: Amen."

CHAPTER 14

1. *Spinoza's Ethics,* R. H. M. Elwes, trans. (New York, Dover, 1951). Unless otherwise noted, following passages quoted from the *Ethics* are from the Elwes translation. Bidney holds that in proposition LXVII Spinoza was intent mainly on opposing the Stoic glorification of suicide. David Bidney, *The Psychology of Ethics of Spinoza* (New Haven, Yale University Press, 1940), pp. 339, 388.

2. W. Macneille Dixon, *The Human Situation* (London, Edward Arnold, 1950), p. 344.

3. "On the Improvement of the Understanding," Elwes, p. 3.

4. *Ethics,* V., note to prop. XLI.

5. *Ethics,* V., prop. XXIX, Schol.

6. There seems to be an analogy between this immortality and the notion of some neurotics that they do not die at all so long as they exist as an idea in the head of someone else.

7. H. A. Wolfson, *The Philosophy of Spinoza* (New York, Meridian, 1958), Vol. II, p. 322.

8. Pantagruel, Book IV, Ch. XXVII. Atropos is one of the three *parcae,* or Roman goddesses of fate, who cuts the thread of life.

9. Frederick Pollock, *Spinoza, His Life and Philosophy* (1889), p. 270.

10. Wolfson, *op. cit.,* p. 274.

11. Edgar Morin, *L'Homme et la Mort dans l'Histoire* (Paris, Corréa, 1951), p. 222.

12. Wolfson, *op. cit.,* p. 311.

13. Nietzsche, *Die Unschuld des Werdens,* Vol. I (Stuttgart, Alfred Kröner, 1956), p. 236.

CHAPTER 15

1. "Principles of Nature and Grace" (1714) in *Leibniz: The Monadology and Other Philosophical Writings,* R. Latta, trans., (Oxford, Clarendon Press, 1898).

2. *Ibid.*

3. One may consider this an anticipation of Weismann's theory of the mortal cells of the body proper (soma) and of the immortal germ-cells; "The immortality of unicellular beings and of the reproductive cells of multicellular organisms is, I believe, a fact which does not admit of dispute" (August Weismann, "The Duration of Life," in *Essays upon Heredity,* Oxford, Clarendon Press, 1889-92, V. II, p. 74).

4. "Principles of Nature and Grace," Latta, trans., *op. cit.,* p. 414.

5. *Ibid.,* p. 420.

6. *Discours de Metaphysique,* édition collationnée avec le texte autographe . . . par Henri Lestienne (Paris, Vrin, 1929), p. 89.

CHAPTER 16

1. Hume, *Unpublished Essays* (London, Longmans Green, 1875), p. 404.

2. Alexander Radischev (1749-1802), O cheloveke, o ego smertnosty y bessmertii (On Man, on His Mortality, and Immortality), 1792, *Isbrannie Filosofskie Sochinenia,* ed. I. L. Shchipanov, Gos. Isd. Polit. Liter., 1949.

3. D'Alembert, writing on Diderot's *Encyclopédie,* says that since death is as *natural* as life there is no ground to fear it.

4. In this, however, he was more reasonable and realistic than some of his contemporaries who dreamed of the possibility of an infinite duration of human life on earth. Sometimes even theological proofs have been advanced to this assertion and John Asgill, in a pamphlet that appeared early in the eighteenth century in London, claimed that according to the covenant of eternal life revealed in the Scriptures man may be translated to eternal life without passing through death. The pamphlet was publicly burned and the author deprived of his seat in Parliament. See also Swift's comments in *Gulliver.*

5. Joseph Priestley, the discoverer of oxygen, anticipated Condorcet. In his *Essay upon the Principles of Government,* 1768, he writes: "Nature, including both its materials and its laws, will be more at our command; men will make their station in the world abundantly more easy and comfortable; they will probably prolong their existence in it and will daily grow more happy."

6. Hume, "Of the Immortality of the Soul," (1777) Essay I of the *Unpublished Essays,* especially pp. 401-406.

7. In recent times, C. J. Ducasse also considers metempsychosis (in a somewhat modified version) the most plausible hypothesis. See Ducasse, *Nature, Mind and Death* (LaSalle, Ill., Open Court, 1951).

8. Essay I, in *Unpublished Essays.*

9. Hume, *On My Life* (London, Hunt & Clark, 1826).

CHAPTER 17

1. *Critique of Pure Reason,* Norman Kemp Smith, trans. (London, Macmillan, 1956), pp. 372-3. (Quoted by permission of St. Martin's Press, Inc., New York, The Macmillan Company of Canada, Limited, and Macmillan & Co., Ltd., London.)

2. Herder: *Vom Wissen und Nichtwissen der Zukunft (6-e Sammlung "Zerstreuter Blaetter,"* 1797).

3. Recension von Herder's "Ideen zur Philosophie der Geschichte der Menschheit" in *Allgemeine Literaturzeitung,* 1785.

4. *Träume eines Geistersehers,* in Kant's Sämtliche Werke (Leipzig, Inselverlag, 1921), V. I, p. 106.

5. Reason is acting in a double capacity, as theoretical or speculative, and as practical.

6. Richard Kroner, *Kants Weltanschauung* (Tübingen, 1914), p. 20.

7. *Critique of Practical Reason* (1788), Lewis White Beck, trans. (Chicago, University of Chicago Press, 1949), pp. 247-8.

8. *Critique of Pure Reason,* pp. 247-8.

9. *Ibid.,* p. 21.

10. *Ibid.,* p. 22.

11. *Ibid.,* pp. 22, 23.

12. *Ibid.,* p. 27.

13. *Ibid.,* p. 28.

14. *Ibid.,* p. 29.

15. *Ibid.,* p. 360.

16. *Ibid.,* p. 379.

17. *Ibid.,* p. 380.

18. *Ibid.*

19. *Ibid.,* p. 650.

20. *Ibid.*

21. *Ibid.*

22. *Ibid.*

23. *Critique of Judgment,* J. H. Bernard, trans. (London, Macmillan, 1914), par. 83.

24. *Critique of Pure Reason,* p. 665.

25. *Ibid.,* p. 521.

26. *Ibid.,* pp. 651, 652.

27. *Critique of Practical Reason,* p. 225.

28. *Ibid.,* p. 226. This modification of the position of *The Critique of Pure Reason* was prompted by the possible objection that happiness, being a state in which all desires are satisfied, is conceivable only for a sensuous being and is incompatible with the idea of man being a creature of two worlds.

29. *Ibid.,* p. 258.

30. *Ibid.,* pp. 259-260.

31. *Religion Within the Limits of Reason Alone,* Theodore Greene and Hoyt H. Hudson, trans. (LaSalle, Ill., Open Court, 1934), p. 149, note.

32. *Vorlesungen ueber die philosophische Religionslehre* (Lectures on the Philosophy of Religion) edited by Poelitz, 2nd ed. (1830), p. 150.

33. *Streit der Fakultaeten* (Berlin edition, 1798), VII, p. 40.

34. In *Berliner Monatsschrift* of June, 1794.

35. J. G. Fichte, "Ueber den Grund unseres Glaubens an eine goettliche Weltordnung," *Philos. Journal,* Bd. VIII, 1798.

36. Fichte, *"Appelation an das Publicum,"* 1799, in *Schriften*

zu Fichte's Atheismus-Streit (her. Hans Lindau, Munchen), 1912, p. 149.

37. Fichte, *Tatsachen des Bewusstseins,* (posthumous, Tuebingen, 1817).

38. Fichte, *Anweisung zum Ewigen Leben,* 1806.

CHAPTER 18

1. W. T. Stace, *The Philosophy of Hegel* (New York, Dover, 1955), p. 514.

2. Karl Loewith, *Meaning in History,* (Chicago, University of Chicago Press, 1949), pp. 53-4.

3. *Lectures on the Philosophy of History,* J. Sibree, trans. (London, 1900), pp. 75 ff.

4. Alexandre Kojève, *Introduction à la Lecture de Hegel* (Leçons sur la Phenomenologie de l'Esprit), 5th ed. (Paris, Gallimard, 1947), pp. 527, 538.

5. In this connection Kojève says of Heidegger that he has taken up the Hegelian theme of death, but has neglected the complementary themes of struggle and work. Marx, on the contrary, took up the theme of struggle and work, but neglected the theme of death. *Ibid.,* footnote, p. 573.

6. "Die Philosophie ist also nicht ein Trost; sie is mehr, sie versoehnt, sie verklaert das Wirkliche, das unrecht scheint, zum Vernuenftigen, zeigt es als solches auf, das in der Idee (Gott) selbst begruendet ist und womit die Vernunft befriedigt werden soll."

7. "Dieser Tod also, das Leiden, der Schmerz des Todes, der ist dies Element der Versoehnung des Geistes mit sich, mit dem was er an sich ist."

8. Edgar Morin, *L'Homme et la Mort dans l'Histoire* (Paris, Corréa, 1951), pp. 264, 265.

9. Hegel, *Vernunft in der Geschichte* (Phil. Bibliothek, Meiner, Leipzig, 1922), p. 66.

10. "Eben Liebe ist diese Identitaet des Goettlichen und Menschlichen, und diese Verendlichung des Bewusstseins 1st bis auf ihr Extrem, den Tod, getrieben; also hier ist Anschauung der Einheit in ihrer absoluten Stufe die hoechste Anschauung der Liebe. Denn Liebe besteht im Aufgeben seiner Persoenlichkeit, Eigentumum."

11. "Der Tod ist die Liebe selbst; es wird darin die absolute Liebe angeschaut. Es ist die Identitaet des Goettlichen und des Menschlichen, dass Gott im Menschen, im Endlichen bei sich selbst ist und dies Endliche im Tode selbst Bestimmung Gottes ist. Durch den Tod hat Gott die Welt versoehnt und versoehnt sich ewig mit sich selbst."

12. Karl Gruen, *L. Feuerbach in seinem Briefwechsel und Nachlass* (Leipzig, 1874), V. 1, p. 26.

CHAPTER 19

1. Even in Lucan's famous phrase, where he speaks of the happiness of dying that gods conceal from men so that they may endure life, this pessimism is obvious.

Pliny the Elder was perhaps the only ancient thinker who showed a longing for death. At the same time he repudiated the belief in immortality as a "confounded folly."

2. The pessimism of Leopardi and Byron belongs to a later period. Their conviction that pain and suffering predominate in life is nevertheless unable to overcome their fear of death.

3. It is prompted by what St. Paul proclaims "the desire to depart and be with Christ." And we find the mystics' desire for death eloquently described by St. Ignatius of Antioch as he prepares for his impending martyrdom in the Roman amphitheatre: "the pangs of a new birth are upon me. . . . Alive as I am at this moment of writing, my longing is for death. Desire with me has been nailed to the cross and no flame of material longing is left. Only the living water speaks within me, saying: hasten to the Father! I have no taste for the food that perishes nor for the pleasures of this life." (*Ignatius,* ad Rom. 6, 1:7, 2-3.)

4. But there was in him also an ecstasy (*Wollust*) of self-annihilation: *"Tod ist die rauschhafte Feier endlicher Hingabe an die Vernichtung des Selbst"* (Death is the ecstatic celebration of the final surrender to the annihilation of the self).

5. "Inward goes the mysterious road. In us, and nowhere else, is eternity with its worlds, the past and the future." *Bluetenstaub,* 1798. Schelling spoke of Novalis' "frivolity toward things."

6. "The world must be romanticized. Thus one retrieves the original meaning. To romanticize is nothing but qualitative involution. The lower self is made identical in this operation with the higher self. . . . This operation is still unknown. By giving to the common a higher meaning, to the usual a mysterious aspect, to the known the dignity of the unknown, to the finite the aura of infinity, I romanticize them." *Fragmente.*

7. *Fragmente,* "Uber Medizin."

8. *Bluetenstaub,* No. 16.

9. Ralph Tymms, *German Romantic Literature* (London, Methuen, 1955), p. 168.

10. Fragments 2671, 2196.

11. Oscar Walzel, *German Romanticism,* Alma E. Lussky, trans. (New York, Putnam, 1932), p. 88.

12. "Are not the mountains, waves, and skies, a part of me and of my soul, as I am of them?" asks Byron.

13. Among the ancients it is Empedocles who comes closest to being a precursor, and indeed he has been clearly acknowledged as

such by Hoelderlin. But Empedocles believed in the transmigration of the soul.

14. However, whether Hoelderlin really said, "Leben ist Tod, und Tod ist auch ein Leben," is doubtful. See *Hoelderlin, His Poems,* Michael Hamburger, trans. (New York, Pantheon, 1952), p. 260.

15. Translated from F. Feigel, *Das Problem des Todes* (München, Reinhardt, 1953).

16. The longing to die of the Romantics is considered by the adherents of Freud's theory of the death instinct as a confirmation of this theory. Critics of the theory on the other hand point out that it "proves" the theory only because its proponents are guilty of *petitio principii:* that which has to be proved—the existence of the death instinct—is stipulated, and then certain observations are interpreted as proving it.

17. Schelling, *Gesammelte Werke,* 1856-61, Bd. 2, p. 248. Schelling remarks that often, instead of *dying,* the expression is *to give up the ghost.* In German the word for ghost is the same as for spirit, namely *Geist,* and Schelling suggests that the spirit one gives up in dying is that of the self-centered desire, and that when Plato spoke of philosophy as learning to die, he meant that it is learning how to overcome one's egotistical will. Salvation, however, consists not in the suppression of the will but in the attainment of the paradisical state of *desireless volition.*

18. Heidegger begins his *Introduction to Metaphysics* (1953) with this question, declaring that "the asking of it *is* philosophizing." Without mentioning Schelling even once, he speaks of it as "the broadest, the most profound, and the 'first' question."

19. Those interested are referred to Karl Jaspers' *Schelling* (München, 1955).

20. Norman Malcolm tells us, also without mentioning Schelling, that Ludwig Wittgenstein "sometimes experienced the feeling of amazement that anything should exist at all and quotes from the *Tractatus* 'not how the world is, is the mysterious, but that it is.'" *Ludwig Wittgenstein* (Oxford University Press, 1958), p. 70.

CHAPTER 20

1. Arthur Schopenhauer, *The World as Will and Idea,* T. B. Haldane and J. Kemp, trans. (London, Routledge & Kegan Paul, 1883, 9th impr., 1948), V. I, p. 419.

2. *Ibid.,* V. III, chap. 16, "On Death and Its Relation to the Indestructibility of Our True Nature," p. 249.

3. *Ibid.,* III, p. 264.

4. In the English translation of the original German title *Die Welt als Wille and Vorstellung,* the rendering of *Vorstellung* as *idea* is unfortunate and misleading, especially since the Platonic

300 / Notes to Chapters

ideas occupy an important place in Schopenhauer's system. It might have been more appropriate to translate *Vorstellung* as *representation* or *presentation*.

5. *The World as Will and Idea,* V. I, § 1 and § 2.

6. *Ibid.,* II, p. 164.

7. *Ibid.,* II, pp. 165-175.

8. *Ibid.,* II, pp. 170-172.

9. *Ibid.,* I, p. 491.

10. Schopenhauer speaks of "theoretical egoism" because he sees the solipsistic position in accordance with his voluntaristic metaphysics as a position where the individual assumes that "his body is the only real individual in the world, i.e., the only phenomenon of will and the only immediate object of the subject, [and] on that account regards all phenomena that are outside his will as phantoms, just as in practical reference exactly the same thing is done by practical egoism." (I, p. 135)

11. *Ibid.,* I, p. 135.

12. *Ibid.,* I, pp. 129, 130.

13. *Ibid.,* II, p. 168.

14. "Which means that the will becomes object, i.e., idea." (*Ibid.,* I, p. 219).

15. *Ibid.,* I, p. 168.

16. *Ibid.,* I, p. 169.

17. *Ibid.,* p. 171.

18. *Ibid.,* I, pp. 190, 191.

19. *Ibid.,* p. 196.

20. *Ibid.,* I, p. 197. Knowledge, however, as a rule remains subservient to the will, since it has indeed "originated for this service and grew, so to speak, to the will, as the head to the body." (*Ibid.,* p. 230).

21. *Ibid.,* I, p. 199.

22. *Ibid.,* II, pp. 180-181.

23. *Ibid.,* II, pp. 168-9.

24. *Ibid.,* II, p. 400.

25. *Ibid.,* II, p. 411.

26. *Ibid.,* II, p. 179.

27. *Ibid.,* II, p. 183.

28. The term *objective world* signifies for Schopenhauer not a world outside and independent of a subject, but the *world of objects* which exist only for a subject.

29. *The World as Will and Idea,* I, p. 414.

30. *Ibid.,* I, p. 336.

31. *Ibid.,* I, pp. 401-403.

32. *Ibid.,* I, p. 252.

33. *Ibid.,* I, p. 365.

34. *Ibid.,* III, p. 256. Schopenhauer calls fainting "the twin-brother of death."

35. This is a poor argument, for whether we should think with terror of the time before we came into the world, or not, the fact is that we do not, but the thought of not being strikes terror into many hearts.

36. *Ibid.*, I, p. 365.

37. *Ibid.*, III, p. 251.

38. *Ibid.*, III, p. 249.

39. What makes Schopenhauer's position really difficult is that since the will is imperishable it is incomprehensible why the fear of destruction should exist at all in the brute, which according to Schopenhauer is conscious of itself as endless.

40. *The World as Will and Idea*, I, p. 362.

41. *Ibid.*, I, p. 515.

42. *Ibid.*, I, p. 356.

43. *Ibid.*, I, p. 363, also: "We may say that no one has really a lively conviction of the certainty of his death."

44. *Ibid.*, I, pp. 363-365.

45. *Ibid.*, III, p. 259.

46. *Ibid.*, III, pp. 274-275. In this argument Schopenhauer already leaves the empirical approach and introduces the metaphysical: "Therefore Plato attributed true being to the Ideas alone, i.e., to the species." But can one identify them? Schopenhauer must have been aware that unless he does so, he cannot assert the imperishability of the species.

47. *Ibid.*, III, p. 267.

48. *Ibid.*, III, pp. 266-281.

49. *Ibid.*, III, p. 260.

50. *Ibid.*, I, p. 353.

51. The same doctrines serve Schopenhauer in overcoming the distressing view of the world that science presents to us.

52. *The World as Will and Idea*, III, p. 287.

53. *Critique of Pure Reason*, pp. 74, 77.

54. *The World as Will and Idea*, III, p. 290.

55. *Ibid.*, III, p. 288.

56. "The contradiction in adjecto which is contained in this expression tells us that we are dealing here with a metaphysical truth which as such is beyond our power of comprehension" writes Deussen, perhaps Schopenhauer's most ardent disciple. Paul Deussen, *Geschichte der Philosophie*, Leipzig, 1917, V. 2, part 3, p. 549.

57. "If, therefore, life as it is, satisfies, whoever affirms it in every way may regard it with confidence as endless, and banish the fear of death as an illusion that inspires him with the foolish dread that he can ever be robbed of the present, and foreshadows a time in which there is no present. . . ." (*The World as Will and Idea*, I., p. 361.)

58. *Parerga und Paralipomena,* 2nd ed., V. II (Berlin, A. W. Hayn, 1862), Chap. 10, pp. 284-302.

59. "The sharp distinction of will from knowledge, together with the primacy of the former, which constitutes the fundamental characteristic of my philosophy, is therefore the only key to the contradiction which presents itself in so many ways, and arises ever anew in every consciousness, even the most crude, that death is our end, and yet that we must be eternal and undestructible, thus the sentimus, experimurque nos aeternos esse of Spinoza. All philosophers have erred in this: they place the metaphysical, the indestructible, the eternal element in man in the intellect. It lies exclusively in the will, which is entirely different from the intellect, and alone is original. The intellect, as was most fully shown in the second book, is a secondary phenomenon, and conditioned by the brain, therefore beginning and ending with this. The will alone is that which conditions, the kernel of the whole phenomenon, consequently free from the forms of the phenomenon to which time belongs, thus also indestructible. Accordingly with death consciousness is certainly lost, but not that which produced and sustained consciousness; life is extinguished, but not the principle of life also, which manifests itself in it. Therefore, a sure feeling informs every one that there is something in him which is absolutely imperishable and indestructible." (*The World as Will and Idea,* III, p. 291.)

60. *Ibid.,* p. 285. "From my premise: the world is my representation follows first of all: first I am, then the world. This one should remember as an antidote against mistaking death for annihilation." (*Parerga und Paralipomena,* v. II, chapter 10, "Zur Lehre" etc.)

61. *Parerga und Paralipomena,* II, chap. 10.

62. *The World as Will and Idea,* I., p. 366. Also: "If a man fears death as his annihilation, it is just as if he were to think that the sun cried out at evening, 'Woe is me, for I go down to eternal night.' " (p. 362.)

63. *Ibid.,* I., p. 515.

64. *Ibid.,* I, p. 428.

65. *Ibid.,* I, pp. 451, 485.

66. *Ibid.,* I, pp. 489-490.

67. *Ibid.,* I, p. 429.

68. And which is "one of the principal elements of our pleasure in the beautiful." *Ibid.,* I, p. 469.

69. *Ibid.,* I, p. 527.

70. *Ibid.,* I, p. 506.

71. *Ibid.,* I, p. 493.

72. *Ibid.,* III, p. 454.

73. *Ibid.,* I, p. 369.

74. *Ibid.*, I, p. 520; "Necessity is the Kingdom of Nature; freedom is the kingdom of grace." (p. 523.)

75. *Ibid.*, I, p. 522.

76. "The peace and quietness upon the countenance of most dead persons seems to have its origin in this. Quiet and easy is, as a rule, the death of every good man. But to die willingly, to die gladly, to die joyfully, is the prerogative of the resigned, of him who surrenders and denies the will to live. For only he wills to die really, and not merely apparently, and consequently he needs and desires no continuance of his person. The existence which we know he willingly gives up: what he gets instead of it is in our eyes nothing, because our existence is, with reference to that, nothing. The Buddhist faith calls it Nirvana, i.e., extinction." (III, p. 308.)

"Death is the great opportunity no longer to be I;—to him who uses it. During life the will of man is without freedom: his action takes place with necessity upon the basis of his unalterable character in the chain of motives. . . . Death loosens these bonds; the will again becomes free; for freedom lies in the Esse, not in the Operari." (III, p. 307.)

77. *Ibid.*, I, pp. 366-367.

78. *Ibid.*, III, pp. 473-474.

79. *Ibid.*, III, p. 302.

80. *Neue Paralipomena*, p. 636.

81. *The World as Will and Idea*, III, p. 306.

82. *Ibid.*, I, p. 270.

83. *Ibid.*, III, p. 260.

84. *Ibid.*, III, p. 286.

85. *Ibid.*, III, p. 461.

86. *Ibid.*, III, p. 463. Freud's view that life is a contest of two opposing forces was anticipated by Schopenhauer: "What really gives its wonderful and ambiguous character to our life is this, that two diametrically opposite aims constantly cross each other in it; that of the individual will directed to chimerical happiness in an ephemeral, dreamlike, and delusive existence. . . ; and that of fate visibly enough directed to the destruction of our happiness." (III, p. 466.)

87. *Ibid.*, III, p. 463.

88. *Ibid.*, I, p. 532.

89. *Ibid.*, III, pp. 470-473.

90. *Ibid.*, I, p. 528.

91. *Ibid.*, III, p. 264.

CHAPTER 21

1. There is frequently some confusion about Feuerbach's writings on death and immortality, especially as regards his *Gedanken*

ueber Tod und Unsterblichkeit. Properly speaking, there is no such work at all. It is merely the title of the third volume of his collected works, published in 1847, which contains (a) *Todesgedanken* (*Thoughts on Death*), written in 1830 and published anonymously; (b) *Die Unsterblichkeitsfrage vom Standpunkt der Anthropologie* (*The Problem of Immortality from the Point of View of Anthropology*), 1846; and (c) a postscript *Ueber meine Gedanken ueber Tod und Unsterblichkeit* (*My Thoughts on Death and Immortality*). Finally, in volume X, entitled *Gottheit, Freiheit, Unsterblichkeit* (*God, Freedom, and Immortality*), there is another postscript, *Zur Unsterblichkeitsfrage vom Standpunkt der Anthropologie* (*Concerning the Problem of Immortality from the Point of View of Anthropology*).

2. *Saemmtliche Werke,* 10 vols. (Leipzig, 1847-1866), V. III, pp. 15, 17.

3. *Ibid.,* III, p. 18.

4. *Ibid.,* III, p. 19.

5. *Ibid.,* III, p. 63.

6. *Ibid.,* III, pp. 20-21.

7. *Ibid.,* III, pp. 26-28.

8. *Ibid.,* III, pp. 57-58, 61.

9. *Theoretische Seelenkrankheit* (*Ibid.,* p. 62). It may be appropriate to insert here the development of the argument concerning body-mind relation as Feuerbach presented it thirty-six years later in *God, Freedom and Immortality* (10th volume of his Collected Writings, 1866), in a chapter "On the Power of the Soul over the Body." After having discussed the effects of the body on the mind he writes: "There are many facts which prove that the resolutions of the will, ideas, imaginings, emotions like joy, hope, love, fear, anger, vexation, terror and grief can and do determine our physical well- or ill-being, our health or sickness, life or death. The facts are correct, but how about the conclusions which spiritualists draw from them? And what about the premises which they take for granted? Don't they presuppose in advance that the soul wills, thinks and perceives for itself, without the body? . . . But is not the soul, as far as it exercises power over the body, not, to say the least, *in* the body, or if one dislikes this 'in' as smacking too much of spatial relationship, is it not united, intimately bound up with the body, being thus actually an embodied soul [*beleibte Seele*]? How is it then possible to dissolve this bond, to isolate the soul . . . and then to conceive as an action on the body what is merely an action with the body and through the body? [*Als eine blosse Wirkung auf den Leib zu fassen, was nur Wirkung mit dem Leib und durch den Leib ist?*] . . . For how is it at all possible to reconcile effects like love, anger, annoyance, fear and terror with an immaterial and uncorporeal and trans-corporeal soul? To be sure there is a considerable difference whether I be-

come sick through a psychological or a physical cause, whether out of fear of contamination, or because of actual contamination, whether I lose consciousness because of an outside pressure on my brain or faint because of a shocking news or sight. But the representation is itself only possible on the basis of a brain and this fits perfectly with the fact that an emotion, as a brain movement, produces a corresponding effect also in the rest of the body. [*Aber die Vorstellung ist ja an und fuer sich nur under der Voraussetzung, nur auf Grund eines Hirns moeglich, und es steht daher im schoensten Einklang damit, dass eine Gemütsbewegung als eine Hirnbewegung auch in dem uebrigen Koerper eine entsprechened Wirkung aeussert.*]" (*Ibid.*, X, pp. 177-8.)

10. *Ibid.*, X, pp. 63-64.

11. *Ibid.*, X, pp. 65, 68-69.

12. *Ibid.*, X, pp. 84-85.

13. *Ibid.*, X, p. 87.

14. *Ibid.*, X, p. 88.

15. *Ibid.*, X, p. 90.

16. As a twenty-two-year-old, after two years of study under Hegel, he writes that "I have now the urge to throw myself into the very opposite." Karl Gruen, *Ludwig Feuerbach in seinen Briefen und Nachlass* 2 vols. (Leipzig, 1874), V. I, p. 16.

17. *Saemmtliche Werke,* III, p. 385.

18. *Ibid.*, II, 386. However, "having the idea of immortality is no proof of the necessity and existence of immortality. It is a valid proof only for those who make their imagination the measure of what is and what ought to be. It is of value only for those who derive the world from thought, from a word, from a spirit." *Essence of Christianity,* Marian Evans, trans. (London, 2nd ed., 1877), p. 241.

19. *Essence of Christianity,* p. 247.

20. *Saemmtliche Werke,* III, p. 71.

21. *Ibid.*, III, p. 37.

22. *Ibid.*, III, p. 70.

23. *Ibid.*, III, pp. 91-108.

24. Feuerbach writes about these and other poems and aphorisms (*Satyrisch-theologische Distichen,* 1830, and *humoristisch-philosophische Aphorismen,* 1834) that in all of them he opposes the truth of life to the truth of philosophy, speculation, and religion, and that he has expressed in them as a poet what many years later he formulated as a philosopher and thinker. (III, pp. 390-1).

25. Life is life only because
there is no other.

26. Ich bin untheilbarer Natur,
Ein Sein, ein Ich, ein Ganzes nur;
Von meinem Sein nicht lassen thu',
Kann Nichts davon, kann Nichts dazu

Den Menschen kannst Du nicht tranchiren
Ad libitum nicht excerpieren.

Der Tod ist nicht ein leerer Spass;
Natur spielt keinen Eulenspiegel,
Sie fuehrt wahrhaften Tod im Siegel.
Es zehrt sich selber auf das Sein,
Und schliesset in das Nichts sich ein.

Die alte Fabel lehret zwar:
Ich kaeme zu der Engelschaar;
Doch das ist Wahn der Theologen,
Die uns von jeher angelogen.
Mein lediges Derselbesein,
Das modert in dem Totenschrein;
Es endet die Identitas. . . .

Doch Ich, Ich steh' nicht wider auf,
Mir schliesst der Tod den Lebenslauf,
Ich muss im Nichts zu grunde gehen,
Soll neues Ich aus mir entstehen.

Der andern Menschheit bess'res Ich,
Vor dem mein Ich ins Nichts entwich,
Das its das wahre Himmelreich,
In das ich nach dem Tode Steig.

Zu denen treibts mich hinzufahren,
Die noch nicht sind und noch nicht waren: . . .
In Euch Ihr lieben Kindelein,
Die Ihr statt unser tretet ein,
Und atmet Eure Lebensluft
Aus unserer kalten Totengruft.

Gleichwie im Fleische der Citronen
Der Saeure herber Saft tut wohnen;
So sitzet wie in seinem Pack
Der Tod in Deinem Knochemark.

Der Tod enthuellt den Grund der Welt,
Der Tod nur die Natur erhellt.
Das Sein wird erst im Tode klar,
Drum ist das Sein im Tode gar.

. . . Ich rath es darum ernstlich Dir,
Wenn es Dir gleich nicht macht Plaisir;
Fall betend nieder vor dem Tod,

Allmaechtig ist die Todesnoth.
Erst lass vom Tode Dich erschuettern,
Von seinem Schrecken Dich durchzittern;
Dann kommt von Selbst in Dein Gedaerme
Des Lebensfriedens linde Waerme.
Erst beitz' im Tod von Selbst Dich rein;
Versoehnung kommt schon hintendrein.

27. *Saemmtliche Werke,* III, pp. 79-80.

28. *Ibid.,* X, p. 235.

29. "Fuerchte Dich nicht von dem Tod! Du verbleibst ja stets in der Heimat, auf dem vertrautem Grund, welcher Dich liebend empfaengt." *Satyrisch-theologische Distichen,* III, p. 130.

30. *Ibid.:* "The only rational memento mori."

<h3 style="text-align:center">CHAPTER 22</h3>

1. Jakob Burkhardt's influence was very considerable, but he is not included among the eight whom Nietzsche specifically names as his guiding spirits. "There are four pairs that have never denied themselves to me when I made my sacrifices," he writes in the 2nd volume of *Menschliches Allzumenschliches:* "Epicurus and Montaigne, Goethe and Spinoza, Plato and Rousseau, Pascal and Schopenhauer. It is with these that I have to come to terms again . . . by them I want to be proved right or wrong. Whatever I say, conclude, think out for myself and others, it is on those eight that my eyes are fixed."

2. *Nietzsche's Works,* Musarion Ausgabe (München, 1922), V. III, p. 138. This is very different from Dürer's intentions. The Knight is the Christian Soldier facing a hostile world, "hampered, but not discouraged by the stings of death, luxury, disease and poverty" in his pilgrimage leading to God. (Erwin Panofsky, *The Life and Art of Albrecht Dürer,* Princeton, Princeton University Press, 1955, p. 152.)

3. *The World as Will and Idea,* V. II, Chap. 17, "On Man's Need of Metaphysics." Metaphysics is defined here as "all knowledge that pretends to transcend the possibility of experience" (p. 364), and Schopenhauer distinguishes two kinds: religion, which can have only indirect truth, and philosophy, which is an "objectively true metaphysics" (p. 368). The difference between them "may be briefly expressed by the words *reasoned conviction* and *faith*" (pp. 365-6).

4. *Froehliche Wissenschaft,* p. 357.

5. *Ibid.,* p. 125.

6. It is important to realize that Nietzsche considers Schopenhauer's identification of will with drive, instinct, and desire as totally mistaken, for will is precisely "what deals with desire as a

master." Nor does Nietzsche consider will a special faculty. Strong will is merely "the clarity of direction" imposed by a dominant motive. *Will to Power,* Aphorisms 84, 95, 46.

7. Letter to Malwida Meysenbug, Jan. 14, 1880.

8. *Ecce Homo* (in connection with Lou Andreas-Salomé's "Hymn to Life," which Nietzsche set to music).

9. *Nietzsche's Werke,* XIX, p. 352.

10. Trans. from Karl Loewith, *Nietzsche's Philosophie der ewigen Wiederkehr des Gleichen* (Stuttgart, W. Kohlhammer, 1956), p. 231.

11. Letter to Overbeck, May 21, 1884.

12. *Werke,* XIV, p. 326.

13. *Ibid.,* XIX, p. 229.

14. *Ibid.,* XIV, p. 326.

15. *Ibid.,* XIX, p. 228.

16. "Die Lehre vom Uebermenschen ist die Voraussetzung fuer die Lehre von der ewigen Wiederkehr, weil nur der Mensch, der sich selbst ueberwunden hat, auch die ewige Wiederkehr alles Seienden wollen kann, und die Entwuerfe zum Willen zur Macht setzen ihrerseits die Lehre des Zarathustra voraus." Loewith, *op. cit.,* p. 59.

17. We find in Eudemus, a pupil of Aristotle, as quoted in Cornford, *Greek Religious Thought* (Boston, Beacon Press, 1950), p. 69, a precise statement of the doctrine of eternal recurrence: "If one might trust the Pythagoreans, who believe in the recurrence of precisely the same series of events, you will be sitting there, and I shall be holding this staff and telling you my story, and everything will be the same."

And in Virgil: *"Erunt etiam altera bella, atque iterum ad triam magnus mittetur Achilles"* (There will be also other wars; and great Achilles will again be sent to Troy).

18. There is also an interesting passage in Schopenhauer (*The World as Will and Idea,* III, p. 267): "Throughout and everywhere the true symbol of Nature is the circle, because it is the scheme or type of recurrence. This is in fact the most universal form in nature, which it carries out in everything, from the course of the stars down to the death and the genesis of organized beings, and by which alone, in the ceaseless stream of time, and its contents, a permanent existence, i.e., Nature becomes possible."

19. *Also Sprach Zarathustra* (Stuttgart, Alfred Kröner, 1956), pp. 241, 244.

20. Lou Andreas-Salomé, *Nietzsche in seinen Werken,* 3rd ed. (Vienna, 1924), p. 222.

21. *Werke,* XVI, p. 253.

22. Loewith, *op. cit.,* p. 126.

CHAPTER 23

1. Henri Bergson, *Creative Evolution*, A. Mitchell, trans. (New York, Holt, 1911), p. 271.

2. Henri Bergson, *The Two Sources of Morality and Religion*, transl. by R. Ashley Audra and Cloudesley Brereton (New York, Henry Holt & Co., 1935), p. 246.

3. Bergson, *Time and Free Will*, (New York, Macmillan, 1913), p. 73.

4. Ludwig Klages, *Der Geist als Widersacher der Seele*, (München, A. Barth, 1932), p. 1358.

5. Klages, *op. cit.*, 2nd ed. (1939), V. I, p. 448.

6. "Zur Metaphysik des Todes," in *Logos*, Tübingen, 1910.

CHAPTER 24

1. Max Scheler, "Tod und Fortleben," in *Schriften aus dem Nachlass* (Berne, Franke, 1933), V. I, pp. 397-413.

2. Herder's views (see p. 139) can be considered to belong to this variety.

3. Scheler, *op. cit.*, p. 397.

4. *Ibid.*, p. 401. However, Scheler considers the criticism by the Kantians—that the spiritualistic phenomena cannot give us any indication of the reality behind them, since it is precisely the integration of phenomena into the context of natural laws that is the criterion of their objective reality—as not valid. (p. 402.)

5. Although Scheler believes in a "realm of eternal spirit" and thinks that its existence "can be denied only by a positivism and biologism which overlooks the simplest things" (*ibid.*, p. 39), this doctrine has no bearing on the survival of the spiritual person: one can accept it and still deny personal survival.

6. What Scheler means by "limit" can be spatial as well as temporal limitation, or the limit of the qualitative contents of the states of the body (*Leibzustaende*).

7. "Wie sich waehrend des Lebens ihre Akte 'hinausschwangen' ueber die Liebeszustaende, so nun sie sich selbst hinausschwinge ueber ihres Leibes Zerfall." (*Ibid.*, p. 45.)

8. "Es ist eine Wesensansicht dass zu einer Person ein Leib gehoert."

9. In support of his view Scheler points out that the views of Goethe (and Kant) are also based on this "spiritual excess-phenomenon." Goethe said to Eckerman that "the conviction of our survival arises for me from the concept of activity, for if I am active to the last, nature is in duty bound to assign to me another form of existence, if the present is no more capable to hold my spirit." Goethe adds that he would not want to dispense

with the happiness of believing in a future existence. ("Ich moechte keineswegs das Glueck entbehren, an eine kuenfitge Fortdauer zu glauben, ja ich moechte mit Lorenzo von Medici sagen, dass alle diejenigen auch fuer dieses Leben tot sind, die kein anderes hoffen.")

10. Scheler holds that neither from the essence of the person nor its acts and the laws regulating these acts can we prove its existence—neither before nor after death. For such attempts would be as mistaken as the ontological proof.

11. *Ein Wechsel des Herrschaftsbereichs der Person und des Schauplatzes ihrer Erlebnisaeusserungen* (*op. cit.*, p. 406). These views were formulated by Scheler in his "middle period" (1912-1922) when he held a personalistic and theistic position and was a convinced Christian. His untimely death has deprived us of what might have been another outstanding contribution to the problem of death from the new position he adopted after an inner crisis led to the abandonment of the theistic and Christian one.

CHAPTER 25

1. Ernest W. Hocking, "Whitehead on Mind and Nature," in Paul A. Schilpp, ed., *The Philosophy of Alfred North Whitehead* (New York, Tudor, 1951), p. 383.

2. "Immortality," in Schilpp, *op. cit.*, pp. 682-700.

3. *Ibid.*, p. 683.

4. *Ibid.*, p. 684.

5. *Ibid.* Whitehead notes specifically that this statement is a direct contradiction to Plato and to the theological tradition derived from him.

6. *Ibid.*, p. 685.

7. *Ibid.*, p. 686.

8. *Ibid.*, p. 687.

9. *Ibid.*, pp. 687-688.

10. *Ibid.*, p. 688.

11. *Ibid.*, p. 689.

12. *Ibid.*, p. 693.

13. *Ibid.*, p. 695.

14. *Ibid.*, p. 699.

15. Julius Seelye Bixler, "Whitehead's Philosophy of Religion," in Schilpp, *op. cit.*, p. 510.

CHAPTER 26

1. Thus Pascal, in spite of his insistence that man cannot be reduced to the epistemological subject or to a thing, is a forerunner of philosophical anthropology and not of existentialism.

2. The difference between man in general and man as the con-

crete person, aware of its finitude and the difference between the statistical and the existential attitudes, is nicely brought out in the anecdote about a patient who, before an operation, asked the surgeon whether the operation was very dangerous and what his chances of survival were. The surgeon replied that the operation was serious, and that approximately fifty per cent of the cases died, whereupon the patient inquired: "Are the fifty per cent already dead?" For the scientific view there are only cases, and death is anonymous. For the patient nothing matters but his own existence, which is threatened by death.

3. These are familiar motifs. One thinks of St. Augustine: "there was in me a great disgust for living, and a fear of dying" (*Confessions,* IV, p. 6) and of Pascal: "When I consider the short duration of my life, consumed in the eternity preceding and following it, the little space I occupy . . . I am frightened. . . . The last act is bloody . . . some earth is thrown on one's head and that's all there is to it for all eternity." (*Pensées,* 205 and 210)
One must, however, be careful, especially when exploring the roots of existentialism, not to apply the term "existential" to these experiences, since one would then be easily tempted to find existentialists where there are none. These experiences alone do not suffice to establish St. Augustine and Pascal as precursors of existentialism. And it remains uncertain whether they can be considered as such even in view of certain elements in their thinking emphasizing the person, the individual.

4. There is also the difference among contemporary existentialists as to their devotion or total disregard of Husserl's phenomenology.

5. *Journals,* Alexander Dru, trans. (New York, Oxford University Press, 1938), entry of May 12, 1839.

6. *Ibid.,* p. 351.

7. *The Sickness unto Death,* Walter Lowrie, trans. (New York, Anchor Books, 1954), p. 150.

8. "Wir sind zu der erschuetternden Erkenntnis gelangt, dass der Mensch von Anbeginn ein Moribundus ist. Diese Erkenntnis befruchtet und durchdringt unser ganzes philosophieren. (Hermann Glockner, *Heinrich Rickert zum Gedaechtnis,* Ztschr. fuer Deutsche Kulturphilosophis, Bd. 3, H. 1, 1936.) Glockner tells us that when he related the above conversation to his teacher Rickert, the latter sharply retorted: "We are in no way moribundi, we are merely morituri!"

9. Emmanuel Mounier, *Existentialist Philosophies,* E. Blow, trans. (London, Rockliffe, 1948), p. 12. Sartre is perhaps the exception. His attitude in the French resistance during the last war with its humiliation of defeat and occupation was that of "better death than this" (*Republic of Silence*).

10. *Stages on Life's Way,* Walter Lowrie, trans. (Princeton, Princeton University Press, 1940), p. 465.

11. Walter Lowrie, the English translator of *The Concept of Dread,* admits that *dread* is not an adequate translation of *Angst* (*Fear and Trembling* [Princeton, Princeton University Press, 1941], note 20, p. 264). Eric Blow, the translator of Emmanuel Mounier's *Existentialist Philosophies,* has similar reservations for his rendering of *angoisse* as *anguish,* and remarks, rather naively, that *"angoisse* seems to mean some sort of mental agitation which, so far, has been observed only by existentialist philosophers, and consequently no word in any language conveys what is meant by it." (!) (Preface, p. lv.) *Angst* is, however, a central concept in psychoanalysis and has been uniformly translated as *angoisse* (not *anxiété*) and as *anxiety.* This latter is not altogether satisfactory, but is preferable to "dread." The use of the term "anxiety" in both psychoanalytic and existentialist literature naturally raises the question of the possible difference between pathological and existential anxiety. Tillich attempted to define pathological anxiety as "a state of existential anxiety under special conditions" and existential anxiety as "a state in which being is aware of its possible non-being." (*Courage to Be,* New Haven, Yale University Press, 1952, p. 65.)

12. Trans. from O. F. Bollnow, *Existenzphilosophie* (Stuttgart, W. Kohlhammer, 1955), p. 370.

13. *The Concept of Dread,* Walter Lowrie, trans. (Princeton, Princeton University Press, 1944), p. 139.

14. Jaspers, "Philosophical Autobiography," Paul A. Schilpp, ed., in *The Philosophy of Karl Jaspers* (New York, Tudor, 1957), p. 9.

15. Jaspers, *Philosophie* (Berlin, Springer, 1932), V. II, p. 220-30.

16. *Ibid.,* p. 228.

17. *Ibid.,* p. 230.

18. Jaspers, *Einfuehrung in die Philosophie,* p. 121. English translation by Ralph Manheim, under the misleading title, *Way to Wisdom* (New Haven, Yale University Press, 1959).

19. Jaspers, *Rechenschaft und Ausblick* (München, Piper, 1951), p. 264.

20. Jaspers, *Einfuehrung in die Philosophie,* p. 33.

21. "The Reply to My Critics," in Schilpp, *op. cit.,* p. 796.

22. Jaspers, *Philosophie,* III, p. 95.

23. Here we shall not go into a discussion of the phenomenological method which Heidegger uses.

24. *"Das 'Wesen' des Daseins liegt in seiner Existenz."* Heidegger; *Sein und Zeit* (Tübingen, Max Niemeyer, 7th ed., 1953), p. 42.

25. Heidegger, *op. cit.,* p. 56.

26. *Ibid.,* p. 69.

27. *Ibid.*, p. 179.

28. "Das Dass seines Da, als welches ihm in unerbittlicher Raetselhaftigkeit entgegenstarrt."

29. *Ibid.*, p. 184.

30. *Ibid.*, p. 186. Heidegger's claim, however, that until he came along "the phenomena of anxiety and fear . . . have without exception never been differentiated" betrays an astounding conceit as well as total and astounding ignorance of Freud's work.

31. Wellek points out that anxiety and care "belong nevertheless to psychological experience and that instead of speaking of *Seinspsychologie* we should realize that we have before us nothing but *psychologism.*" (A. Wellek, "Struktur, Charakter, Existenz," *Philos. J.,* 1949, p. 442.)

32. "Nur solange (menschliches) Dasein ist, gibt es Sein."

33. "Der verfallenden Nichtigkeit der Welt."

34. "Das Nichts, davor die Angst bringt, enthuellt die Nichtigkeit die das Dasein in seinem Grunde bestimmt, der selbst ist als Geworfenheit in den Tod."

35. Heidegger, *op. cit.*, p. 240.

36. "Das Dasein stirbt faktisch, sofern es existiert."

37. Heidegger, *op. cit.*, p. 245.

38. "Die Seinsweise, in der das Dasein zu seinem Tode ist." *Ibid.*, p. 247.

39. Heidegger remarks that the medico-biological investigation of *demise* could possibly yield results that might be important ontologically, if there is also proper orientation toward an existential interpretation of death, and he wonders whether sickness and death must not be understood even medically, as existential phenomena.

40. Heidegger, *op. cit.*, p. 248.

41. "Die Moeglichkeit der schlechthinnigen Daseinsunmoeglichkeit." *Ibid.*, p. 250.

42. "Feige Furcht, Unischerheit des Daseins und finstere Weltflucht." *Ibid.*, p. 254.

43. "Das Vorlaufen . . . bringt es (das Dasein) vor die Moeglichkeit . . . es selbst zu sein . . . in der faktischen, ihrer selbst gewissen und sich aengstenden Freiheit zum Tode" (p. 266). Karl Lehmann points out that Heidegger speaks as if there were two different kinds of death: the natural phenomenon, that does not concern man as existence, and the specific human death; and this latter death is again divided into the death which I can understand existentially, and the death to which *I* as existence, have to take position. He also holds that Heidegger's existential analysis, by considering only death, but not also birth, does not really concern itself with the whole of existence, which is not thrown into the world, but is to be conceived as a link and, possibly, as a purpose-

ful entry into the world. K. Lehmann, *Der Tod bei Heidegger und Jaspers* (Heidelberg, Evang. Verlag, 1938).

44. The critique of unauthentic life is not original with Heidegger. Pascal and Bossuet have rebuked the *divertissements,* the faked, artificial life man usually leads.

45. Regis Jolivet, *Le problème de la mort chez M. Heidegger et J. P. Sartre* (Paris, Editions de Fontenelle, 1950).

46. A. Sternberger, *Der verstandene Tod. Eine Untersuchung zu Martin Heideggers Existentialontologie* (Leipzig, S. Hirzel, 1934), p. 47.

47. Rudolph Berlinger, *Das Nichts und der Tod* (Frankfurt, Klostermann, 1954 [?]), p. 181.

48. Ewald Wasmuth, *Vom Sinn des Todes* (Heidelberg, Lambert Schneider, 1959), pp. 50-51.

49. *Ibid.,* p. 53. Wasmuth's views are those of the Christian philosopher. He is radically opposed to the interpretation of life through the lifeless, because when lifeless Nature serves as a model, belief in immortality becomes impossible (p. 41).

In admitting that "all life is mortal, all life can be killed" (p. 35), and holding that "death is the limit of life, not part of life," he maintains, nevertheless, that beyond the transitoriness of the individual, the imperishable life, which does not know death, "shows" itself (p. 65). But what is the use of catching a glimpse of the Imperishable in us if it cannot help to eliminate death? (p. 87). Still, the transformation of death (which is Nothingness that waits for every one of us in the future) into the gate of life, is possible. It is "the mystery of the revelation of God in Jesus Christ" (p. 105), a mystery before which our author falls silent, "since it does not behoove philosophy to interpret the starry heavens of faith" (pp. 105 and 120).

50. R. Guardini, *Die letzten Dinge* (Werkbund Verlag, 1940), p. 12. English translation: *The Last Things,* Charlotte Forsyth and Grace Branham (New York, Pantheon, 1954).

51. Heidegger, *Erlaeuterungen zu Hoelderlin's Dichtung* (Frankfurt, Vittorio Klostermann, 1944), pp. 14, 18, 23; *Was ist Metaphysik?* (Frankfurt, Vittorio Klostermann, 1949), p. 28.

52. *The Republic of Silence,* A. J. Liebling, trans. (New York, Harcourt, Brace, 1947).

53. *L'Etre et le Néant* (Paris, Gallimard, 45th ed., 1955), p. 616.

54. *Ibid.,* p. 617.

55. *Ibid.,* pp. 621, 623.

56. *Ibid.,* p. 624.

57. *Ibid.*

58. *Ibid.,* pp. 624, 625.

59. *Ibid.,* pp. 628, 629.

60. *Ibid.,* p. 630.

61. "Bien au contraire, il nous semble, que la mort, en se découvrant à nous comme elle est, nous libére entièrement de sa prétendue contrainte." *Ibid.,* p. 630.

62. *Ibid.,* p. 631.

63. By "facticity" of the "for-itself" Sartre means "the double contingency which comprises a necessity," whereby if it is necessary that I *be,* as "being *there*" it is contingent that I be at all, since I am not the foundation of my being. On the other hand, if it is necessary that I be "committed" to a certain point of view, it is contingent that it be this one and not another. *Ibid.,* p. 371.

64. *Ibid.,* p. 631: "Il est absurde que nous soyons nés; il est absurde que nous mourions; d'autre part, cette absurdité se présente comme une alienation permanente de mon être-possibilité qui n'est plus *ma* possibilité, mais celle de l'autre."

65. "Je ne suis pas libre pour mourir, mais je suis un libre mortel." *Ibid.,* p. 632.

66. "Par-dessus le marché." *Ibid.,* p. 633.

67. *Ibid.* Maurice Natanson has attempted to clarify Sartre's idea of death through his idea of "situation." *American Imago,* V. XVI, 4, 1959.

68. *L'Etre et le Néant,* p. 57.

69. *Ibid.,* pp. 561-563.

70. *Ibid.,* p. 569.

71. *Ibid.,* p. 639.

72. *Ibid.,* p. 640.

73. *Ibid.,* p. 641.

74. This very impressive term, since it purports to combine the two most provocative developments in philosophy and psychology of our time, has very little in common with Freud's psychoanalysis; this can be seen from Sartre's statement that his "existential psychoanalysis rejects the postulates of the Unconscious." *Ibid.,* p. 658.

75. *Ibid.,* p. 708.

76. *Ibid.,* p. 85.

77. Jolivet, *op. cit.* Morin, however, compares Heidegger and Sartre to a Stoic and Epicurean respectively. The former attempts to base his attitude to death on an absolute anthropological adherence to it, and by riveting his gaze to it continuously. Sartre, on the contrary, bases his attitude to death on the instant of liberty where the "stranger death" is absolutely ignored and despised (*L'Homme et la Mort dans l'Histoire* [Paris, Corréa, 1951], p. 294). "Sartre subordinates death to such an extent that he forgets the reality of the anxiety of death." *Ibid.,* p. 297. "Liberty is his philosophical prison. . . . And whereas one can reproach Heidegger, who sets up death as the meaning of life, for making of it a senseless sense (*un sens sans sens*), one can also reproach

Sartre for making out of freedom a foolish sense (*un sens insensé*)
Ibid., p. 298.

78. Like Heidegger and Jaspers he repudiates, however, the label of Existentialist.

79. Similarly, the death of a parent greatly affected Hegel, Schopenhauer, and Nietzsche.

80. M. M. Davy, *Un Philosophe Itinérant: Gabriel Marcel* (Paris, Flammarion, 1959), p. 51. It is in this respect, perhaps, that he differs from Pascal, with whom he has otherwise much in common.

81. *Etre et Avoir* (Paris, Aubier, 1935), p. 120.

82. At the philosophical congress in Paris, 1937.

83. F. Heinemann, *Existentialism and the Modern Predicament* (New York, Harper, 1953), p. 134.

84. *Mystère de l'être* (Paris, F. Aubier, 1951), v. I, p. 46.

85. *Etre et Avoir*, p. 11.

86. *Ibid.*, p. 12.

87. *Ibid.*, p. 126.

88. *Ibid.*, p. 158.

89. *Journal Métaphysique* (Paris, Gallimard, 1927), p. 289.

90. *Mystère de l'être*, v. I, p. 154.

91. Translated from Davy, *op. cit.*, p. 316.

92. Also in *Etre et Avoir*, p. 137, footnote.

93. Translated from *Davy*, *op. cit.*, p. 299.

94. Marcel, *Homo viator* (Paris, Aubier, 1944), p. 66.

95. *Etre et Avoir*, p. 135.

96. *Ibid.*, pp. 159-60.

97. *Ibid.*, p. 126.

98. *Ibid.*, p. 145.

99. *Ibid.*, p. 35. Lately he finds this statement too categorical.

100. *Etre et Avoir*, p. 148.

101. *Ibid.*, p. 159.

102. "My being is for me a mystery." *Ibid.*, 161.

103. Heinemann, *op. cit.*, p. 145.

104. *Ibid.*, p. 171.

AFTERWORD

1. There is, of course, a third possibility: the inability to accept the religious solution leads the philosopher to a total disregard of the problems presented by death and to the denial that they fall within the province of philosophy. But this possibility does not belong in the present context where we are concerned exclusively with instances where death is a subject for philosophy.

2. As I. M. Bochenski does in his *Die Europaeische Philosophie der Gegenwart* (Bern, Franke, 2nd ed., 1951), published in Eng-

lish as *Contemporary European Philosophy*, Donald Nicholl and Karl Aschenbrenner, trans. (Berkeley, University of California Press, 1957), p. 198.

3. Joseph Jacobs, *Fortnightly Review*, London, 1899.

4. Fournier D'Albe, *New Light on Immortality* (London, Longmans, 1908), p. 1.

5. Maxim Gorky, *Reminiscences of Tolstoy.*

6. Georg Simmel, *Fragmente und Aufsaetze.*

7. Quoted in René Schaerer, "La Philosophie Moderne Devant la Mort," in *L'Homme en face de la Mort*, collected essays (Neuchatel, Delachaux & Niestle, 1952), p. 133.

8. Morin, *L'Homme et la Mort dans l'Histoire*, p. 242-43.

9. Nicolai Hartmann, *Zur Grundlegung der Ontologie* (Meisenheim am Glan, A. Hein, 1948), ch. 30.

10. Max Scheler: *Tod und Fortleben*, in *Schriften aus dem Nachlass*, 1933.

11. Bertrand Russell, "A Free Man's Worship" (1903); "Why Men Fight" (1916), in *Mysticism and Logic* (New York, Doubleday Books, 1957).

12. Nicolas Berdyaev: *Dream and Reality* (New York, Macmillan, 1951), p. 292.

13. Like "the uses of death" of which Sidney Hook speaks in his address *Pragmatism and the Tragic Sense of Life*, namely "the assurance that no evil and suffering lasts forever" and that "it washes the earth clean." *Proceedings and Addresses of the American Philosophical Association* (Yellow Springs, Ohio, Antioch Press, 1960), p. 12.

14. Voltaire, *Dictionnaire Philosophique*, article "Tout est bien."

15. "Life is cheap, but (at the same time) nothing is as precious as life." Malraux, *Les Conquerants.*

16. Bertrand Russell, "My Mental Development," in Schilpp, ed., *The Philosophy of Bertrand Russell* (New York, Tudor, 1944).

17. As a mere "failure of nerve." And it should be noted that there is a great difference between the concern with the problems of death and "the agony over death" and the "hysterical lament that man is not immortal" to which Sidney Hook seems to reduce it (*op. cit.*, p. 12).

Name Index

Abelard, Peter, 93
Aeschylus, 42
Agrippa, King, 84
Alexander of Aphrodisias, 95
Alexander the Great, 64
Anacreon, 32
Anaxagoras, 40
Anaximander, 34, 35, 150
Andreas-Salomé, Lou, 203
Angelico, Fra, 24
Aristotle, 37, 48, 51, 53-57, 67, 68, 72, 95, 105
Artaxerxes III, 56
Augustine, St., 76
Aurelius, Marcus, 72-76
Averroës, 95

Bell, E. T., 118
Benz, Ernest, 66
Berdyaev, Nicolas, 271
Bergson, Henri, 209-10, 215, 269
Berlinger, Rudolph, 238
Bixler, J. S., 220
Blanqui, Louis, 202
Bonaventura, St., 104
Bosch, Hieronumus, 91
Bowra, C. M., 32
Brentano, Clemens, 159
Browne, Sir Thomas, 211
Bruno, Giordano, 97, 103-08, 156, 183
Brunschvicg, Leon, 255, 270
Burnet, John, 31, 34
Byron, George Gordon Lord, 202

Camus, 272
Cebes, 47
Charlemont, Lord, 138

Christina, Queen, of Sweden, 111
Cicero, 53, 98, 102
Clemenceau, Georges, 272
Condorcet, Marquis de, 135-36, 193
Confucius, 271
Copernicus, 117, 142
Cornford, F. M., 23, 24, 31, 37, 47
Cratylus, 51
Creuzer, Friedrich, 158
Crito, 43
Cusanus, 105, 106, 261

Dante, 96
Democritus, 41, 58, 59, 68
Descartes, René, 111-15, 129, 131, 135, 212
Diels, Hermann, 34
Dilthey, Wilhelm, 103
Dixon, W. Macneille, 122
Donne, John, 18, 87
Duns Scotus, John, 104
Dürer, Albrecht, 199

Eliot, T. S., 272
Empedocles, 40, 46
Epictetus, 71-72, 173, 251
Epicurus, 41, 58-61, 62, 66, 272
Euripides, 42, 47

Faulkner, William, 272
Fechner, Gustav Theodor, 212, 213
Festus, Roman Resident, 84
Feuerbach, Paul von, 186-98, 237
Fichte, J. G., 149, 150, 156, 157, 158